# BATTLES OF THE RUSSIAN NAVY 1793–1815

# BATTLES OF THE RUSSIAN NAVY

## 1793–1815

PHILIP MACDOUGALL

PEN & SWORD
MARITIME

First published in Great Britain in 2026 by
PEN AND SWORD MARITIME
*an imprint of*
Pen and Sword Books Ltd
Yorkshire – Philadelphia



Print ISBN 978 1 03613 677 2
ePUB ISBN 978 1 03613 679 6
ePDF ISBN 978 1 03613 681 9



A CIP record for this book is available from the British Library



Typeset in Times New Roman 10/12.5 by
SJmagic DESIGN SERVICES, India.
Printed and bound in the UK by CPI Group (UK) Ltd.

The Publisher's authorised representative in the EU for product safety is Authorised Rep Compliance Ltd., Ground Floor, 71 Lower Baggot Street, Dublin D02 P593, Ireland.
www.arccompliance.com

*For a complete list of Pen & Sword titles please contact*
PEN & SWORD BOOKS LIMITED
George House, Units 12 & 13, Beevor Street, Off Pontefract Road,
Barnsley, South Yorkshire, S71 1HN, England
E-mail: enquiries@pen-and-sword.co.uk
Website: www.pen-and-sword.co.uk

or

PEN AND SWORD BOOKS
1950 Lawrence Rd, Havertown, PA 19083, USA
E-mail: uspen-and-sword@casematepublishers.com
Website: www.penandswordbooks.com

FSC
www.fsc.org
MIX
Paper | Supporting responsible forestry
FSC® C013604

# CONTENTS

# MAPS

Map 1: Baltic Sea Region

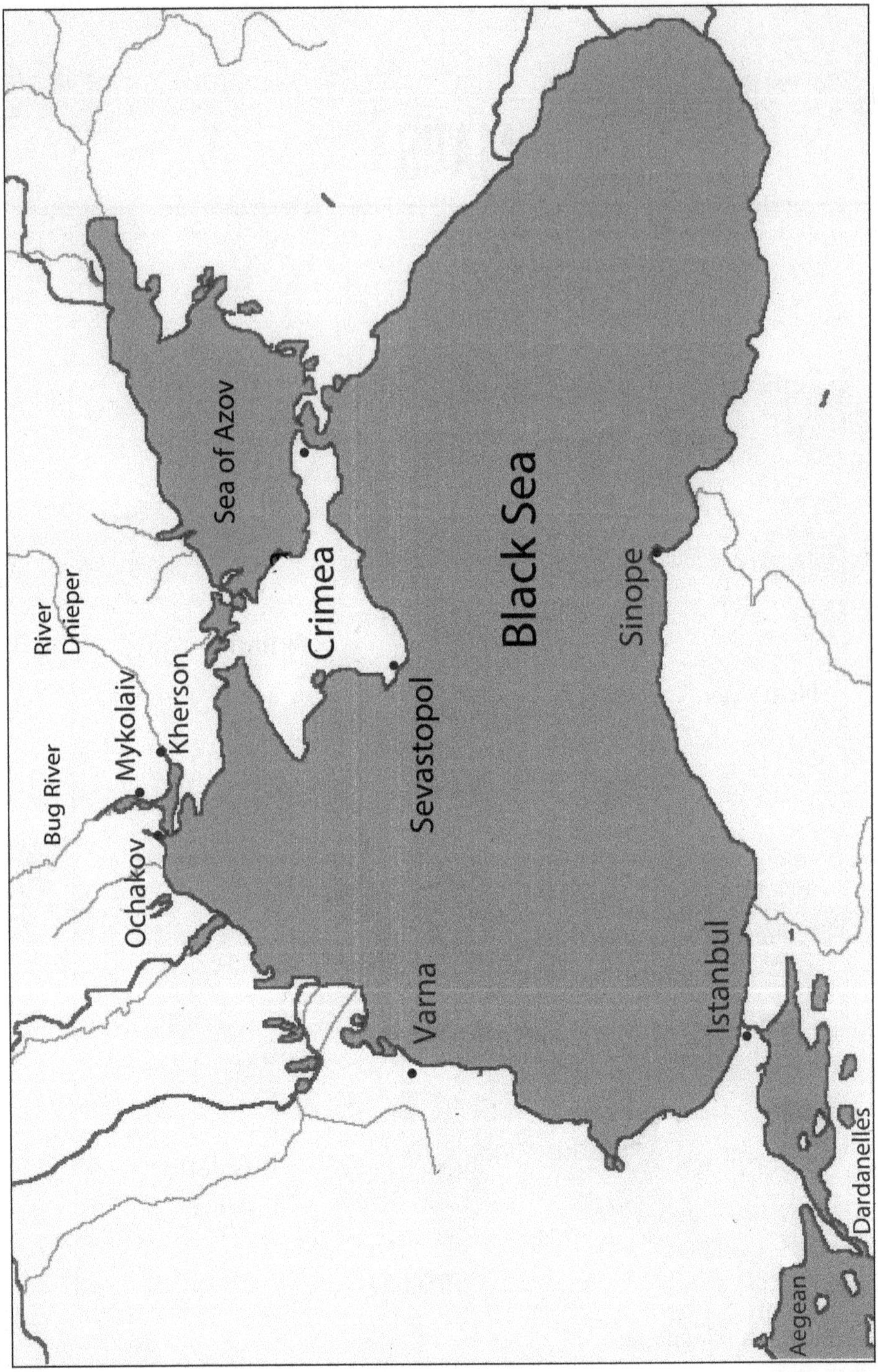


Map 2: Black Sea Region

# ILLUSTRATIONS

11. In having acquired the draught plans for the British 100-gun warship *Victory*, several near-identical ships were built in Russian shipyards. This drawing is of *Rotislav*, a 'Ches'ma' class battleship closely resembling *Victory.*
12. The River Medway looking towards the dockyard at Chatham. During the opening years of the French wars and following Napoleon's invasion of Russia, Chatham was home to ships of the Russian Baltic Fleet.
13. Greig, Aleksey Samuilovich. The son of Samuel Greig, Aleksey served as a naval commander throughout most of the French war period, leading an attack unit during the Battle of Athos and commanding the sailing and rowing flotilla during the Siege of Danzig.
14. Fyodor Fyodorovich Ushakov. The most revered of all Russian admirals, his statue stands immediately in front of the naval Cathedral of Saint Nicholas in Kronstadt.
15. Horatio Nelson, the British admiral and Russophobe who clashed with Ushakov in the Mediterranean.
16. The two massive fortresses defending the town of Corfu, the old fortress and the new fortress, which were successfully taken by Ushakov in 1799.
17. Fortifications surrounding the Maltese city of Valletta. Taken by Napoleon, the subsequent siege and blockade of the island was very much at the centre of the antagonism existing between Ushakov and Nelson.
18. Emperor Paul I. It was Paul's assassination that ultimately ensured that war between Britain and Russia did not break out. It was Paul's belief that Britain was only waging war against France to achieve advantage at the expense of Russia.
19. Various Russian cannons on the quayside of Tallinn harbour, some of them possibly once incorporated into the defence of Tallinn at the time that British attacks on the port were feared.
20. Alexander I, an emperor with little regard for the navy.
21. Dmitry Nikolayevich Senyavin. A highly successful naval commander, Senyavin was tactically adept, gaining victories in the Dardanelle Strait and Athos against the Ottoman Fleet.
22. Dubrovnik. Alongside Kotor, Dubrovnik was one of several key strategic points on the east side of the Adriatic captured by Senyavin during 1806.
23. Kilitbahir Kelesi. Defending the Dardanelles Passage, and consequently any attempt at a seaborne attack upon Istanbul from the Mediterranean, were fortresses and batteries located on both its European and Asian sides. The fortress of Kilitbahir provided a powerful defence on the eastern, or Asian, shore.
24. Kale Sultanieh. Standing on the opposite shore and facing Kilitbahir Kelesi stood Kale Sultanieh. Between them they could provide a potentially crippling cross-fire.
25. The naval Cathedral of Saint Nicholas in Kronstadt. Inside are various memorial panels regarding battles and other events relating to the Russian Navy.
26. Among the commemorative panels lining the wall within Saint Nicholas Cathedral are several that record the French Revolutionary and Napoleonic period. Shown here are panels for 1804 through to early 1806. In March 1807, it is recorded that in capturing the island and fortress of Tenedos, six officers and seventy-three lower

ranks were wounded on shore while on the ship *Rafail*, two officers were killed and one midshipman and six seamen were wounded.

27. The burning in August 1808 of the seventy-four-gun *Vsevolod* outside the port of Paldiski following her unsuccessful bid to outsail *Implacable* and *Centaur* of the British Navy.
28. Belem Tower, Lisbon. It was in the deep anchorage close alongside Belem Tower that Senyavin's squadron took up moorings during the failed attempt to reach the safety of the Baltic following Alexander's alliance with Napoleon.
29. Napoleon Dock, Antwerp. Here at Antwerp, a huge warship building programme was implemented by Napoleon, with Russian warships used to undermine this construction programme by assisting the British Navy in an ongoing blockade of the mouth of the Scheldt.
30. Daugava River, Riga. In the wide anchorage of the Daugava, several hundred merchantmen annually collected to take on stores from the warehouses lining the banks of the river. To prevent those ships and stores falling into French hands during Napoleon's invasion of Russia, both British and Russian warships actively collaborated.

# KEY PERSONALITIES

**Alexander I (1777-1825).** Emperor of Russia from 1801 until his death in 1825, during which time he gave limited attention to the value of Russia having a strong ocean-going navy.

**Arbuthnot, Charles (1767-1850).** British ambassador to the Ottoman Empire between 1804 and 1807

**Ball, Captain Sir Alexander John (1757-1809).** As commander of the seventy-four-gun third-rate *Alexander*, he played a key role in Nelson's blockade of Malta, serving later as the island's civil commissioner and *de facto* governor.

**Beg, Abdülkadir.** Holding the equivalent rank of vice admiral, and always known in Russian documents as Kapudan Abdülkadir Beg, he command an Ottoman squadron assigned in 1798 to work alongside a Russian squadron commanded by Ushakov.

**Catherine II (1729-1796).** Better known as Catherine the Great, she ruled the Russian Empire between 1762-1796. For her the Russian Navy was an important asset to which she gave much attention.

**Chichagov, Pavel Vasilyevich (1767-1849).** Served under Paul I as minister of naval forces but previously captain first class of the sixty-six-gun *Retvizan* during the Anglo-Russian period of naval co-operation in the North Sea.

**Crown, Roman Vasilievich (1754-1841).** Served in the North Sea during the late 1790s with the rank of captain first rank. Returned to British waters in 1812 commanding a squadron of ships sailing out of Arkhangelsk with the rank of vice admiral. Of Scottish parentage, he first served in the British Navy before transferring to the Russian Navy in 1788.

**Elliott, Hugh (1752-1830).** British ambassador to Naples, 1803-06.

**Elphinston, John (1722-1785).** British naval captain recruited by Catherine II to lead, with the rank of rear admiral, a squadron of Russian warships into the Mediterranean, subsequently participating in the Battle of Çeşme (1770).

**Greig, Aleksey Samuilovich (1775-1845).** The son of Samuel Karlovich Greig. Born in Kronstadt, he initially trained as an officer in the British Navy before returning to Russia.

Under Senyavin, he led one of the tactical units during the Battle of Athos (1807), later commanding the sailing and rowing flotilla during the Siege of Danzig (1813).

**Greig, Samuel Karlovich (1735-1788).** Born in Scotland, he was one of several British naval officers invited by Catherine II to help modernise the Russian Navy. Playing a significant role in the Russian victory at Çeşme (1770), he later oversaw reconstruction of the naval base at Kronstadt. He died of typhoid while commanding the Baltic Fleet during the Russo-Swedish War (1788-1790).

**Kartsov, Pyotr Kondratievich (1750-1830).** As a rear admiral, he led a squadron of ships into the North Sea from Kronstadt and survived the wrecking of his flagship *Prince Gustav*. Following a few months of service in the North Sea under Makarov, he was then raised in rank to vice admiral and ordered to take a small squadron into the Mediterranean to join Ushakov. Upon the accession of Alexander, he was appointed to the Admiralty board.

**Khanykov, Pyotr Ivanovich (1743-1813).** Sometimes in English Hanickoff. Of a noble family, Khanykov first entered the navy in 1759 and as a midshipman gained experience with the British Royal Navy between 1762-1765. Participated in the Battle of Çeşme (June 1770) and in Catherine's war against Sweden. As a vice admiral, he commanded the squadron sent to England to serve alongside Admiral Duncan and in 1799, following his return to Russia, he was promoted by Paul to the rank of full admiral and given command of the Baltic Fleet. With the threatened attack on Kronstadt in 1801, Khanykov supervised the improvement of the harbour defences. He was dismissed in 1808 following an unsuccessful confrontation with an Anglo-Swedish Fleet.

**Korobka, Maxim Petrovich (1759-1836).** As a rear admiral he led a unit of eight ships that left Kronstadt for the security of England in 1812. During the following year he participated in the blockade of the French and Dutch coasts, intercepting military and transport ships. At the end of 1813, he returned to Arkhangelsk.

**Mackenzie, Thomas (1740-1786).** As a lieutenant commander, he gained distinction at the Battle of Çeşme with promotion to rear admiral in 1783 when he was appointed to the Black Sea Fleet overseeing construction of the Sevastopol naval base. Of Scottish parentage, his father, also named Thomas, had held rank as a rear admiral in the Russian Navy.

**Makarov, Mikhail (1735-1813).** As a lieutenant, Makarov was present at the Battle of Çeşme, and during the war with Sweden he was present at the battles of Gogland and Öland, commanding *Vseslav*. As a rear admiral, Makarov initially served under Khanykov in the squadron of Russian ships blockading the Dutch coast under Admiral Duncan, but later replaced Khanykov as the senior Russian commander. He was promoted to the rank of vice admiral in 1797, acting alongside Duncan in the landing of troops on the Dutch coast. A full admiral from 1801, he was appointed to the admiralty board by Alexander I and in January 1810 to the head of naval commands in St Petersburg.

**Mordvinov, Nikolay Semyonovich (1754-1845).** Russia's first naval minister and a notable anglophile. Entering the navy at the age of 12, he gained further experience of the sea in England, serving on British ships in North America between 1774-1777. During Catherine's second Ottoman War, he commanded an in-shore flotilla during the bombardment and assault on Ochakov. On the formation of ministries by Alexander I in 1802, he took the post of minister of naval forces, but only held this position for three months.

**Nauckhoff, Rear Admiral Henrik Johan (1744-1818).** Promoted to rear admiral in 1796, he commanded the Swedish Fleet during the war against Russia that broke out in 1808.

**Nelson, Horatio (1758-1805).** Widely regarded as one of the greatest naval commanders in history, he provided inspirational leadership and the implementation of strategies and tactics that brought about several decisive British naval victories. In Russia he is frequently compared with Ushakov, who was also an inspirational leader who used tactics that Nelson later adopted.

**Peter I (1672-1725).** Better known as Peter the Great, he ruled Russia from 1682 until his death in 1725. A naval enthusiast, he is regarded as founder of the Russian Navy.

**Pitt, William, the younger (1759-1806).** Prime minister of Britain during most of the French Revolutionary war period. He became uncomfortable with territorial gains made by Catherine prior to the outbreak of the French wars, arming a naval squadron in 1791 that was intended to bring about a Russian withdrawal from some of Catherine's newly acquired territories. While the fleet never sailed, Russian historians regard this as an important factor in a later developed animosity by a few British naval officers, including Nelson, towards Russia.

**Potemkin, Prince Grigoriev (1739-1791).** Appointed by Catherine II as governor general of Russia's southern provinces, he created the Black Sea Fleet alongside its land-based infrastructure.

**Sébastiani, Horace François Bastien (1771-1851).** French ambassador to the Porte, 1806-1807.

**Senyavin, Dmitry Nikolayevich (1763-1831).** Senyavin took part in the Battle of Cape Kaliakra and the Mediterranean campaign of Ushakov, going on to adopt and refine Ushakov's combat tactics while commanding the Russian Fleet in the Ionian and Adriatic (1805-1807), defeating the Ottoman Fleet in two separate engagements.

**Smith, John Spencer (1769-1845).** The British plenipotentiary to the Ottoman Porte between 1795 and 1801.

**Spencer, George John, 2nd Earl (1758–1834).** First Lord of the Admiralty under Prime Minister William Pitt, serving between 1794 and 1801.

**Stroganov, Pavel Alexandrovich (1774-1817).** Served as Russian *chargé d'affaires* in London in 1806, following Semyon Vorontsov's resignation.

**Tate, George (1745-1821).** British born, he served under Khanykov in the North Sea, and as a vice admiral in 1796 and 1797 commanded the Russian squadron in the North Sea. He was again in British waters in 1812. His father, also named George, served in the Russian Navy under Peter the Great.

**Tomara, Vasily Stepanovich (1746-1819).** Russian plenipotentiary to the Ottoman Porte.

**Traversay, Ivan Ivanovich (1754-1831).** French Creole by birth, he served first in the French Navy before taking up an invitation by Catherine II to enter the Russian Navy, with Alexander I appointing him commander-in-chief of the Black Sea Fleet. He replaced Chichagov in January 1810 as minister of naval forces.

**Troubridge, Thomas (1758-1807).** As commander of the seventy-four-gun British third-rate *Culloden,* he served off Malta under Nelson during the autumn of 1798, and was ordered by Nelson to sail for Zante and Cephalonia in the hope that he could take possession of these islands before Ushakov. Later he was given secret instructions to sail to Civitavecchia, the nearest port to Rome, ahead of the Russians so that 'the eternal city' could be taken in the name of Nelson and not Ushakov.

**Ushakov, Fyodor Fyodorovich (1745-1817).** Patron saint of Russia's present-day navy. During Catherine's second war against the Ottomans, Ushakov developed a series of tactics, that both built upon and greatly improved those as practised by other navies, including the British Navy. In that war he gained four victories at Fidonisi (1788), Kerch Strait (1790), Tendra Island (1790), and Cape Kaliakra (1791). A naval compact agreed with the Porte in 1798 saw Ushakov working alongside the Ottoman commander Abdülkadir Beg in a successful campaign fought against the French.

**Vorontsov, Count Alexander Romanovich (1741-1805).** Imperial chancellor during the early years of Alexander I's reign.

**Vorontsov, Count Semyon Romanovich (1744-1832).** The Russian ambassador to London between 1785-1800 and 1801-1806.

**Whitworth, Charles, 1st Earl (1752-1825).** The British ambassador to the court of St Petersburg from 1788 until his expulsion from Russia by Paul I in 1800. Unproven is the possibility of him using Secret Service money to fund the assassination of Paul I.

# INTRODUCTION

*Battles of the Russian Navy 1793 – 1815* is the first book in English to concentrate solely on the actions of the Imperial Russian Navy during the French war period of 1793 to 1815. It is a period of history commonly referred to as the French Revolutionary and Napoleonic Wars, but for the purpose of this book, and when referring to those wars, I have sometimes referenced them as the French Wars. During those wars, the Russian Navy was active in the Mediterranean, Baltic, and North seas, proving itself to be a significant force that in serving Russian war aims directed itself not only against the naval forces of France but also those of Sweden and the Ottoman Empire. Resulting from shifting alliances and changing rulers, Great Britain and her navy also became an occasional enemy.

At the time, Russia possessed the third largest navy in the world. Those of senior rank often held a great affinity towards the British Navy through either being former British naval officers or having undergone a period of training in Britain. Attendance at the naval academy in Portsmouth followed by service on a British warship was a feature common to many who gained high rank in the Russian Navy. Ships of the Russian Navy also had much in common with the British Navy, either because they were designed by British shipwrights or were, in the case of one class of warship, based on plans stolen from Britain.

The navy of Russia that entered the war against France was one that had been created, or more correctly recreated, by Catherine the Great, Empress of Russia from 1770 to 1796. From the very outset of her reign, she took great interest in naval affairs, recognising that a strong ocean-going navy could bring great wealth to Russia through the securing of new territories to foster a growth in trade. In this she was supported during the middle and later years of her reign by Scottish-born naval admiral Samuel Greig, who became supreme commander of her Baltic Fleet. Unfortunately, upon his death there was no one of his calibre to replace him.

In many respects Greig symbolises the problem that faced the Russian Navy during the late eighteenth and early nineteenth centuries, that of the occasional arrival of a naval genius such as Greig, but who was then succeeded by someone of greatly inferior calibre. While Fyodor Fyodorovich Ushakov and Dmitry Nikolayevich Senyavin alongside Greig can be regarded as representing the genius side of the Russian Navy, others such as Pavel Vasilyevich Chichagov and Ivan Ivanovich Traversay led the Russian Navy in a downward spiral. As well as being subject to the variable talents of those appointed to command positions, the navy was also dependent on the whims and fancies of the changing rulers of the empire and whose authority was absolute. While Catherine had shown great interest in naval affairs, her interest waned in her declining years, allowing those she appointed to misuse naval funds and squabble among themselves. Following her death she was succeeded by her son Paul, who reigned as Paul I. He ensured a brief period of rejuvenation, for while it cannot be disputed that Paul had many failings, not least of which was his uncontrolled anger and sometimes rash illogical decisions that gained him many enemies, his time as emperor was one that greatly benefited the navy. If his reign had lasted as long as that of his mother, then the Russian Navy might well have become a major asset that could have allowed Russia to dominate not just in the Baltic and Black Sea, but also the Mediterranean. However, his reign, no more than five years, was cut short by assassination, in which British involvement cannot be ruled out. In turn Paul was succeeded by his son, Alexander I, whose interest in the navy was minimal. Instead, he directed his thoughts only to how the navy could act in the best interests of the army. In this he was fully supported by those he appointed, receiving questionable advice from Chichagov and Traversay.

Russia effectively had two navies. The largest was the Baltic Fleet based on Kronstadt and St Petersburg and the second a significantly smaller Black Sea Fleet. While both were theoretically under the command of the Admiralty Collegiate in St Petersburg and, latterly, a minister of naval forces (later minister of the navy), the Black Sea Fleet had considerable independence and was differently organised. In part this was because of the considerable distance of Sevastopol, the home base of the Black Sea Fleet, from St Petersburg. Of equal significance was that Catherine, during her reign, had allowed Russia to the south to be ruled by her former favourite and lover, Prince Grigoriev Potemkin, with this high level of independence becoming the adopted practice of her immediate successors. While other navies had separate fleets, a centralised command structure always ensured a high degree of similarity and competence existing between one fleet and another. For Russia this did not prevail, lessons learnt and practised by one fleet were rarely shared with the other. Indeed, throughout most of the 1793-1815 period, the Black Sea Fleet, while not possessing the strength of the Baltic Fleet, developed a series of strategies and tactics that proved highly effective and were much advanced upon those practised by other navies, including the British Navy. This cannot be said of the Baltic Fleet. At best this fleet failed to shine while at worst it was nothing less than a dismal failure. The difference in performance was especially noticeable during the opening years of Alexander's reign when the Baltic Fleet failed even to put to sea, and in consequence gave no support to merchant shipping threatened by French privateers. In sharp contrast, and during this same period, ships either emanating from the Black Sea or joining the Black Sea Fleet from the Baltic, were inflicting considerable pain on the French in the Adriatic. It is a theme that will be considered in detail as it usefully highlights the value of a sea-going navy and what Russia could have achieved if more attention had been given to the better development of a powerful blue water maritime force.

In the writing of this book, I have placed heavy reliance upon Russian language sources, both primary and secondary, alongside additional primary and secondary material written in English, French and Turkish. These are listed in the bibliography. In using Russian sources, this has allowed for an understanding of attitudes prevalent among Russian naval officers of the period as well as views held by later Soviet and Russian historians. Between them, but not all, they offer criticisms of Britain and in particular use made by the British government of the naval alliance forged during that wartime period. This is something rarely, if ever, discussed outside of Russia. In making use of these sources, it allows further light to be thrown on why Russia, as a long-term ally of Great Britain during the eighteenth century, became a bitter enemy during the nineteenth century, with one writer, Barbara Emerson, referring to those later years as 'the First Cold War'. During the 1793-1815 war, Russia and Britain strived to gain much from the struggle at sea, and for this reason as allies, but allies with differing strategic objectives, there was between them conflict. This, in turn, paved the way for times of open and declared hostility. On the front line, admirals of those two navies when required to work alongside each other sometimes clashed, with perceived insults festering. At other times when those appointed were more adept in the art of diplomacy, any feather-ruffling was rapidly smoothed over and easily forgotten.

At the outset of the war, a Russian squadron was sent to the North Sea to work alongside and under the command of a British admiral, this representing an early, but not the earliest, example of full inter-naval co-operation between two nation states. Fostered under wartime conditions and with no previous naval exercises to ensure effective harmonisation, it is surprising how well it worked. Mistakes made in that attempt at naval unity, such as allowing seamen of one nation to openly insult those of the other, are now a rarity when navies work alongside each other, but were then given too little attention. Also, when it came to the distribution of the spoils of war, always a highly contentious issue with possible future consequences, it will especially play on the mind of the one who gained least as well as those who become the spoils of war. Malta, the Ionian Islands, Sicily and Egypt were all areas that at one time or another were during the French war period in contention between Russia and Britain, with Russia coming to regard itself as short-changed in each of those territories. To this might be added Russia's concerns as to what lay behind Britain's maritime explorative voyages into the North Pacific in the years preceding the French Wars, and Russia under Paul giving serious thought to depriving Britain of India through an invasion of the latter.

Throughout I have dispensed with footnotes, as I wish the book to be as readable as possible and not viewed as an academic tome. It is for this reason I have adopted the use of a shortened discussion of sources located at the end of the book, which also contains useful additional detail, sometimes of a more technical nature. These discussion sections run in unison with each chapter and might best be referred to after the reading of the respective chapter. In writing *Battles of the Russian Navy 1793 – 1815* I am especially grateful for the assistance and support provided by the staff of the Belarus National Library in Minsk as well as the staff of the Central Naval Museum, St Petersburg. As always in the books I have written, thanks must also be given to the staff of the National Archives (Kew) and the National Maritime Museum (Greenwich).

Finally, a short note on the use of dates and place names. While elsewhere in Europe the Gregorian calendar had been adopted by the late eighteenth century, Russia adhered to the Julian calendar until 1918 and during the late eighteenth century Russian dating was behind Europe by eleven days and then, in 1800 by twelve days. For this reason, there is a difference in dates as expressed in British sources as compared with Russian sources. To avoid over-complication, I have used dates given according to the Gregorian calendar unless quoting from a published extract that used the earlier calendar. Where a number in brackets is given following the name of a ship, this refers to the number of guns carried by that ship and allows for a quick comparison of the strength of one ship when pitted against another, as in *Helena* (74), *Helena* being a third rate carrying seventy-four guns. Regarding place names, I have used the modern-day name but where that differs from the name used during the period of the French wars, I have on first use added the earlier name in brackets. Conversely, if the French wartime period name is used in a contemporary quote, I have used the name as quoted, but with the modern-day name given in brackets.

Philip MacDougall, Ph.D.
Chichester and Minsk

# PROLOGUE

# BUILT BY AN EMPRESS

At the outset of the wars fought between 1793 and 1815, the Russian Empire could boast of possessing one of the world's largest and most powerful navies, a navy that also had some very recent combat experience. Within the previous thirty years, ships of the Imperial Russian Navy had successfully fought actions against the Ottoman Empire (the Russo-Turkish Wars of 1768-1774 and 1787-1792) and Sweden (the Russo Swedish War of 1788-1790). In effect, the Russian Navy had more recent combat experience than any other of the world's navies, including those of Great Britain, France and Spain.

This was the navy of Catherine II, otherwise known as Catherine the Great, Empress of Russia. It was a navy of over 800 vessels, of which sixty-seven were first class battleships known as 'ships of the line', although it must be admitted that the largest portion of Catherine's fleet was formed of in-shore river craft. By comparison, the navy of Great Britain consisted of around 600 vessels and that of France of just under 300, but these navies possessed a greater number of ships of the line alongside other deep-water vessels (see Table 1 on next page). If measured in terms of ships by size and the total number of guns carried, Catherine's navy had a world ranking of fourth, placing her navy behind Great Britain, France and Spain. According to Robert Fulton, writing in 1792, ordnance carried by ships of Catherine's navy numbered 9,000. By comparison, those of Great Britain carried 14,000, France 12,000 and Spain 10,000.

Catherine, following a coup mounted against her husband Peter III, had ascended the Imperial Throne on 28 June 1762. Proving herself remarkably focused, even prior to the coup, she declared in a memorandum that it would be her intention to elevate the Russian Empire, 'to a degree of power above all the other empires in Asia and Europe.' For this she recognised the need to create a favourable balance of trade that could finance the Russian military in achieving this objective. Her assessment of Russia's current trading position made dismal reading, recognising that while an export trade existed, this remained entirely in the hands of foreigners. On ascending the throne she wrote:

> *The Russian merchantry, although enjoying great privileges and possessing within the country all the necessary resources, has failed to establish consulates and offices abroad, thus leaving all the profits of foreign trade to foreign merchants.*

**Table 1: The major fleets of Europe, c1790.**

| Nation | Total vessels | Ships of the line | Frigates | Sloops, corvettes, gunboats and other small craft | Total cannon | Total seamen |
|---|---|---|---|---|---|---|
| **Russia** | **803** | **67** | **36** | **700 various** | **9,000** | **21,000** |
| Britain | 661 | 195 | 210 | 256 sloops | 14,000 | 100,000 |
| France | 291 | 118 | 69 | 141 various | 12,000 | 78,000 |
| Spain | 222 | 72 | 41 | 109 sloops | 10,000 | 50,000 |
| Holland | 187 | 44 | 43 | 100 sloops | 2,300 | 15,000 |
| Ottoman Empire | 180 | 30 | 50 | 100 galliots | 3,000 | 14,000 |
| Denmark | 118 | 38 | 20 | 60 chebecks | 3,000 | 12,000 |
| Sweden | 79 | 27 | 12 | 40 galleys | 2,300 | 13,000 |
| Venice | 58 | 20 | 10 | 58 various | 1,000 | 14,000 |
| Portugal | 53 | 10 | 14 | 29 various | 1,500 | 1,000 |
| Naples | 32 | 10 | 10 | 12 various | 1,000 | 5,000 |

Source: Fulton, Robert (1810) *Torpedo War, and submarine explosions* (New York: W. Elliot), 45.

In this respect she was showing a determination to make Russia more like western Europe through the development of trade and industry, with a navy that could establish through conquest or a strong presence overseas territories designed to extend Russia's ability to trade across the world.

For such an ambition, the navy that Catherine had acquired was simply not fit for purpose, a fact she confirmed in June 1765 while reviewing the fleet at Kronstadt:

> *We have many ships and a great empire, but we have neither fleet nor seamen...I must admit, that they look more like a herring fleet which departs from Holland every year, and not in truth a fleet fit for war; not a ship holds its rank.*

By that date, Catherine had already taken steps to correct the appalling state into which the Russian Navy had fallen, initiating a major shipbuilding programme. In parallel to this, she also gained British government consent to allow both promising officers to train in England and the right to recruit into her navy experienced officers from the British Navy.

The first operational use of Catherine's navy was against the Ottoman Empire in a war that broke out in 1769. In a bold and imaginative plan, several squadrons of Russian ships drawn from the Baltic sailed into the Mediterranean, and for which purpose the North Sea, English Channel, Western Atlantic and Western Mediterranean had all to be traversed. Given the poor state of some of the Russian ships, a result of skill shortage in the Russian dockyards, many would not have reached the Mediterranean had they not taken refuge in the British naval dockyard at Portsmouth, receiving here extensive repairs. At Menorca too, which was then in British hands, Russian ships were given additional support, revictualling in Port Mahon and sending their sick and wounded to the island's naval hospital. The object behind this entry into the Mediterranean was to land troops on the Peloponnese Peninsula, then known as Morea, where it was intended to incite an uprising of Greek speakers against their Ottoman-Turkish overlords. While this proved unsuccessful, the Russian troops, in receiving little support from the Greeks, were quickly returned to the ships from which they had been offloaded. However, one outstanding naval victory was achieved in the harbour of Çeşme (pronounced Cheshmeh) where a large part of the Ottoman Fleet was destroyed. Unable to believe that the Russians were capable of such a deed, the defeated Ottomans took the view that it was a battle primarily inspired by the British Admiralty and that most of the ships claiming to be Russian were in fact British. While it is true that some of the officers on board the Russian ships were British, part of Catherine's recruitment programme, the majority were not. Even today, visitors to Çeşme are reliably informed that it was not a Russian Fleet that sealed the Ottoman defeat, but one primarily made up of British warships. Following that victory, the Russian Navy secured temporary dominance of the eastern Mediterranean, successfully blockading the Dardanelles and preventing Constantinople (Istanbul) receiving supplies from the south other than by land. Lacking a permanent base in the Mediterranean and with no long-term advantage to be gained, Catherine's ships were eventually forced to return to the Baltic.

One obvious consequence of this first Russian naval expedition into the Mediterranean was that it was now even clearer that Russia needed to acquire fleet bases in areas of naval operation, correctly realising that facilities offered by the British could not be permanently relied upon. After all, if the Imperial Fleet made permanent advances into the Mediterranean, or elsewhere in the world, the British would inevitably see Russia as a rival, with war the most likely outcome. In fact, within a short time the two did exhibit a degree of unfriendliness towards each other, this during the American War of Independence/American Revolutionary War (1775-1783). While Catherine was no supporter of the American colonists in their bid for independence, believing them to be infringing on the rights of a legitimate government, she took exception to British naval interception and the searching of ships carrying items out of Russia on the assumption they might be carrying goods defined by Great Britain as illicit war cargoes bound for an enemy port. Following a rash of seizures by the British Navy of ships carrying Russian merchandise into ports hostile to Great Britain, Catherine agreed to join with Sweden and Denmark in what was termed a League of Armed Neutrality. Each of the participants, upon joining the league, pledged their co-operation, including, if necessary, by force, to protect the merchant shipping of all league members. With Russian squadrons dispatched to the Mediterranean, Atlantic and North Sea to enforce this decree, the prospect of a clash with Britain was certainly possible. But with Britain not wishing to antagonise Russia, there was little further interference by Britain with ships of the league.

The war fought against the Ottomans might not have achieved all that Catherine had hoped, failing to create a land-front on the Peloponnese, but elsewhere substantial gains were made. A military push on the southern fringes of areas already occupied by Russia had brought to Catherine part of the Yedisan region that lies on the Black Sea, immediately to the north of the Southern Bug and Dnieper River estuaries together with further sections of territory around the Sea of Azov. Possession of these territories was confirmed by the Treaty of Küçük Kaynarca, signed in 1774, which concluded Catherine's first war with the Ottoman Empire. Of even greater significance was that the Küçük Kaynarca treaty gave to Russia the right for her naval and commercial vessels to freely enter the Black Sea and which, in turn, could be used to create a much-enlarged overseas trade network. For this purpose, Catherine founded the new cities of Mykolaiv, Kherson and Mariupol, and to which came not only Turkish and Greek merchants but others drawn from around the Mediterranean. It was the Treaty of Küçük Kaynarca that delivered the Crimea to Catherine, over which she claimed full sovereignty. In 1783, the naval base at Akhtiar (Sevastopol) was founded. In a second war fought against the Ottomans (1787-1792), Russia went on to strengthen her position in the Black Sea, with Catherine set on taking even larger slices of Ottoman territory and Istanbul her ultimate objective.

In the various wars fought against the Ottoman Empire, thought had always to be given to the possibility of a further war breaking out against Sweden, which would then force Russia to fight on two fronts. Prior to a series of successful campaigns carried out by Peter the Great (r. 1682-1725) during the Great Northern War fought between 1700 and 1721, Sweden had been the dominant power in the region, possessing at one time virtually the entire Baltic coastline. Losing much of this territory to Peter, successive Swedish monarchs harboured a desire to regain those lands, maintaining for the purpose a sizeable army and navy. It was at times when Russia was at war with the Ottomans that she became especially vulnerable to an onslaught from Sweden, even more so if part of Russia's Baltic Fleet was dispatched into the Mediterranean. While no threat from Sweden had existed at the time of Catherine's first war against the Ottomans, this was not so in 1788 when her second Ottoman war broke out. Again, she planned to send ships into the Mediterranean, calling upon her Admiralty to mobilise eighteen sail of the line for this purpose. It was a fleet that never arrived, as it was required to remain in the Baltic following Sweden's entry into an alliance with the Ottoman Empire.

For Catherine this proved fortuitous as, upon the outbreak of war with Sweden, Russia had a fleet in readiness while Sweden had no fully prepared fleet. Gustav III (r.1771-1792), the Swedish king, in fighting this war, wished first to capture St Petersburg by means of a combined land and sea attack. But this failed through the Swedish Fleet, being both much smaller than the Russian Fleet (see Table 1) and in only a partial state of readiness. Following a sea battle fought off Hogland on 17 July 1788, the Swedish

Fleet was forced to retire to Sveaborg, with Russia left in control of the Baltic. On 26 July of the following year, off Öland, a second battle was fought. Generally regarded as indecisive, it did have the outcome of forcing the Swedish Fleet to take refuge in Karlskrona, where it remained. Only in 1790, the final year of the war, did the Swedish Fleet, under the direct command of Gustav III, act more aggressively, mounting attacks upon Reval (Tallinn) and Kronstadt, but on both occasions successfully repelled by a stronger Russian force.

While the fleet Catherine had prepared for a further onslaught upon the Ottomans in the Mediterranean did not sail, the war also being fought simultaneously against the Ottomans did gain for Russia the fortress of Ochakov at the mouth of the Dnieper, which provided Russia with unrestricted access into the Black Sea. For William Pitt, Britain's prime minister, this was a point of concern, fearing that in having access to the Black Sea, Catherine was on the cusp of altering the entire balance of power in the East. If she further broke through into the Mediterranean, Russia would then become a direct threat to Britain's own position in that sea. His wish was that Catherine should abandon Ochakov and, to force the issue, he proposed sending into the Baltic a fleet of warships that would, if Catherine failed to agree, bombard the Russian Fleet bases of Riga and Kronstadt. In the end, this fleet did not sail. Pitt failed to convince Parliament of his own fears while the public in general showed little appetite for such a war. As to any future deterioration in the relationship between Russia and Great Britain, such was put on temporary hold by the cataclysmic events occurring in Paris that united the two in opposition to an outbreak of revolutionary fever.

# PART ONE

# Organisation, structure and readiness for war

On the outbreak of war with France in 1793, the Russian Empire covered 8 million square miles (2.7km$^2$) of land, with Catherine having added, or about to add, 200,000 square miles (518,000km$^2$). This was a truly vast territory stretching from the White Sea in the north, the Baltic to the west, the Black Sea to the south, and the North Pacific to the east. While creating great opportunities for imperial expansion by way of the sea, the vast distances between each of these maritime regions resulted in the need for Russia, for the purpose of defence and further territorial expansion, to ideally possess four separate and distinct maritime forces. However, this was beyond the financial capabilities of Russia, with it being impossible for each of these regions to expand their sea-going forces exponentially. Seen as having only limited value were the small number of ships operating in the White Sea and North Pacific and where the naval ports of Arkhangelsk and Okhotsk were located. Despite being ice-bound for much of the year, Arkhangelsk's proximity to a vast supply of timber did give it importance for the construction of ships, while Okhotsk gave support to colonies established in Alaska and the Aleutian Islands. Instead, money that might usefully have been directed to Okhotsk to develop trading links with other nations possessing a Pacific coastline, namely China and Japan, was used exclusively for maintaining and expanding a greater naval presence in the Baltic and Black Sea. In the Baltic, there was a constant fear that a resurgent Sweden might make a renewed attempt to reclaim lands lost in earlier decades, while the Ottomans clearly resented Catherine's Black Sea coastline acquisitions.

# CHAPTER 1

# PORTS, DOCKYARDS AND NAVAL BASES

Without naval bases and the industrial complexes that formed around them, it would be impossible for any navy to set sail. Apart from facilities required for building, fitting and refitting ships for sea, such complexes needed additional amenities for the provision of food, water and medical supplies. Ensuring the freshness of certain foods, naval bases of the eighteenth and nineteenth centuries often had within their working areas slaughterhouses, mills and bakeries. Accommodation for seamen was an additional requirement, particularly in the Russian Navy of the eighteenth century when those of the lower deck were expected to serve for life, although reduced by Paul to twenty-five years. During winter, when Riga, Reval (Tallinn) and Kronstadt, the three main naval ports of the Baltic Fleet, were ice-bound and the fleet unable to put to sea, crews were housed in barracks. To improve those facilities, alongside Catherine's ambitious plans for expanding the navy, she had to confront a massive financial shortfall, a problem not helped by bureaucratic inefficiency and corruption. This required her borrowing large sums, initially from Dutch bankers. Eventually, this became impossible, the interest rates too much of a burden. Instead, recourse was made to the printing of large amounts of paper money, the rouble-assignat, but this, by 1796, had lost two-thirds of its silver equivalent. The outcome was that some of Catherine's more ambitious schemes for the reconstruction and improvement of Russia's decaying naval bases, as well as her ship construction programme, had to be drastically curtailed. In addition to Riga, Reval and Kronstadt, other land-based naval facilities for use by the Russian Navy in northern waters existed at Rogerwick (Paldiski) on the Pakri Peninsula of modern-day Estonia, alongside Arkhangelsk on the White Sea and the Admiralty at St Petersburg. To the south, and upon Russia gaining entrance into the Black Sea, the fleet was supported by facilities at Kherson, Mykolaiv and Sevastopol. To the far east, on the Sea of Okhotsk, existed one further naval port, but considered at that time to be of limited value.

## Arkhangelsk

Under Peter I, due to Arkhangelsk at that time serving as Russia's only entry point into the oceans of the world, this previous commercial port became Russia's first naval base. Here, fourth and fifth rates, alongside frigates destined for the Baltic Fleet, were built in the Solombala shipyard located on an island at the mouth of the North Dvina. Ice-bound from October to May, for Arkhangelsk lies only 130 miles south of the Arctic Circle, Arkhangelsk also had the disadvantage of being surrounded by shallow waters. Not surprisingly, upon Peter's acquisition of a Baltic coastline, Arkhangelsk ceased to have any real value as an operational port, with Catherine basing there no more than four of her larger ships of war that were, when necessary, available to join the Baltic Fleet by first sailing into the North Sea.

## Kronstadt

Kronstadt, which lies in the Gulf of Finland on land taken from Sweden during the Great Northern War, was the primary naval base of the Baltic Fleet, serving also as a commercial port. Some 32 kilometres (20 miles) west of St Petersburg, the naval base stands at the mouth of the Neva on the eastern end of the island of Kotlin, an island 7.5 miles long (12.1km) by about 1 mile (1.6km) broad. Of sufficient size to accommodate the entire Baltic Fleet, Kronstadt had, in common with Arkhangelsk, the drawback of being icebound in winter, although for a shorter period. In addition, the approach to Kronstadt was hazardous due to a series of sandbanks and shoals that extended 1.5 miles (2.4km) towards Tolbaaken Rock, a further hazard. Prior to Catherine's accession, and despite its value to both commerce and the navy, Kronstadt had been much neglected, the channels leading into the port rarely dredged, its buildings, workshops and other facilities falling into an advanced state of decay. Sir Charles Knowles, a British admiral recruited by Catherine in 1770 as her intendant-general to provide advice on how to update and improve her navy, upon first coming to Kronstadt was horror-struck, describing the harbour, yard buildings and ships as all to be in a ruinous state and the dockyard bursting with rubbish accumulated over several decades. On the building slips were several vessels that should have been launched years before, but through work upon them having long ceased, their timbers were fungus-ridden and rotten. Following his appointment, Knowles immediately set about overhauling the yard, introducing a range of new facilities that included three dry docks, of which two were completed by the end of 1774. Knowles through age, he was over 70 by the time of arriving in Russia, remained in Catherine's service for just three years, with his position assumed by Samuel Greig, another former British naval officer. Greig was much admired by Catherine, having played a leading role in the naval battle fought at Çeşme. As well as overseeing the work begun by Knowles, Greig initiated a series of new projects that included enlarging the sea walls and constructing a naval prison and a quarantine hospital. Greig also brought about the construction of new accommodation for officers (small houses surrounded by gardens) and barracks for twelve corps of seamen. A particular feature of the barracks was that within the outer courtyard was a model of a fully rigged ship intended to assist in teaching new recruits the tricks of seamanship and allowing old timers to retain their dexterity during the winter period when ships were unable to put to sea. As for the commercial port, Greig adapted it more advantageously to the needs of commerce, deepening the harbour and completely separating it from the naval port. Unfortunately, the war with Sweden that broke out in 1787 brought a sudden end to these ongoing improvements, with Greig placed in charge of the fleet that engaged the Swedish Navy at Hogland. He may well have returned to Kronstadt had he survived the war, but he succumbed to a fatal illness in October 1788. Consequently, and with Russia having fallen into even higher levels of debt, Catherine reduced overall expenditure on Kronstadt so that by the time of the wars with France, the naval base had once again fallen into disrepair. A situation that was to continue for several years.

## The Admiralty

Lying within the city of St Petersburg, opposite the Peter and Paul Fortress, alongside the Neva and close to the Winter Palace, the Admiralty was the navy's showpiece yard. With a river frontage of around 250m and a depth of 130m, it was not substantial in size, referred to by Charles Lord Whitworth, Britain's envoy-extraordinary to Russia during the reign of Peter I, as a 'little yard' where 'all sorts of boats and small craft are built'. The city, fortress and Admiralty were all founded by Peter the Great on land taken from Sweden, as with Kronstadt. Modelled on the British naval yard of Chatham, which Peter visited in 1698, Daniel Defoe, writing during the early seventeenth century, described the Admiralty as being 'fitted with wet and dry docks, storehouses and magazines of naval preparations, vast and incredible'. Less of a naval base, the Admiralty was primarily a building yard, it being difficult for ships, other than smaller vessels, to navigate the shallows of the Neva unless completely stripped of their internal furnishings to reduce their overall draft. To transfer to Kronstadt, a typical third rate once launched at the Admiralty required the aid of a lifting machine known as a camel, which fully embraced the ship to give it sufficient lift to pass over the shallows. For the use of camels, a more detailed explanation is given on page 164.

## Riga and Tallinn

The cities of Riga and Tallinn were once part of the Hanseatic League. Later, both fell under Swedish control. It was during the Great Northern War that Riga and Tallinn were acquired by Russia, with Riga most cherished as a commercial port and Tallinn as a naval port. In this respect, Tallinn's greatest value was through being to the west and further into the Baltic than St Petersburg and, as such, free of ice for two or three months longer than the Gulf of Finland, where Kronstadt lay and into which the Neva flowed. It had a vast and safe harbour where, under Catherine, it was customary for ten ships of the Baltic Fleet to be stationed, with some also at Riga. While the latter possessed naval barracks, a naval hospital and storehouses for the fleet, Tallinn was better positioned through being closer to the primary fleet base at Kronstadt. In May 1792, Catherine gave her approval for a major expansion of the naval facilities at Tallinn, with this work having only just begun upon the outbreak of war with France and that included barracks for the accommodation of 6,000 seamen.

## Paldiski

The Pakri Peninsula, including Paldiski, was further territory acquired by Peter I during the Great Northern War, with construction of a naval port at Paldiski beginning in 1716. At that time Paldiski was seen as a potential main fleet base as, unlike the other ports available to the Baltic Fleet, it was mainly ice-free during winter. Central to a scheme adopted by Peter was construction of a breakwater between Paldiski and the off-shore island of Välke-Pakri, which was designed to create an area of protected water sufficient to accommodate the entire fleet, with the mainland and Välke-Pakri heavily fortified. On the death of Peter, the entire project was put on hold, although Catherine II did attempt its completion, but was unable to provide sufficient funding.

## Okhotsk

Okhotsk, which lies in the Russian Far East alongside the Sea of Okhotsk, was the home base of the Okhotsk military flotilla, a small, heavily underfunded naval unit. Its responsibility was that of protecting Russia's interest in the Far East and Pacific, a factor that took on increased importance upon France and Britain undertaking explorative expeditions into the North Pacific. From Okhotsk, Vitus Bering had set out in the 1720s to discover whether America and Asia were joined by land. By Catherine II's time, the North Pacific had effectively become a Russian lake with colonies established on the Kamchatka Peninsula, Aleutian Islands, Alaska and eventually further to the south in British Columbia and the Californian seaboard. During the French wars, Okhotsk played no part in the fighting, but might have taken on value if France or Great Britain, through entry into the Pacific, had begun to threaten those established Russian colonies.

## Kherson and Mykolaiv

Following the founding of the city of Kherson by Catherine in 1778, a shipbuilding yard at the mouth of the Dnipro was established, alongside a trading port and fortress. Prior to the relocation of the Black Sea Fleet to Sevastopol a few years later, Kherson served as the base of the Black Sea Fleet. While overshadowed by Sevastopol, the dockyard continued to build ships, with its facilities greatly expanded under Catherine. At Mykolaiv (Nikolaev), on the banks of the Ingol River, 89 miles inland from the Black Sea, a further building yard was established in 1789 but eventually superseded by Kherson as the main construction yard for ships joining the Black Sea Fleet.

## Sevastopol

Aktiar, renamed Sevastopol by Catherine in 1784, lies on the south-western tip of the Crimean Peninsula and was, and remains, Russia's primary base for the stationing of the Black Sea Fleet, the bay well protected from the elements and providing a depth of water suitable for mooring the navy's largest warships. Prince Grigoriev Potemkin, Catherine's one-time favourite and lover and who, as governor general, ruled southern Russia on Catherine's behalf, considered Sevastopol as 'the best harbour in the world'. A survey carried out in November 1782 by Captain First Rank I.M. Odintsov showed Sevastopol and its inlets to be suitable 'for fifty warships and other vessels'. In March of the following year, a second and more detailed survey indicated Sevastopol to possess:

> *Four bays protected from winds by the mountains, and a fifth, a roadstead stretching in length to seven versts (4.64 miles) and in width to one and a half versts [0.99 miles] with a depth of ten fathoms [60 feet] with a silty bed.*

Despite Potemkin's declaration of Sevastopol as 'the best harbour in the world', to which Francisco de Miranda, the future liberator of Venezuela, while accompanying Catherine on a tour of the Ukraine, gave equal praise, assessing it as a harbour that could safely hold 100 vessels, it was not without problems. Those building the yard and later assigned to its ships would find themselves ravaged by disease and plague, at that time endemic to the region. As for the ships entering the harbour, their timbers would be attacked by a boring mollusc, *teredo navalis* (ship worm), that would slowly reduce them to an unseaworthy state. It was a problem previously little encountered by the Russian Navy, ship worm at that time not present in the Sea of Azov or the eastern Baltic due to these waters having lower levels of salinity.

As a naval base, Sevastopol was for Russia of inestimable strategic importance, the key to Catherine retaining possession of her new territories bordering the Black Sea and a springboard for taking further Ottoman territory. John Paul Jones, a man best known to the world as 'the founder of the American Navy', and who gave his services as a naval commander to Russia during Catherine's second Ottoman War, was one who underlined the importance of Sevastopol, but considered that further bases must be established for the purpose of turning the Black Sea into a Russian lake:

> *I have always believed that Russia requires a port on the Asiatic side, opposite the Crimea, to protect the fleet from flaws of wind and currents, and to be, as it were, a sentinel post on the Turks. I have thought of Sinope for this purpose, and I spoke of it to the empress and Prince Potemkin; but, being better informed, I found a more suitable situation, where I am certain such a post could be securely established at small cost, and beard the whole Ottoman Empire. This place is a peninsula between Sinope and Constantinople [Istanbul].*

Appointed to oversee the naval facilities under construction at Sevastapol was Rear Admiral Thomas Mackenzie. He arrived at Sevastapol in May 1783, initially giving attention to laying out the moorings in the roadstead and the construction of a careening wharf. This latter was situated in one of the inlets for the purpose of allowing a ship to be heaved over for the cleaning of the underwater hull with the inlet gaining the name Keel Bay. In both this and other construction work on the new naval base, Mackenzie was assisted by Nickolay Ivanovich Korsakov, a Russian engineer who was particularly well-regarded by Potemkin for work already undertaken elsewhere in southern Russia.

By August 1783, Sevastapol had seen completion of a timber dry dock, apparently built in little more than a month, together with a house for the admiral, a smithery for the making of anchors, and a landing pier. To this, MacKenzie was writing in November of that year of:

> *Houses, headquarters, officers' accommodation, sailors' barracks, local materials and provision stores all close to completion.*

While the naval base was fully completed by 1791, and the Black Sea Fleet by then fully at home in the harbour, MacKenzie himself had succumbed to a bout of ill-health, possibly malaria, that had brought an end to his life four years earlier. To complete the work, MacKenzie was succeeded by Rear Admiral Fyodor Fyodorovich Ushakov and later by Rear Admiral Dmitry Senyavin, both to play significant roles in the wars fought against France.

## Sveaborg

Captured from Sweden in May 1808, the heavily fortified Sveaborg (Suomenlinna) group of islands that are located south-east of Helsinki provided a further base capable of use by the Baltic Fleet, its capture giving Russia total dominance over the eastern Baltic. Here, within the fortified area that had been built for the defence of Helsinki, was a naval base that included two dry docks, one of which was designed to hold four ships of the line, together with mast houses, a masting crane, ropery and stores.

# CHAPTER 2

# FLEETS, SQUADRONS AND SHIPS

At the outset of her reign, Catherine inherited a fleet of thirty-two ships of the line and no more than ten frigates, but with many of these in such a poor state of repair, within two years of her accession seventeen, mainly those of fifty guns or more, had to be broken up. Given her desire to rebuild the Russian Navy, and to a much higher standard, she soon authorised a substantial shipbuilding programme. By 1793, and the outbreak of war with France, a total of 118 ships of the line and fifty-eight frigates had either been built or were under construction. Of this number, forty per cent were no longer available to Catherine's navy, either condemned through age or lost at sea. In addition, during this same period Catherine acquired six ships of the line and two frigates, these captured during the war against Sweden. The building programme brought about by Catherine was one that greatly exceeded the number of ships built by any previous ruler, including Peter the Great. Under Peter, during the latter twenty-two years of his reign, when the building of a 'blue water' navy had become one of his major concerns, the number of launchings per year averaged 2.93 ships of the line and 1.7 frigates. Catherine, by comparison, between the beginning of her reign and the war with France, was launching an average of nearly four ships of the line each year and near on two frigates. Nevertheless, while this rate of construction appears impressive, and certainly exceeded that of France, it was completely overshadowed by Britain, undeniably the world's largest navy, launching during the same time an average of 5.4 ships of the line and 3.1 frigates. Even had she been desirous of doing so, Catherine in no way could have overseen the launching of a similar number of ships. In terms of financial outlay alone, such a programme would have crippled the Russian economy.

Apart from finance there were other factors working against a more substantial increase in the size of Catherine's navy, factors that greatly increased the cost of building and maintaining ships in Russia. Corruption was endemic. Money set aside for the building and maintenance of ships was frequently embezzled by officials. And stores purchased were stolen from within the yards by the workforce. At sea, one such example was that ships built at the Solombala yard in Arkhangelsk, in being brought round to the Baltic, would every so often 'lose' their main anchor weighing a ton in a non-existent storm, but sold by the officers to Dutch merchants. Potemkin, in May 1783, drew attention to one senior official, Ivan Gannibal, commander of naval artillery and a member of the Admiralty Collegiate, complaining:

*Everything is neglected. There is no proper record of anything...none of those who were supposed to be watching were in their place...Everyone was removed and everything was in the hands of Gannibal's secretary... whom [Gannibal upon his retirement] took away with him, leaving neither the forest nor the money here.*

Materials needed for the construction of ships, when brought into the yards, was often improperly stored, and through early rotting was soon unfit for the purpose. Referring to Kherson shipyard, Alexander Semyonovich Katasanov, director of the School of Naval Architecture in St Petersburg, wrote:

*Oak and pine, timber for ships and different types of boards, all without exception, are located in an open area, where they are damaged by rot and cracks from rain, moisture, and extreme heat.*

As for ships already built, once launched they received little maintenance, and rotting timbers and other blemishes were often ignored or covered over with paint. In 1824, but with his observations equally pertinent to the earlier wartime period, the intendant of the Baltic Fleet, Vice Admiral Vasily Golovin, observed:

*Our ships, placed in order and deceptively painted on the outside, contain puddles of rainwater, heaps of dirt, thick layers of mould and infectious air inside, filling their entire holds. New and old ships stand in the harbour for a year or two without caulking, from which their grooves fill with water during the rains, which, freezing in the winter, tears them apart even more, and melts in the spring, and imparts a hole and rottenness to all parts of the ship.*

A Russian Admiralty estimate carried out in 1802 indicated that the thirty-five ships and fifty-one smaller sailing vessels built at St Petersburg during the previous forty years had cost 4.36m roubles. But in Britain, for a similar shipbuilding programme, the cost would have been less by 1.06m roubles. And this despite wages being comparatively higher in England. It was also added that Russian ships when compared with their British counterparts were of mediocre reliability and durability and, consequently, needed frequent repairs or replacements.

A further factor that hindered a more expansive shipbuilding programme was the availability of slipways on which warships could be built. For the construction of ships for the Baltic Fleet, the three naval yards of Kronstadt, St Petersburg and Arkhangelsk possessed between them no more than ten slipways, whereas Great Britain, in her six naval yards (Portsmouth, Sheerness, Chatham, Deptford, Woolwich and Plymouth), could boast twice as many. During the later years of Catherine's reign more facilities became available, these for the rapid creation of a Black Sea Fleet. But even here the availability of slipways was limited. Adding to the actual gap in shipbuilding facilities between Russia and Britain was that of Britain making considerable use of commercial shipyards where ships were built under contract. Russia had no commercial yards capable of building large warships.

Of those three yards, Kronstadt, with three building slips, was used for the construction of first rates. This was less by choice than of necessity, as both the Admiralty and the Solombala yard at Arkhangelsk were constrained by difficulties of transferring larger ships, once launched, to the Baltic. The necessity of using camels to lift ships being transferred from St Petersburg to Kronstadt along the Neva has already been mentioned, but camels had also to be used for third rates at Arkhangelsk. The harbour here, through being shallow with a sandbar at its entrance, was a hazard to larger ships unless lifted to reduce their draught. Once free of the harbour, ships from Arkhangelsk destined for the Baltic underwent a two-month voyage, having to round the Scandinavian peninsula before sailing the length of the Baltic. As for the small number of ships that were built at the Solombala yard for permanent stationing at Arkhangelsk, no more than four at any one time, these were given flattened hulls to ensure they could more easily navigate the shallower waters around Arkhangelsk, but in consequence had poor sea-keeping qualities

Geographical location and climate were further problems that especially beset the Admiralty, Solombala and Kronstadt naval yards. Harsh winter conditions and long nights impacted upon the overall progress of work, although the long daylight hours of summer provided partial mitigation. The distance of Kronstadt and the Admiralty from the centre of the Russian Empire, and from where shipbuilding materials were frequently brought, meant that the supply of timber for ships under construction came at great cost, with oak from approximately 6,000 trees required for completion of a third rate and even more for a first rate. Oak timber, which only thrives in temperate zones, of which St Petersburg lay to the extreme north-west, was usually sourced from Crown lands on the right bank of the Volga in the forests of Kazan. It was then floated along the length of various connecting rivers, taking around two years to reach those yards. It was a process that affected the value of these timbers, gaining moisture that was rarely given sufficient time to season before being used in the construction of ships. Those harsh winters created one further problem. Ships under construction suffered deterioration of their timbers while standing in frame on the building slips. As for ships launched into the Neva from the Admiralty, through this being a freshwater river, and to prevent further deterioration, they had to be immediately transferred to Kronstadt, as remaining too long in fresh water led to their hulls decaying sooner than in salt water.

Of course, the question might be asked as to why all ships for the Baltic Fleet were not built at Kronstadt, so offsetting the difficulty of transporting them to that yard, with Arkhangelsk constructing only ships needed for the White Sea. Primarily, this relates to the vulnerability of Kronstadt to enemy attack. Lying as it does at the mouth of the Neva, it would not have been impossible for an enemy to mount a successful attack on its facilities, which the Swedish king Gustav III had attempted in 1790, and Britain's Horatio Nelson, following the bombardment of Copenhagen in 1801, had planned (see Chapter 10). Thus, the Admiralty at St Petersburg, safely positioned 6km from the open sea of Neva Bay, and Arkhangelsk positioned close to the Arctic, were deemed far more secure. In addition, Arkhangelsk did have the advantage of being the nearest of the Russian yards to the Ural Mountains, where abundant supplies of iron ore were located and used in the production of anchors and other items. Arkhangelsk was also near forests that could supply timbers, such as fir and larch, used in the construction of ships, although the closest larch forests were gradually being exhausted through over-use, fire and waste.

In effectively building her navy from the ground up, Catherine had not only to undertake the rebuilding of her naval yards but to ensure she had a sufficient corps of artisans to undertake her ship construction programme. In this she was helped by inheriting three outstanding English ship constructors who had already been recruited: the brothers Alexander and James Sutherland, and John Lambert Yeames. One significant design of first rates that Yeames provided for Catherine was the 'Ches'ma' class, named after the successful battle fought against the Ottomans. Closely resembling the 100-gun *Victory* launched at Chatham in 1765, *Ches'ma* was launched at the Admiralty yard in 1783. Catherine herself was successful in recruiting one further shipwright from England, John Coleman, who came to Russia in 1784. Coleman oversaw construction of several ships of the line including four of the 'Ches'ma' class. Of Russia's own ship constructors, I.V. James at Arkhangelsk oversaw the building of nine sixty-six-gun third rates and three frigates before transferring to the Admiralty yard, where he began work on constructing first and third rates, including the 100-gun *Trekh Ierarkhov*, the second of three 'Ches'ma' class ships to be launched at that yard. At Arkhangelsk, and replacing James upon his transfer to St Petersburg, was M.D. Portnov. He remained there for twenty years, constructing a total of twenty-three sixty-six-gun ships. Also at Arkhangelsk, Portnov oversaw construction of fourteen seventy-four-gun third rates and two forty-four-gun ships. At the Admiralty, and working alongside James, upon his transfer there were two further Russian shipwrights, V.A. Selyaninov and G. Ivanov, both of whom played a significant role in constructing first rate ships of the 'Ches'ma' class. Other native Russian shipwrights responsible for ship constructions were G. Maltsev and V. Gunion, both employed at Arkhangelsk.

Assisting Russian constructors in the learning of their trade was that of the most promising students spending time in England working under the supervision of master shipwrights in one of the naval yards. Danila Masal'skiy, in returning to Russia in 1779, brought with him the dimensions of *Victory*, allowing Yeames and James to draw up plans for *Ches'ma* and the ships that immediately followed. A few years later, another Russian shipwright, Vasili Vaslov, while working at Portsmouth, obtained a complete copy of *Victory*'s design drawings, allowing the final four ships of the 'Ches'ma' class to adhere even more closely to the design layout of *Victory*.

Another technical innovation acquired from Russian shipwrights undergoing training in England was the technique of sheathing ships' hulls with thin copper plates. This had the advantage of increasing the service life of a ship through giving it protection from rot and molluscs (ship worm) that ate into the timber. A further advantage was that it helped keep the underside of a ship free from weeds and other accumulations, allowing ships that were coppered to sail much better. It is generally accepted that the innovation of coppering, at a time when this technology was generally unknown outside of Britain, was directly responsible for a victory gained by Admiral Rodney in 1780. While patrolling off Cape St Vincent, his copper-bottomed ships easily overhauled a squadron of Spanish ships with hulls that had not been so treated. While France and Spain might not have possessed the technology at that time, Russia under Catherine was aware of its use and would soon gain full knowledge of how the copper sheets were applied using copper zinc-bolts.

In early 1780, orders from the Admiralty Collegiate had been sent to Kutygin, one of the Russian apprentices in England, to learn what he could of the technique and to acquire some sheets of copper to be sent to St Petersburg for testing. Following the arrival of those sheets a second shipwright apprentice, Danila Masalovsky, was instructed while in the dockyard at Portsmouth to master the skills of copper hull sheathing, sending back to St Petersburg in August an extensive report describing the technology in detail. Suitably impressed as to the value of coppering, Catherine, in consultation with the Admiralty Collegiate, issued on 3 November a decree introducing copper sheathing in the Russian Fleet. To provide an uninterrupted supply of copper, new mines were opened and a factory to produce copper plates was established in the dockyard at Kronstadt. However, none of this could be done overnight, the necessary workings taking time, and consequently too late for the provision of sheathing for ships that in 1795 were sent into the North Sea to work alongside a British squadron under Admiral Duncan. Instead, those ships were coppered in England at the Chatham yard when taken into dry dock for the cleaning of their hulls.

In general, Russian ships, having limited repair facilities and a general shortage of shipwrights, resulted in many vessels having a much shorter service life than might otherwise have been. For the Black Sea Fleet this was a major problem. Here it had become necessary to rapidly build ships to ensure that in the event of a new war with the Ottoman Empire this new area of territorial expansion could be effectively defended. Construction, not just of ships but a supporting land-based infrastructure, had to be undertaken at breakneck speed. Overseeing this work was Potemkin, and the speed in which the new fleet was created was truly impressive and revealed to Catherine during a triumphal procession of the Crimea in 1787. From Potemkin's palace that overlooked Sevastopol, she was initially denied a view of the harbour as the windows facing the bay were deliberately obscured by curtains. On Potemkin's command, as if on stage at the theatre, the curtains were drawn back to reveal 'a numerous and formidable fleet' which, according to Joseph II, the Holy Roman Emperor, one of many dignitaries present on the occasion, consisted of 'at least twenty ships of the line and frigates all aligned in battle order facing the very place where the monarchs dined.'

In witnessing these ships, it was impossible not to be impressed. Francisco de Miranda, the future leader of an independent movement in South America and friend of Potemkin, considered that neither the timber nor the design of the ships could be bettered. In his view, they were superior to any built in Spain or France, constructed 'in the English manner'. Lady Craven, a later visitor to Sevastopol, was another admirer of the new fleet, her reasoning though was less than scientific, basing her view on the fact that at the head of the fleet was Vice Admiral Count Nikolay Semyonovich Mordvinov, an anglophile who had served four years in the British Navy and 'much more like an Englishman than any foreigner' she 'had ever met'. The Holy Roman Emperor, while impressed with the rapidity in which the fleet had been constructed, took a more objective approach, describing the ships as built of green timber, adding that they were worm-eaten.

Of those various witnesses to the new fleet, it was Joseph II who came closest to the truth. In so rapidly constructing the fleet, too many corners had been cut, primarily through using unseasoned timbers and an inadequate number of shipwrights. Furthermore, it was a problem that was to persist for at least another decade. At Kherson in May 1790, the first ship laid down at that yard, the sixty-gun frigate *Sviataia Ekaterina*, was never launched. Instead, and through the use of unseasoned timber, dry rot set in, resulting in her having to be broken up while still on the slipway. Making matters worse was that the building slip had also been built using the same unseasoned timbers, and also had to be entirely rebuilt.

More successful in the sense that they were launched and subsequently served at sea were eight sixty-six-gun 'Aziia' class frigates built during Catherine's sovereignty. Setting aside two of those ships built at Kherson, one wrecked at sea and the other captured by the Ottomans after she ran aground, the average service life of the remaining ships between launch and final disposal was just over twelve years, as compared with the fifteen years of Aziia class frigates built at Arkhangelsk during the same period. Ushakov, the admiral who succeeded MacKenzie at Sevastopol, provides further evidence of the poor quality of ships built at Kherson, based on his experience of commanding those same ships at sea during an expedition into the Adriatic (see Chapter 4). In a letter dated August 1798 written to Rear Admiral Paul I.G.G. Kushelev, major general in the navy, Ushakov submitted the following information:

> *The ships and frigates in the last war [Catherine's second Ottoman war] were built with great haste, just so that they would be ready for action, and because of the hasty construction, they are not so strong and are somewhat weaker, and sometimes many rotten parts are already showing.*

In another letter, this one dated March 1799, Ushakov wrote:

> *Of the squadron entrusted to me, half of the ships and most of the frigates have a great leak; from some ships, especially the Epiphany, the Trinity and some frigates, the upper planking falls off; the planks sometimes float out from under them to the top; this is because they are badly sheathed*

> *and fastened with thin nails. The nails are so corroded and decayed that only one remains in them, and when they split a board to take it out, all the nails crumble...The grooves and joints from under the upper planking are open and because of this the ships and frigates have a great leak, the ships Bogoiavlenie Navarkhiia Voznesenie Gospodne, Troitsa [Sviataia Troitsa], Magdalena [Maria Magdelana], St Peter [Sviatoi Pyotr], require immediate correction by keeling.*

It was on 6 January 1790 that the first ship, the fifty-two-gun *Sviatoi Mikhail*, was laid down at Nikolaev. She was another ship that would end her days prematurely through having been built with unseasoned timbers, sold out of service for this reason just twelve years later. Upon the launch of *Sviatoi Mikhail* at the end of October, the same building slip three weeks later saw the laying down of *Legkii*, a small lightweight frigate of twenty-six guns. But due to a shortage of available timbers, it took twenty-five months before she could be launched. Again, *Legkii* was a ship with a short lifespan, serving a mere nine years before ordered in 1804 to be broken up.

For the building of this new fleet, shipwrights undertaking the work were initially drawn from yards already existing in the south, Krichev and Novopavlovsk. Apart from their numbers being inadequate for the quantity of ships required, their experience was limited to the construction of river craft used for the conveyancing of materials along Russia's vast network of waterways. Sometimes they had also been called upon to build armed galleys and other rowing vessels, but at no time had they gained the experience of building ships of the size that were required for service on the Black Sea. To assist, more than 200 shipwrights were relocated to the southern yards from Kronstadt and the Admiralty. However, the marshy grounds surrounding the new yards combined with inadequate sanitation within the newly built townships took their toll on these new arrivals, with large numbers of shipwrights and yard labourers succumbing to plague and other diseases, forcing ever more less skilled workers to replace them. Only upon the later expansion of the new city and the introduction of better sanitary arrangements did the life expectancy of a naval shipwright in the south begin to increase.

# CHAPTER 3

# ORDNANCE

Russian warships, in common with other European navies, were equipped with iron muzzle loading cannons, although bronze ordnance did equip some Russian war ships. For Russia, there was no shortage of iron, the mineral-rich Ural Mountains providing vast quantities that made Russia the world's largest exporter of iron ore. During the late eighteenth century, Britain was one country heavily dependent on Russia for the supply of iron, importing between 1790 and 1801 iron bars to an annual value of around £200,000, which represented around half of Britain's iron imports. The other major supplier was Sweden. Nevertheless, despite the availability of iron ore in Russia, ordnance manufactured during the early years of Catherine's sovereignty was of poor quality, with many recorded incidents of serious injury to gun crews by barrels bursting at the vent. It was a problem of which Catherine became aware, informed in 1772 that of 100 cannons presented by Russian founders, only ten met the necessary quality.

Apart from poor quality ordnance, a further problem arose from warships armed with a mixture of guns on any single deck that in battle created confusion. Mixed ordnance on a ship's gun deck had once been a universal practice, but in France, Sweden and Britain, this had been phased out by the end of the seventeenth century. Other than Russia, the Ottoman Navy still adhered to the practice, a result of their guns, apart from those manufactured in Türkiye, being reused ordnance captured in battle or the purchase of what was available from other countries. Guillaume-Antoine Olivier, a French entomologist who journeyed into the Ottoman Empire between 1792 and 1798, in a description he gave of one unnamed Ottoman warship of the mid-1790s, highlighted the resulting problem. It can be imagined that the same would occur on Russian warships:

> *The guns were of a different calibre, and they were served without order or preparation: the shot brought for loading the cannon were frequently either too large or too small, which did not allow a ship of the greatest force to defend itself against a single frigate.*

In theory, the mixing of ordnance during Catherine's sovereignty should never have occurred. Just two years after she became empress, a set of naval regulations was issued, emphasising conformity of ordnance on gun decks. But these regulations generally went unheeded. In part, this resulted from a general shortage of guns of the regulated sizes, but further complicated by the issuing of a range of non-regulated guns. In 1767, only 36-, 18-, 8- and 6-pounder long guns were specified, However, by the beginning of the French wars, ships were being issued with howitzers, carronades, light 3-pounders (known as falconets) as well as 30- and 12-pounder long guns.

While predominantly of iron, the equipping of some ships with bronze cannons also set Russia apart from other major European powers. The reason was that bronze cannons, which could be highly ornamented and polished, added stature to certain selected ships. Those carrying an admiral's flag. It is worth adding that bronze was also better for ordnance manufacture, but being more expensive to manufacture had fallen out of favour with most nations. Amongst all else, bronze cannons were lighter with greater residual strength. This lightness in weight permitted ships armed with bronze cannons to fire a heavier weight of shot than those armed with iron ordnance. Also, bronze cannons had a much longer service life. One example of a bronze cannon held by the Royal Armouries in England was still in use 250 years after its date of manufacture in 1601.

The long gun, so named to distinguish it from other types of naval ordnance, varied in length from around 3m (9.84ft) for 36- and 24-pounders to 2.5m (8.2ft) for an 18-pounder. While a typical iron manufactured 36-pounder had a weight of around 3,250kg, smaller 18-pounders weighed just over 2,000kg. When firing solid iron shot, and it was the weight of the shot that was used to indicate the size of these guns, the object was to pulverise and damage the hull and decks of an enemy ship. In addition, long guns could be loaded with bar and chain shot (shot connected by chain or a solid bar for destroying the rigging of an enemy ship) and grape shot (canvas cartridges filled with small balls) designed to incapacitate or kill enemy personnel.

The range of a long gun varied according to the amount of gunpowder used to propel the shot and the resulting velocity of that shot, but generally had a range of between 450m (14,76ft) to 1,000m (3,281ft). If manned by an effective and well-trained crew, the rate of fire was at least two shots per minute, although crews operating smaller guns

**Naval ordnance regulations, 1767.**

| **Rating of ships** | **Ordnance calibre** | | | |
|---|---|---|---|---|
| | **Lower deck** | **Middle deck** | **Upper deck** | **Forecastle and quarterdeck** |
| First rate of 100 guns | 36 | 18 | 8 (12 if bronze) | 6 |
| Third rate of 80 guns | 30 | 18 | 8 | 6 |
| New ships of 66 guns | 30 | | 12 | 6 |
| Older ships of 66 guns | 24 | | 12 | 6 |
| Frigates of 32 guns | | | 16 | 6 |
| Prams of 36 guns | | | 36 | 18 |

could double this rate of fire. However, accuracy was a problem caused by windage, or the difference between the diameter of a shot and the diameter of the bore. With neither being precision made, excess windage caused the ball to bound along the barrel and leave the muzzle in an unpredictable direction, with any real degree of accuracy only possible at close range. Here, bronze cannons had a further advantage over those of iron. Being easier to cast to tight tolerances decreased barrel windage and gave bronze cannons greater accuracy.

The howitzer was a gun almost unique to the Russian Navy, for no other navy of the period had chosen to introduce howitzers as standard. Unlike long guns, which fired directly at a target, a howitzer was fired at a high upward angle, allowing projectiles to fall into the interior of an enemy ship rather than firing into the enemy ship's hull or shredding its sails. Developed in Russia, the howitzer was called a 'unicorn' (*yedinorog* in Russan), a name derived from each gun bearing on the flat end of the breech a unicorn in relief, and the handles of the gun also cast in the shape of a unicorn. As used at sea, a unicorn had the ability to not only fire solid and grape shot, but also explosive cast iron shells that could be filled with gunpowder or incendiary materials. First introduced into the Russian Navy during the Seven Years War, it was at that time considered possible that unicorns could replace all other shipboard ordnance. Unicorns also had the advantage of greater accuracy and range, the result of a conical-shaped powder breech that allowed for better seating of the ball in the bore and which reduced windage. If used effectively, the plunging fire of a unicorn shot or shell containing explosive material could quickly spread fire along a wooden deck and onto the rigging and sails, so bringing total destruction to an enemy warship. That unicorns were not commonly used in other navies resulted from these guns generally viewed as unreliable and unsafe, a fragile gun that was sometimes more dangerous to those using it than to the enemy.

Rated in poods, a Russian unit of weight equal to about 36 pounds, both one pood and half pood unicorns were used on board Russian warships, positioned in batteries amidship. One pood unicorns would normally be positioned on a gun deck primarily armed with 36-pounders and a half pood battery on a gun deck of 24-pounders. While it was most common for ships to have batteries of only one or two unicorns, some ships, especially those operating in the Black Sea, were given a much larger number, ninety-gun second rates and the forty-six-gun frigate *Kazanskaya Bogoroditsa* carrying twelve, while the fifty-gun frigate *Grigorii Velikiia Armenii* had as many as eighteen.

Carronades – powerful, short range, smoothbore, cast-iron cannons – were used by the Russian Navy from the late 1780s onwards. Half the weight of an equivalent long gun, they could throw solid iron balls of up to 68lb (21.7kg) to an effective distance of 500m. In close combat they were lethal but completely outranged by the standard long guns of the period, with ships normally carrying only a small number of carronades for use in the final stages of a sea fight. Invented in Britain by Lieutenant General Robert Melville (1723–1809), and sometimes known as 'the smasher', it became better known as the carronade through being produced by the Carron Iron Works of Falkirk in Scotland. Manufactured in 68-, 42-, 32-, 24-, 18-, 12- and 6-pounder calibres, its

**Naval ordnance regulations, 1805.**

| | Long guns | | | | Carronades | | | | | Falconets | Unicorns |
|---|---|---|---|---|---|---|---|---|---|---|---|
| | **36-pdr** | **24-pdr** | **28-pdr** | **8-pdr** | **6- or 24-pdr** | **24-pdr** | **18-pdr** | **12-pdr** | **8-pdr** | **3-pdr** | **1 pood (36-pdr) or ½ pood (18-pdrs)** |
| 100-gun ships | 30 | 32 | 32 | | 20 | 4 | | | 6 | 6 | 6 |
| 74-gun ships | 28 | 30 | | 18 | | | | | | 6 | 3 |
| 64-gun ships | 26 | 28 | | | 14 | | | | | 6 | 3 |
| 44-gun frigates | | 28 | | | 16 | | | | | 2 | 2 |
| 36-gun frigates | | 26 | | | 10 | | | | | 2 | 2 |
| 24-gun frigates | | 18 | | | 6 | | | | | 2 | 2 |

mounting for shipboard use was on a traversing sliding carriage and, because of their relative lightness, were usually mounted on the upper decks, where heavy long guns would otherwise make a ship top-heavy. The one and not inconsiderable disadvantage of carronades was that while throwing a heavy shot the range was reduced, allowing an enemy armed with long guns to stay out of range of a carronade-armed ship. How Russia came into possession of carronades, guns that came to be manufactured in Russia, resulted from a series of careful manoeuvres that spun off an existing connection with the Carron company prior to the company having begun the manufacture of carronades.

This connection with the Carron company first arose during the 1770s when Russia was looking for a supply of ordnance to replace the poor quality guns that were at that time produced in Russia. Both Sweden and the Ottoman Empire, Russia's main opponents at sea, had ordnance of greater reliability, the Swedes through using superior quality iron and the Ottomans by the continuing use of bronze. Having already recruited the British admiral Sir Charles Knowles into her service, Catherine in 1772 informed him that 'for the past two years' she had been making every effort to acquire a skilled cannon founder but without success. In response, Knowles arranged for the purchase of 396 12-pounder guns from the Carron Iron Works, intending also with this large-scale purchase of single calibre guns to curtail the use of gun decks carrying a mixture of ordnance. Gaining permission from the British government to export these guns, the Carron company supplied an initial batch of forty-five. These arrived in June 1772 with the full contract completed by the end of 1773. Although the 12-pounders as ordered were of lighter weight than those customarily used to equip large warships, Knowles considered that as Russian-built ships were bulky, the lighter guns would assist their sailing qualities.

Unfortunately, the choice of Carron was to prove problematic, the guns supplied being of poor quality, with the British Navy having to remove similar Carron-supplied guns from all their warships. Knowles was almost certainly unaware of this emerging problem but soon discovered the deficiency of Carron-manufactured ordnance when a goodly proportion of those exported to Russia failed under examination or test firing. This could well have been the end of the Carron Iron Works as a manufacturer of ordnance had it not been for the employment of Charles Gascoigne as the company's resident manager. Following his appointment, Gascoigne set about rectifying the problem caused by the company's too sudden entrance into the manufacturing of ordnance. Upon the advice of John Smeaton, a leading civil engineer, Gascoigne oversaw the introduction of a new process of manufacture, introducing an assay furnace to bring about a reduction in carbon and other impurities that were being absorbed during the smelting process. Solid casting followed by the drilling of the bore was also introduced, replacing the earlier method of casting guns around a wooden core.

The realisation of the dramatic improvements brought to the Carron works by Gascoigne ensured that Russia did not lose faith with the company, making further purchases of Carron-manufactured ordnance in 1785. Influential in ensuring the continued connection of the Russian Navy with the Carron company was Samuel Greig. Having strong family connections in Scotland, Greig was aware of improvements in the ordnance manufactured by Carron, conceiving the idea of bringing Gascoigne to Russia to 'establish an artillery foundry' producing ordnance to the same standards as had now been achieved by Carron.

To Simon Romanovich Vorontsov, the Russian ambassador in London, Greig wrote that Catherine was fully supportive of the idea and would provide Gascoigne with suitable financial incentive that included a promised annual payment of £2,500 and a share of the profits once he was established in Russia. It was Semyon Vorontsov who was now instructed to surreptitiously set about contacting Gascoigne, and for this he used two intermediaries, Count Stepanov and a Mr Dickson. The former was a Russian naval officer who acted as a courier and the latter a relative of Greig who was living in Edinburgh and tutoring Greig's children. To maintain secrecy, Greig suggested that Stepanov should contact Dickson and that it should be Dickson who first approached Gascoigne, asking that he meet with Stepanov:

> *And since my children are staying with Mr Dickson, your courier [Count Stepanov] can say in Edinburgh that he is going to his house to see my children, which will remove all suspicion of his real mission.*

While a simple letter written to Gascoigne may have been easier, Vorontsov explained to Stepanov that any letter from the Russian ambassador to Gascoigne and sent through the post was likely to be intercepted, with Vorontsov adding a small refinement to the plan as suggested by Greig:

> *Kindly find Mr Dickson, who is tutor to the sons of Admiral Greig in Edinburgh, and tell him to arrange a meeting with Mr Gascoigne for you, but in such a way that it seems as if by chance that he is somewhere promenading and to not happen in the presence of strangers.*

To further ensure that nothing would leak out, Vorontsov felt it essential that everything be explained orally to Armstrong, and that Stepanov should 'not give him anything on paper', adding, 'I ask you to burn this letter.'

Despite Vorontsov claiming that Stepanov 'fixed everything', with Gascoigne agreeing to come to St Petersburg, problems soon arose. That Gascoigne would also be taking with him several artisans skilled in the manufacture of ordnance together with the appropriate machinery meant that such a venture could not be kept secret for long. Upon learning of these plans, the directors of the Carron Iron Works reacted with absolute fury. Not unnaturally, they feared that Gascoigne, in establishing an ordnance factory in Russia would not only be depriving the company of a very profitable trade but would be handing to Russia highly advanced technology as developed in Britain. According to Vorontsov in a further letter to Greig:

> *This matter ended very badly for the directors of the Caron company, about whom all the members of it, as well as all the other iron manufacturers and machinists throughout Great Britain, became so agitated that all his tools were detained. Most of all, the famous and well-known [Matthew] Bolton informed the government that by violating local laws he was transferring to a foreign land, a branch of trade that had hitherto united Great Britain, and which hitherto Great Britain had enjoyed.*

The government, for its part showed far less concern, with Prime Minister William Pitt, following a meeting with Gascoigne, giving approval to the export of machinery and of artisans knowledgeable in the manufacture of ordnance also going to Russia, apparently viewing the whole affair with 'great complacency'. Admittedly, Pitt was to become less of a friend to Russia just a few years later, fearing that Catherine was becoming over-powerful following her later successes in wars against Sweden and the Ottoman Empire, but at that time Pitt was more concerned with the need to strengthen an existing bond between Great Britain and Russia that had come close to falling apart at the time of the American War of Independence/American Revolutionary War and her support for the League of Armed Neutrality. Any further falling out with Russia could easily lead to Russia introducing an embargo on trade with Britain and becoming more favourably disposed towards France. Such an eventuality would result in Britain being denied such essential materials as hemp, flax and iron, raw materials that were essential for the building and keeping at sea both Britain's merchant fleet and ships of war.

Initially, Gascoigne, who arrived in St Petersburg on 26 May 1786, was accompanied by a core group of twelve skilled men, including his chief assistant, Adam Armstrong, along with various precision instruments makers and machinists. Furthermore, the British government did nothing to prevent additional recruitment into Russia of other skilled ordnance workers, as well as fulfilling further requests made by Gascoigne for the provision of coking coal, firebricks, fire clay, sample materials, blast furnaces and parts for a steam engine. Samuel Garbett, a co-founder of the Carron company and the father-in-law of Charles Gascoigne, estimated that between 1784 and 1786, almost 170 workmen and their families migrated from Scotland to Russia. In addition, Catherine, through a representative in London, Ivan Lizakevich, recruited further industrial workers from Birmingham, these coming to Russia in 1786. This massive transfer of technology to Russia was to be described by a later writer in the following terms:

> *Gascoigne's departure for Russia and his subsequent activities there constitute one of the largest, best organised, and most successful of the clandestine attempts to plant a competing industry in a foreign country to be undertaken during the eighteenth century.*

With the assistance of those who joined him from Britain, Gascoigne was able to create a Russian ordnance industry producing guns of great quality that would allow Russia to cease purchasing ordnance from Great Britain. Sent to the Petrozavodsk region, Gascoigne was placed in charge of the Konchezerskii iron foundry originally established by Peter the Great and a more recently established Aleksandrovskii cannon works, re-organising the operation of these two complexes. Among guns produced was the carronade, Gascoigne having brought with him the detailed plans for its production, which allowed Russia to begin installing carronades on her own ships, a technically advanced product that was only later to find its way onto French, Spanish and American ships as well as those of other navies of the world. Within a few years, the Aleksandrovskii cannon works became the major supplier of ordnance to the imperial navy and just a few years later Gascoigne also set up a branch of the Petrozavodsk works close to the naval base on Kotlin Island, which was responsible for repairing and maintaining cannons taken from ships returning to Kronstadt.

* * *

Ordnance can only be as good as those who manned and fired the guns and here Russia suffered a particular weakness. While those of the lower deck were enlisted for long-time continual service, as opposed, as was the case with the British Navy, for the duration of the ship upon which they served, they were given little opportunity to practice their gunnery skills. Warships of Catherine's navy frequently remained in harbour for lengthy periods, with their captains unwilling to risk their vessels at sea other than during the calms of mid-summer or when there was no enemy to confront. For the Baltic Fleet, this was partly dictated by climatic conditions, the seas around all its naval bases freezing in winter, giving crews little opportunity to practice their gunnery skills under sail with training restricted to the short summer season. Even then many ships did not leave harbour as to do so was viewed by some ship commanders as an inconvenience.

This lack of gunnery training was demonstrated to Catherine in 1765 when she was present at a fleet exercise conducted between Krasnaya Gorka and Kronstadt on the southern shore of the Gulf of Finland. Confiding to Panin, her minister of foreign affairs, she told of seeing from her imperial yacht ships of the fleet firing all day at a target that was never hit. Asking Panin not to share with anyone the absolute truth of what she had witnessed, she proceeded to elaborate:

> *They fired cannonballs and bombs without them reaching the target until 9 o'clock in the evening, when finally, bored and having the eardrum of my ears offended by this racket which was as useless as it was ridiculous, I asked the Admiral to come on board with me, where I took leave of him, begging him not to persist in burning what remained of this city. For they had taken the precaution, before firing at the city, of attaching trails of powder in different places, which did not fail to have the effect better than the cannonballs and bombs that had failed to hit anything.*

Even when at sea, ship commanders gave little attention to the need for gunnery practice. In recognising this, John Elphinston, a British naval captain recruited by Catherine to lead one of her warship squadrons into the Mediterranean prior to the Battle of Çeşme, enforced a routine of constant practice during the long voyage, knowing that if this had not explicitly been required then few, if any, of the captains of his squadron would have undertaken regular gunnery practice. In writing a journal of the voyage Elphinston noted:

> *I exercised the squadron every day at the great guns, in forming lines of battle, at small arms and firing at a mark; when the wind would permit; without hindering our voyage, and by the time we got the length of Minorca, they were tolerably expert, and some of the recruits, excellent marksmen.*

To this, he underlined one often ignored value of well-trained gunnery officers:

> *The chief employment of your officers in time of action, is to prevent noise and confusion, and to see that the guns are well pointed, as nothing gives the enemy more courage than when they see the shot idly thrown away; on the contrary, nothing disheartens more, than to see your shot take place.*

# CHAPTER 4

# THE STRUCTURE OF COMMAND

At the pinnacle of the naval command structure was the Admiralty Collegiate, later converted into a ministry, but with any major decision relating to the navy entirely in the hands of the ruling sovereign. The only exception was Catherine's devolution of power to Potemkin when she appointed him governor general of southern Russia. Acting on her authority but with a high degree of autonomy, Potemkin created a powerful fleet in the Black Sea Fleet alongside a land-based supporting infrastructure. Following Potemkin's death in 1791, command of the Black Sea Fleet fell to Vice Admiral Mordvinov, who was later to become minister of naval forces. While individual Russian emperors varied in the degree of interest they took in naval affairs, both Catherine, as already demonstrated, and Paul, her successor, adopted a hands-on approach.

While Paul will be returned to, it is useful here to consider the intensity of interest that Catherine had in her navy and how this played out.

Elphinston, in his journal, as already mentioned, confirms her involvement in naval affairs, writing that between his first arrival in St Petersburg on 8 July 1769 and his sailing to the Mediterranean three months later, Elphinston had four meetings with Catherine, two of which were in private. No other European ruler of such high status met directly with their naval officers other than with those holding senior ministerial positions, nor was this intimacy with senior naval officers replicated in Russia, other than by Peter the Great.

Writing in his journal, Elphinston indicates the meeting to have been in her private apartments, with the empress 'in a state of undress,' meaning that she was robed in her night attire. Initially she enquired as to when the ships he was to command would be ready to sail, and on being told that this was unlikely to be before the end of the year she became extremely annoyed. On learning that the reason was both an inadequate supply of stores and a lack of co-operation among junior officers, she called for the immediate attendance of the president of the naval collegiate, Count Ivan Chernyshev, who was commanded in her name to rectify both problems. Within days, the necessary stores began to arrive and officers who had previously shown a degree of disrespect towards Elphinston were now offering their full co-operation. Another issue raised by Catherine, and demonstrating the intensity of her interest in matters relating to the navy, was the unexpected return to Tallinn of one Mediterranean-bound warship, the eighty-gun *Svyatoslav.* Asking Elphinston if he could give a reason for this, he suggested, based on what he knew of the ship, that before leaving Kronstadt 'no proper alteration had been paid to placing her ballast, and the stowing her hold.'

On 16 September, Elphinston was again commanded to meet the empress, although on this occasion members of the Admiralty Collegiate were also present. Catherine returned to the subject of when *Svyatoslav* would sail. Elphinston explained that following the necessary alterations that were now underway on her ballasting and stowage, *Svyatoslav* could sail with his squadron to the Mediterranean.

A further example of Catherine's enthusiasm for naval affairs is shown by her relationship with Samuel Greig. With him she also had frequent meetings, bestowing upon him a dacha close to her grand summer palace of Peterhof, so that he was more available to attend those meetings. Greatly mourning his premature death in October 1788, she struck a gold medal in his memory, declaring him to be a great loss to Russia. A state funeral for him was also arranged, and Greig was buried in the Lutheran cathedral of the Virgin Mary in Tallinn, with his mausoleum designed by Catherine's architect Giacomo Quarenghi.

Originally the Admiralty Collegiate was established by Peter the Great in December 1718, one of nine collegia each responsible for different areas of government. Specifically, the Admiralty Collegiate oversaw the building and equipping of ships, maintaining naval bases, harbours and wharves, ropes and canvas work personnel and training, medical care, naval campaigns, and navigation. Headed by a president, usually a long-standing naval officer with the rank of admiral, its voting members, apart from the president, included a vice president and several councillors. Attached to it was a supporting office staffed by a secretary, minutes secretary, translators, clerks, and copyists.

A difficulty that arose from the collegia system was the presidents of each collegiate, through direct appointment by the sovereign, were all-powerful within their spheres of interest and desirous of extending their authority as far it would stretch. The result was that they showed little inclination to work with each other, especially affecting the relationship between the collegiates of the Admiralty and that of foreign affairs. Instead of mutual co-operation, there was a disconnect. In an extreme situation, the direction taken by the foreign affairs collegiate, on the approval of the sovereign, might lead Russia towards a war situation that required an urgent deployment of the fleet, but without any input from the Admiralty as to the availability of ships and how suitable they were for the purpose.

Russians holding the most important sea-going commands within the imperial navy were drawn from those of noble birth, with families attached to the navy in the same way that other families were associated with the army. While not compulsory, opportunity existed for those intending a career in the navy to attend the officer naval school at St Petersburg that had been founded in 1701 by Peter the Great. Here were taught English, algebra, geometry, trigonometry, astronomy, navigation, and surveying, with a model yacht used to illustrate some of the taught programme. To overcome a shortage of naval officers to meet the needs of the navy, Catherine oversaw an expansion of the school, with its student capacity, in what had now been retitled the Naval Gentry

Cadet Corps, increased from an original 360 to 600. Of those graduating and deemed the most capable, arrangements were made for them to continue their practical studies in England, serving on British warships for two to five years, with some also attending the naval academy at Portsmouth. One who gained such experience was Vice Admiral Vasily Mikhailovich Golovnin who served during the years 1802 to 1805 under admirals Nelson, Collingwood and Cornwallis, seeing action at Trafalgar. Golovnin, on returning to Russia, compiled a code of naval signals based on the English pattern, but he is most celebrated for two voyages circumnavigating the globe.

It had certainly become clear to Catherine that much was needed to improve the quality of the naval officer corps. Off Krasnaya Gorka in June 1765, she had witnessed that appalling display of gunnery incompetence, aware that while it had not been the officers firing the guns, it was they who had failed to ensure that the men under their command were properly trained through regular gunnery practice. However, what she had witnessed on that occasion was not just poor gunnery but also a display of total ineptitude in areas of seamanship, adding to her earlier remarks given in confidence to Panin, that upon the imperial standard being hoisted on her yacht:

> *[That] as the ships began to pass and salute, two of them perished – it was through the fault of their captains, one of them fell with his stern across the rigging of the other, and this when only a short distance from my yacht. For a good hour they struggled to free their sides and finally succeeded, but in doing so greatly damaged their masts and rigging. Then the Admiral wanted them to form line astern, but not a single ship could manage this, although the weather was very fine.*

A further means by which Catherine improved the quality of her seagoing naval commanders was by recruiting, either on temporary loan or for long-term service, experienced foreign naval officers. From Great Britain had come Sir Charles Knowles, John Elphinston and Samuel Greig, but also Robert Dugdale and George MacKenzie. John Paul Jones, of Scottish descent, was another recruited by Catherine, although he is better known as the founder of the American Navy, something he achieved prior to coming to Russia. In addition, French, Swedish, Norwegian, and Dutch officers joined the ranks of the Russian Navy, with Jan Hendrik van Kinsbergen, a Dutch naval officer, commanding in the Black Sea a flotilla during her first Ottoman war. Two especially notable foreign-born seagoing officers who played significant roles during the French war period were George Tate and Jean-Baptiste de Traversay. Tate was born in England, but his father, also named George, had previously served in the Russian Navy before settling in the USA. Tate, who began the war as a rear admiral, was to serve throughout the war commanding Russian naval units serving in British waters. Traversay, a creole born on the French Caribbean Island of Martinique, served first in the French Navy before taking up an invitation by Catherine to enter the Russian Navy. Here he served in the Baltic Fleet before transferring to the Black Sea Fleet as its commander-in-chief.

While Samuel Greig died shortly before the outbreak of the war with France, his son Aleksey Samuilovich Greig also served in the Russian Navy during this period, and though born in St Petersburg, he had strong connections with Britain. It was in Edinburgh that he received his early education before entering the British Royal Navy. Returning to Russia in 1796, he went on to serve in both the North Sea and the Mediterranean.

The recruitment of foreign officers, or the sending of young Russians abroad for training, was one that solved for Catherine the insufficient number of competent seagoing officers that she had encountered at the beginning of her reign. As a long-term policy such recruitment could only have limited benefit, for if fully integrated into Russian service it inevitably reduced promotional opportunities for native-born Russians, so discouraging their wish to enter the naval officers corps. According to Pavel Vasilyevich Chichagov, a future naval minister and who himself had close connections with Britain:

> *If the government can do without Russians, by welcoming all the adventurers of the earth to distribute to them the places and the wealth of the country, the nationals will not feel the need to educate themselves. Why in fact, should they do so, if they are deprived of the opportunity to exercise their talents?*

As it happens, and despite the number of senior personnel recruited, most senior commanders were Russian, some of them the most talented of the period. First and foremost comes Fyodor Fyodorovich Ushakov. Appointed commander of the Black Sea Fleet in 1790, he went on to lead an important expedition into the Adriatic, and in co-operation with an Ottoman squadron cleared the French out of the strategically important Adriatic region (see Chapter 8). During Catherine's second war against the Ottomans, Ushakov won four notable battles, Fidonisi (1788), Kerch Strait (1790), Tendra Island (1790), and Cape Kaliakra (1791). In these he developed a series of tactics, that both built upon and greatly improved those as practised by other navies, including the British Navy. Well versed in the standard tactics of attacking an enemy fleet in linear formation, he chose instead to attack in battle formation, allowing commanders to act independently and with concentration on the enemy flagship. At Cape Kaliakra, the attack he mounted was on a fleet anchored in shore and in a similar position to the French at Abū Qīr Bay in 1798. Learning from Ushakov was another important Russian-born seagoing commander, Dmitry Nikolayevich Senyavin. Serving under Ushakov, he went on to refine and develop Ushakov's tactics in two battles fought against the Ottomans in 1807 (see Chapter 12).

# CHAPTER 5

# THE LOWER DECK

For recruitment of the lower deck, a particular problem for the Baltic Fleet was that of lacking a ready pool of trained hands when ships were about to sail. Other European navies were not in the same position, for most had a substantial merchant marine that could provide, when required, a large force of ready trained sailors. Instead, for Russia the vast majority of those serving on the lower deck, particularly in the Baltic, were serfs drawn from country estates who had little knowledge or interest in the sea. Once drawn into the navy, they would gain a few skills during a lifetime of servitude, but overall, training was limited and any sea-time at best minimal, giving the serfs recruited little sense of seamanship. For this reason, ships of the Baltic Fleet often sailed with a proportion of untrained or semi-trained seamen alongside a few with experience of the sea, the latter primarily there to train the rest of the crew. Sprinkled into this might also be foreign merchant seamen, including those from Britain, who had been induced in some way to join the Russian service. This latter was not always a voluntary arrangement, foreign seamen were sometimes abducted, as happened in Britain using press gangs. Alternatively, there were occasions when the captain of a merchant ship found several of his crew bribed to join a Russian ship, with those crew members he had lost replaced by Russians who he was now expected to train up as seamen for future service in the Russian Navy.

In the Black Sea, the situation was very different. While serfs were certainly employed on warships, the number was considerably less. In part this was because the population of serfs in southern Russia was much smaller, around twenty-five per cent of the total population of Ukraine, Crimea, and southern Belarus, as compared with the serf population in the north that was much closer to seventy per cent. However, rather than relying on the forced recruitment of less available serfs, the Black Sea Fleet could look to recruiting a much higher number of trained seamen or those otherwise familiar with the sea. Unlike the Baltic, where the British merchant fleet was dominant to such an extent that a Russian-owned merchant ship was something of a rarity, this was not so in the Black Sea. Here, the British presence was negligible, allowing for the growth of a Russian mercantile fleet that, following the annexation of Crimea and Russia's entry into the Black Sea, steadily expanded to meet the growth in regional trade. By around 1805 there were more than 900 merchant ships in the Black Sea flying the Russian flag, although not all were Russian-owned or manned by majority Russian crews. While an increasing number of Russians were being drawn to the sea, the majority of those manning these ships were either Greek or Albanian, men who were also willing to enter the Russian Navy. As Christians of the Orthodox faith, they had a special affinity towards Russia, seeing Russia as a means of freeing themselves from the oppression of their ruling Muslim Turkish overlords.

Compounding the differing operational efficiency of the two Russian fleets was the amount of time ships spent at sea. For both the Baltic and Black Sea, those of the lower deck, when not at sea, were accommodated in barracks constructed at the various naval bases. The system was that of each man joining an assigned battalion of seamen that remained as a constant unit, the men of a particular battalion serving on the same ship and quartered alongside each other when ashore. The long winters of the north meant that ships of the northern commands had to remain in harbour until the Baltic or White sea became ice-free. Instead of this being a period of training on shore, in their winter barracks crews were often given tasks totally unrelated to the sea, despite the existence of the model ship and rigging for sails that Greig had introduced at Kronstadt. Instead, officers often used the men they commanded to carry out duties to their advantage, including work on private estates. When officially sanctioned by the Admiralty Collegiate, a charge was made for the loan of men from the naval battalions to work either on country estates or city building projects. For the Black Sea Fleet, and with Sevastapol being a warm water port, training in winter presented far fewer problems, allowing ships to be more frequently at sea and giving both officers and men much greater sea time. This is one reason why, during the French war period, the Black Sea Fleet was much more effective in its operations than the considerably larger Baltic Fleet. Another, and equally important factor, was that those commanding the Black Sea Fleet were better officers, conscientious in carrying out their duties, those of highest rank ensuring that all inferior officers fully performed the duties assigned to them. Here, Ushakov and Senyavin must again be mentioned, both upon being appointed to the Black Sea overseeing a constant routine of training that increased the combat readiness of the fleet.

Also accounting for the difference in the performance of the two fleets were levels of morbidity and mortality among the men of the lower deck, with the Baltic Fleet often severely incapacitated by outbreaks of disease, especially typhus and scurvy, while the Black Sea Fleet was relatively free of such contagions. In the Baltic, there was much more that the officers could have done to alleviate this situation, as when in barracks or at sea, they showed little interest in the health, welfare, or behaviour of their men. Conversely, at Sevastopol, Ushakov and Senyavin recognised the need for efficient care of seamen, ensuring the men had a good diet, adequate clothing, and medical support. As an explanation for this difference, it is necessary to consider the social composition of the two fleets.

Whereas, the Baltic Fleet was heavily reliant on the recruitment of peasants and serfs, the Black Sea Fleet had a large pool of already trained seamen drawn from the Greek and Albanian diaspora. In directing the affairs of the Baltic Fleet, a vast chasm existed between the aristocratic officers of the upper deck and the serfs and peasants of the lower deck, a chasm much greater than anything existing in the Black Sea Fleet or, indeed, any other eighteenth-century navy. For the Russian aristocrat, the serf was regarded as the lowest of the low, viewed as little more than a slave; the property of the major landowner who, in fulfilment of a duty required of them by the emperor, had released them for service into the navy. Sometimes the officer commanding them was part of the same landowning family to which the serfs he commanded belonged. Aleksandr Radischev, a Russian social critic, writing during the reign of Catherine, wrote of serfs in naval service being 'valued worse than cattle,' adding:

> *No pains were taken to care for their health or their provisioning; their lives counted for nothing; they were deprived of their fixed and proper pay...most of the new recruits died because of neglect by their superiors.*

Perhaps, for the Baltic Fleet, levels of morbidity and mortality might have been greatly reduced if Samuel Greig, Catherine's favourite admiral, had survived the war with Sweden. Of Scottish rather than Russian heritage, and having very limited aristocratic connections, he lacked an innate sense of superiority, possessing a degree of empathy towards the lower deck irrespective of their social standing. Not only did he, as superintendent of the Kronstadt naval base, encourage officers to regularly inspect the living areas of the men, both on land and at sea, but he sought other ways to improve their health. At Kronstadt he brought in well-trained surgeons to care for the sick and injured, also establishing a hospital that was highly praised by John Howard, the English prison reformer, when on a visit to Kronstadt in 1781. According to Howard, the hospital contained:

> *Many spacious rooms, all perfectly clean; whilst the appearance of the patients lodged in them gave plain proofs of the care and attention with which they were treated.*

In returning to Kronstadt eight years later, by which time Greig had died, the hospital was in a state of disrepair. According to Howard's nineteenth-century biographer:

> *On the 9th and 10th of September [1789] he [Howard] visited the marine hospital at Kronstadt, which he now found in a much worse condition than when he had formerly inspected it. The sick mariners in the hospital, and the slaves in the prison, had indeed alike reason to regret that they had not the opportunity of deriving further benefit from the attendance and humanity for which the natives of Great Britain are deservedly celebrated, as the death of Admiral Greig put a stop to many improvements which he had commenced, in accordance with his favourite maxim, "If I cannot do what I would, I will do what I can."*

In further unravelling this difference in operational performance between the Baltic and Black Sea Fleets, a little more attention needs to be given to Ushakov and Senyavin and the reasons behind their differing attitudes to the men they were commanding. The potential for them, as serving naval officers, to replicate the attitudes and behaviour of officers appointed to the Baltic Fleet certainly existed. Both had served in the Baltic before appointment to the Black Sea and had witnessed the prevailing cultural norm of officer contempt towards the lower deck and a consequent lack of concern for the wellbeing of the men. While both Ushakov and Senyavin were, as was inevitable in Russian society, of aristocratic background, neither was the product of the most senior aristocratic families. This partly explains their appointment to the Black Sea, as sons of the upper aristocracy would wish, and gain, appointments that kept them within proximity of St Petersburg, the centre of the empire. Ushakov was on the bottom aristocratic rung through being the son of a retired sergeant of the Russian imperial guard, although Senyavin was slightly better placed, the son of a former vice admiral who had once governed Kronstadt, but Senyavin learning from Ushakov during many years in which he served as his second-in-command.

The social gap between these two officers and the men they commanded was further reduced by the nature of those who comprised the lower deck of the Black Sea Fleet. Made up of fewer serfs and peasants, the social chasm between officers and men was less difficult to overcome, making it easier for officers appointed to the Black Sea to better understand what motivated their men and what was needed to ensure their effectiveness. In addition, and tutored by Ushakov and Senyavin, they became much more aware that a crew debilitated by ill health would make it impossible for a naval ship to successfully perform assigned combat tasks. Enforced by Ushakov was a regular inspection of ship crews and a concern that corners never be cut in the supply of fresh victuals and other essentials. It was Ushakov who oversaw construction of a hospital at Sevastapol, but unlike the one built by Greig at Kronstadt, this hospital was not allowed to fall into decay. Upon his leaving Sevastopol, it was retained by Senyavin and later successors as an important feature of the naval base. The prevalence of malaria in and around Sevastapol could well have undermined the medical safeguards that Ushakov introduced, especially as the cause of this disease was unknown. In the belief that it was a product of foul air emanating from the surrounding marshlands, and unaware that it was the product of mosquitoes, Ushakov had the naval barracks removed from the low-lying ground upon which it had been built. Instead, he had it placed on higher ground at a distance from the mosquito-infested low-lying marshes. In so doing, and for reasons unknown to him, Ushakov ensured a consequent reduction in the numbers laid low by this frequently fatal disease.

# CHAPTER 6

# BATTLE TACTICS AND BATTLE PRACTICE

In terms of battle practice and fleet exercises, the ships of the Baltic Fleet, apart from several squadrons sent into the North Sea to co-operate with the British Navy, rarely put to sea during the French Revolutionary and Napoleonic Wars. This was in stark contrast to the Black Sea, the ships of that fleet frequently at sea both for purposes of training and wartime operations. In the Black Sea, training was taking place all year round, encouraged of course by Sevastopol being a warm water port. It was a squadron from the Black Sea that not only conducted a highly successful campaign against the French in the Adriatic and Ionian seas, but also gave assistance to British naval operations in the Mediterranean. A few years later it was the ethos of the Black Sea Fleet that lay behind two victories gained in the Aegean against the Ottomans. While most of the ships that fought in those battles were drawn from the Baltic, the commander and many of the ordinary seamen were men previously imbibed with the service culture of the Black Sea. As for events in the Baltic, the only successes gained at sea were in response to Napoleon's invasion of Russia and achieved not by the large battleships of the fleet, but by the smaller vessels and rowing boats of the inshore navy, a totally separate force working alongside the army.

One battle in which ships of the Baltic Fleet might have participated was Camperdown, a British victory won by Admiral Adam Duncan on 11 October 1797. Only a few months earlier, numerous units of Russia's Baltic Fleet had been working closely alongside Duncan's ships in blockading the Dutch coastline, with Holland at that time in alliance with revolutionary France. If those Russian ships had still been present in the North Sea, they might well have joined Duncan's battle formation, allowing for an accurate assessment of their combat performance. Given, however, that on first arriving in British waters, the Russian squadron had demonstrated poor seamanship compared with the British Navy, the addition of Russian ships might well have disadvantaged Duncan. In any sea battle, station-keeping and cohesion are critical, and at Camperdown the Russan ships may have fallen behind the fast-moving British ships as they descended upon the Dutch, or simply become entangled with other ships be they friend or foe. Against the Swedish Navy, during the war that broke out in 1788, the Baltic Fleet had proved relatively able. But later in 1807, when the Swedish Fleet was reinforced by two powerful British seventy-four-gun third rate warships, the Russian ships under the command of Admiral Pyotr Khanykov, turned tail and ran (see Chapter 16).

Having fought full-scale fleet actions, both during Catherine's second Ottoman War and the French war period, the fighting tactics adopted by those who commanded the Black Sea Fleet is much clearer. Through the transfer of officers between the two fleets, it is possible that the Baltic Fleet, if placed in a similar situation, might have replicated those same tactics developed by Ushakov during his time of commanding the Black Sea Fleet and then refined by Senyavin. Although, when ships from the Baltic were dispatched into the Mediterranean, the Baltic-trained commanders were more hesitant when attacking the enemy, unable to fully recognise that both Ushakov and Senyavin were extremely capable and much ahead of the game. Ushakov was building on tactics previously used by Rodney and Howe of the British Navy and later adopted by Nelson. He rejected the doctrine of forming a line of battle in which ships were positioned in a linear formation against an enemy that would adopt a similar aligned formation with ships of similar strength firing continuous broadsides into each other. Instead, Ushakov advocated the use of a concentrated force upon only part of the opponent's battle line, but initially attempted to disrupt the enemy's command and ability to control the battle through an attack at full sail on their flagships. While the whole concept of linear battle formations was certainly questioned by other naval commanders, Ushakov was the first to abandon it in favour of a pre-planned head-on attack by ships under full sail.

It was by the 1670s that the leading naval powers had developed the 'line of battle', it being formally adopted in England by 'Fighting Instructions' dating to March 1653. The creation of a blue water navy by Peter the Great saw the linear formation in battle officially presented in Russia's first naval code issued in 1720 entitled *Book of Naval Charter: About Everything that Concerns Good Management About the Fleet's Time at Sea.* In using the linear formation, fleets divided into three columns – van, centre, and rear – with each ship in theory, if not in practice, distanced from the next by approximately one cable (185m). In the resulting slugging match, it was only possible for one fleet to gain a major victory over the other if the ships of one of the two fleets failed to maintain strict formation. In giving thought to how a great victory could be achieved, several tactical possibilities began to see the light of day, of which 'breaking the line' by an attacking fleet to windward was one that slowly evolved in practice. Here, the largest and fastest ships of the fleet would descend upon the rear column, breaking the line by cutting it off from the centre and van. To provide support for those ships under attack, the defending fleet's centre and van would need to double back to enter the ongoing battle, a manoeuvre that would take some time as a fleet sailing in line of battle would be under light sail, and each ship would have to reverse course by tacking or wearing. Unless well-practised, such a movement would result in confusion and possible collisions. If nothing else, it was time consuming and before reaching the point of battle would be initially engaged by other ships of the attacking squadron. By the time of reaching the rear column, and assuming it by then to have been overwhelmed, it would constitute no remaining threat to the attacking fleet. This then left the possibility of capturing or disabling the disorganised ships of the van and centre. However, as every commander also knew, something should always be left to chance, for nothing could be certain. Stray or well-aimed shots knocking down masts and yards of both friend and enemy alike, or maybe a sudden and unexpected change in wind direction.

In Russia, influenced by Ushakov's successes at Kerch, Tendra and Cape Kaliakra, the tactic of breaking the line gained official recognition in a Naval Fleet Charter issued in 1797 by Emperor Paul that detailed not just its use in battle but how it could be combatted if used by an attacking fleet. However, during his time of service in the French wars, Ushakov had no opportunity to make further use of the tactics he had developed. Instead, Senyavin in 1807 successfully adopted those same tactics and twice under full sail successfully attacked an Ottoman fleet formed in line of battle (see Chapter 14). Most important was that of some of the attacking ships through concentration upon one part of the enemy's line passing through the line to attack the enemy formation on both sides. This ensured the enemy was completely outgunned as any return fire would be hindered by no ship having a crew of sufficient size to fire all guns at the same time from both sides.

It was neither Nelson nor Ushakov who innovated breaking the line, nor were they the first to use it in practice. Others had implemented the tactic, but were unable to fully exploit its possibilities through failing to adequately prepare their subordinate commanders in the intent to break the enemy line or encourage individual initiative. Here, both Nelson and Ushakov were the exception, with Nelson's success at Trafalgar heavily based on his sharing and discussing such tactical ideas with his ship commanders, his 'band of brothers', alongside rigorous training of the fleet. Unfortunately, Ushakov's use of the tactic is most frequently ignored by British naval historians, a point frequently noted by Russian historians. Instead, British naval historians concentrate on its use by Nelson at Trafalgar and the failure of earlier admirals, such as Rodney and Howe, in their attempts to break the line, being less effective but imaginative in concept. Sam Willis, in a 2008 publication, otherwise a sound account of naval tactics, in commenting upon the Batte of Trafalgar states correctly that Nelson went at the enemy at full sail, but adds 'contrary to tradition'. Of what tradition is Willis referring? Ushakov had adopted the tactic of attacking the enemy at full sail seventeen years earlier so had already gone 'contrary to tradition'.

In undertaking these tactics, where ship commanders had to use their own initiative where to best place themselves during the battle as it unravelled, the fleet commander had to have total faith in the ability and resolution of those he commanded. Here Nelson had a clear advantage over Ushakov, while Nelson's captains were unfailingly faithful to the ideas he pursued, a result of Nelson fully unveiling to them his plans and frequently discussing them with his band of brothers. While it is unclear as to the extent both Ushakov and Senyavin confided in their ship commanders use of those tactics, it is also clear that some were ill-prepared to close with the enemy in the way that both Ushakov and Senyavin were expecting. Some even failed to support their fellow captains when under heavy enemy fire that required their assistance and support. To correct this, Ushakov and Senyavin were dependent on issuing instructions by way of signalling flags during the battle itself, and which were often claimed as unseen during the fog of gunfire.

At Trafalgar, Nelson had no need of signalling as each captain knew exactly what was required.

Aside from fleet engagements, Ushakov also perfected the operational methods used by units of the Black Sea Fleet when supporting landings of military forces from the sea. In this, his greatest success was in the Ionian Sea where the squadron he was commanding captured from the French the heavily fortified town of Corfu, an action preceded by his naval forces first making successful landings not only on the island of Corfu, but also each of the other Ionian Islands. In a series of operations, the cannonading of enemy batteries and strongpoints from his ships out at sea had often been followed by the positioning of artillery in high mountain or hilltop positions that allowed them to control the entire battle zone. Edward Brenton, a British naval captain contemporary to those times, noted that British naval gun crews conducted similar feats, blandly stating, and thereby ignoring the achievements of Ushakov, that 'few but English would have attempted to place guns in such a position'. Subsequent British naval historians have failed to bring greater accuracy to this statement through an amendment that might have stated 'few but English *and Russians*' would have made the attempt. A few years later, and against the French, a few similar operations were successfully carried out by Senyavin (see Chapter 13). Against the Ottomans, similar assaults on land were attempted in the Black Sea between 1809 and 1810 (see Chapter 15), but these were far less successful, a result of the enforced economy cuts made upon the navy by Alexander.

For the Baltic Fleet, operations were conducted to support the large-scale landing of troops, but these were poorly realised in outcome. Landings at Den Helder of 20,000 Russian troops in 1799, and working in conjunction with the British, would not have been logistically possible if it had not been for support offered by the British Admiralty. Lacking a merchant fleet, Russia simply did not have enough of her own ships that could be used as transports, resulting in the conversion of some older Russian warships, with the help of British shipwrights, being converted into troop transporters, with the bulk of the 20,000 carried on British merchant ships. On a second occasion, the need arose to transport 25,000 troops from Sveaborg in Finland to defend Riga against an advancing French army. Earmarked to undertake this relatively simple project, little more than 300 nautical miles, was a fleet of warships to be sent into the Baltic from Arkhangelsk. Yet it proved impossible to achieve. The ships never arrived, and following a delay of several months, a small fraction of the original force were brought to Riga by inshore rowing craft (see Chapter 18).

## PART TWO

# Against revolutionary France

Britain and Russia were natural allies during the eighteenth century. The two countries were heavily dependent on each other for trade. Huge imports of raw materials from Russia were fuelling Britain's industrial growth, while creating for Russia a highly beneficial balance of trade. Admittedly, some in Britain feared the increasing might of Russia, believing that the technical support that Britain was giving to Russia was creating a future behemoth that might one day prove a dangerous enemy. Countering such thoughts was the great distance between the two nations, this at first putting such fears to rest. Following the outbreak of revolution in France, an event that greatly shocked Catherine, but made worse by the guillotining of Louis XVI, she willingly hurled Russia into a convention of friendship with Great Britain. Signed in London on 25 March 1793, it was designed to destroy the newly created French republic and reinstate the Bourbon monarchy. Out of this came a naval and military alliance that would see Catherine sending a squadron of warships to work alongside a British fleet blockading the Dutch coastline. Since 1795 and a successful intervention by French revolutionary forces, the Netherlands, now the Batavian Republic, had become a client state of France. The Batavian Navy, or armed privateers, using the Texel roadstead stretching along the coastline of Texel Island, could easily slip into the North Sea and attack British convoys entering and leaving the Baltic. Following Catherine's death in 1796, Paul agreed to provide naval support for a combined attack on the Texel roadstead for the purpose of eliminating this threat.

# CHAPTER 7

# A RUSSIAN SQUADRON IN THE NORTH SEA

Deal, a seaside town lying on the east coast of Kent, faces directly on to the Downs, a sheltered stretch of water where sailing ships once assembled awaiting a fair wind that would give them passage south and west into the English Channel or to the north. It was also in the Downs that incoming merchant ships collected a pilot for the Thames and outgoing merchant ships dropped their pilots. Naval ships also assembled here. In wartime these might be fleets bound for the Mediterranean or the Atlantic or smaller squadrons providing convoy escort for outward bound merchant ships. At Deal, a naval shipyard and hospital had been established to support naval forces either stationed or temporarily active on the Downs. For this reason, and for the inhabitants of the town, ships were commonplace, an everyday sight that was taken for granted.

Yet on occasions, something did happen at sea that drew the attention of those who lived and worked in Deal. Sometimes it might be the drama of boats setting out to rescue those on a ship that had run aground on the nearby and wickedly treacherous Goodwin Sands. At other times, during this wartime period, it might be a performance laid on by French privateers enacting a daring attack on an unsuspecting merchantman. Tacking and jibing through the mass of shipping, privateers sailing out of Boulogne frequently attempted the capture of one or two merchantmen, hoping momentarily to avoid the attention of the naval guardships. But during the summer of 1795, something much more intriguing caught the attention of those living in Deal: the arrival of Catherine's promised squadron of warships.

Consisting of twelve men-of-war and eight frigates, this heavyweight of naval ships came into the Downs on Thursday 7 August. Forewarned by the forty-four-gun Russian frigate *Arkhangel Mikhail*, which had entered the Downs on the previous day, a crowd of onlookers were assembled and gazing inquisitively at the incoming ships. It was something completely new, something never previously witnessed – a Russian navy arriving to work alongside the Royal Navy in British home waters. More than that, those ships were to be totally integrated into the British Navy, taking their orders from a British admiral.

Many were there simply to see the ships of Catherine's navy and the colourful flags they displayed, possibly also to acquaint themselves with the men of such a strange and distant country. Others were more discerning, especially those who had once served in the British Navy. They wanted to see the layout of the ships, the curve of their timbers and whether in sailing into the Downs, those who manned them were as skilled as British seamen. Would they hold proper formation, furl their sails in unison, and drop anchor in the proper fashion? With telescopes raised, many looked eagerly out to sea, watching Catherine's ships as each reached its assigned anchorage. In command was Vice Admiral Pyotr Ivanovich Khanykov, a seasoned sailor who as a midshipman had been among volunteers sent by Catherine at the beginning of her reign to experience seamanship in the British Navy. Later Khanykov, as a lieutenant, served at the Battle of Çeşme and as a captain first class in the Swedish War. His promotion to vice admiral was made in September 1793.

Supporting Khanykov were two rear admirals, Mikhail Makarov and the British born George Tate whose father had served under Peter the Great. Another who should be mentioned is Captain First Class Pavel Chichagov, a future minister of naval forces and commanding the sixty-six-gun *Retvizan*, a ship generally regarded as the best in the squadron. Originally a Swedish warship named *Rättvisan,* she had been launched at Karlskrona in September 1783. That she was now in Russian service resulted from her having been captured during the recently concluded war against Sweden. Her builder, Frederik Henrik af Chapman, was the leading naval constructor of the age, his ship designs the result of careful scientific analysis to establish displacement, load capacity, stability, and flow resistance. In fact, so outstanding were his ships that the British Admiralty had long been desirous of getting their hands on one of his designs, something the Russians allowed when *Retvizan* was later taken to Chatham dockyard for repair work. On that occasion, the lines of *Retvizan* were carefully recorded and later assimilated in some of the British Navy's own ship designs.

While the Russian captains felt that in arriving at the anchorage they had put on an impressive display, they heard nothing but criticism from the more knowledgeable of the observers on shore. According to Chichagov, 'one ship did not lower or tighten the sails at the right time, another dropped anchor on the opposite side to where it should have been dropped', and these he wrote were among 'a thousand observations of detail that put us back in our place'. He felt it all to be a little unfair, noting in his private journal that the Downs was always tormented by winds and tides that were not easy for Baltic sailors who were accustomed to a comparatively peaceful sea. An additional problem, according to Chichagov, was that on several of the Russian ships were English pilots who were 'unable to make themselves understood and so could not prevent certain blunders and awkwardness which did not escape the spectators on shore.'

Whatever Chichagov and the other Russian officers might have thought, and whatever excuses they made for their poor performance, the simple truth was that they could not match the skills of British seamen. Fashioning peasants and serfs from men of the land into valued seafarers was no easy task and required months, if not years, of intensive training. Moreover, those Russian ships were new out of port, having been at sea for no more than a few weeks. While some of the lower deck might have served during the Swedish War, many had never previously set foot on a ship. Only during the voyage to

England had they begun learning the skills of seamanship. Their shortcomings became even more obvious when, just a few days later, they sailed out of the Downs in company with Duncan's North Sea Squadron. For Chichagov, the truth was now all too clear, 'from the very day on which the signal was given to us to raise sail,' he later wrote, 'the torture of my arrogance also began.' Painfully, he added, 'all the manoeuvres of the English ships were better than ours and required no more than a quarter of the time required by us.'

**Ships of Vice Admiral Hanickoff's squadron, 1795.**

| | Guns | Commanders |
|---|---|---|
| *Pamiat' Evstafii* (Memory of Evstafii) | 74 | Vice Admiral Pyotr Ivanovich Khanykov<br>Captain First Rank Sanatin |
| *Sviataia Elena* (Saint Helen) | 74 | Rear Admiral Chev Mikhail Makarov<br>Captain First Rank Bacanov |
| *Pyotr* (Peter) | 74 | Rear Admiral Chev Tate<br>Captain First Rank Barqulov |
| *Gleb* (Gleb) | 74 | Captain First Rank Thesiger |
| *Retvizan* | 66 | Captain First Rank Chichagov |
| *Europa* (Europe) | 66 | Captain First Rank Barisov |
| *Parmen* (Parmen) | 66 | Captain First Rank Chevalier Alexander Cruise |
| *Iona* (Iona) | 66 | Captain First Rank Farutchov |
| *Nikanor* (Nikanor) | 66 | Captain First Rank Prince Troubetskoi |
| *Pimen* (Pimen) | 66 | Captain First Rank Kolfcoltsov |
| *Graf Orlov* (Count Orlov) | 66 | Captain First Rank Batchmanov |
| *Philippe* (Philip) | 66 | Captain First Rank Smirnov |
| *Venera* (Venus) | 44-frigate | Captain Second Rank Bodesko |
| *Riga* | 44-frigate | Captain Second Rank Backdov |
| *Arkhangel Rafail* (Archangel Raphael) | 44-frigate | Captain Second Rank Treskene |
| *Reval* | 44-frigate | Captain Second Rank Clockachov |
| *Arkhipelag* (Archipelago) | 44-frigate | Captain Second Rank von Muller |
| *Kronshtadt* (Kronstadt) | 44-frigate | Captain Second Rank Chernyavin |
| *Arkhangel Mikhai*l (Archangel Michael) | 44-frigate | Captain Second Rank Brown |

As they departed from the Downs, again numerous telescopes along the shoreline had the Russian ships under scrutiny. Now it was even clearer how badly they were performing. Not one of the Russian ships could hold its position, soon falling behind the closely held British formation. Duncan, in seeing this, and fearing that he would lose sight of Khanykov's ships, gave a signal to his own ships to reduce sail and allow the ponderous Russian squadron to draw abreast. Chichagov declared himself to have been mortified, as were all his fellow captains, especially as they knew they were still within sight of the shoreline where 'every telescope in the Downs was trained upon us.' Having made so little progress, and with the day ending, the Russians witnessed one more display of British naval artistry: Duncan, according to custom, signalling the whole fleet to reef top sails, with each of his ships lowering its sails simultaneously. According to Chichagov, the speed was so quick that on the Russian ships 'the crews had hardly reached the shrouds', completing this manoeuvre in around fifteen to twenty minutes, while on board Duncan's ships it had taken 'one and a half or at most three minutes.'

To be fair, even a British fleet when rapidly recruited at the outset of a war was inclined to slowness and poor co-ordination. Maybe not as noticeable as that of Khanykov's squadron, for always on a British warship a proportion would have learnt their skills as merchant seamen. Nevertheless, those under his command soon learned, helped by English officers attached to some of the Russian ships. In a report to Catherine, written on 25 September 1795, Khanykov tells of his men, even within that short period of time, performing their assigned tasks with much more alacrity. In his view, the union with Duncan's squadron was highly beneficial for his men. In his words, they were 'jealous of the agility and resourcefulness of the English' and, in wishing not to be their inferior were 'in things like taking reefs, adding and subtracting sails, and in everything else' had become 'so sophisticated that what used to done in ten or twelve minutes, they now do in three or four minutes.' Confirming this rapid adoption of their seagoing skills, Chichagov wrote of his men on *Retvizan*, 'taking three to five minutes' to undertake tasks that had previously taken 'ten or twelve minutes'.

Bringing together two naval units with the expectation that they would work side-by-side in the fight against a common enemy requires patience, tact, and a willingness on the part of both to work in harmony. In this, Duncan proved an ideal choice as the agreed overall commander. Unlike some of his brother officers, he showed no contempt or indifference towards the Russian ally. Instead, he would frequently heap praise on Khanykov and the men he commanded, especially once the steep learning curve had been scaled and the Russian ships were matching or even exceeding the speed of his own ships. In September, Duncan was writing to Earl Spencer, First Lord of the Admiralty, that the Russian ships were sailing better than the British ships, telling him that 'our sailors could do no better.' Spencer expressed surprise, especially as the Russian ships were 'long out of dock and uncoppered' while the British ships of the combined fleet had only recently left the dockyard at Chatham. Spencer vainly searched for a possible reason, and one that did not reflect badly on those manning the British ships, suggesting 'it may have been owing to their [Russian ships] carrying more sail in the night or some such circumstance.' Almost certainly the Russians, in seeing how out-matched they had once been, had shown determination in proving themselves, while one of their ships, the Swedish-built *Retvizan*, was of a superior design to any of Duncan's ships.

Other British naval commanders were less favourable to ensuring the success of this international naval co-operation. While it was customary for squadrons of ships when first coming within sight of each other firing the required number of guns in salutation, the return salute on British ships was always less by two. This was not the Russian practice, which saw the firing of an equal number of guns when the respective squadron commanders were of equal rank. Khanýkov, while at anchor in the Downs, saluted his equal in rank, Vice Admiral Peyton, with seventeen guns, but to the astonishment of the Russians, Peyton returned two shots less. To the Russians this was an affront, while the British found it to be perfectly in order. Peyton's explanation was that in previously agreeing to an equal salute, he had meant an equal salute to an English vice admiral, and while Peyton was correct, he later made no attempt to pacify Khanykov by way of expressing any form of regret. In London, Vorontsov, the Russian ambassador, was informed of this 'insult', taking up the matter with Earl Spencer at the Admiralty and Spencer informing Duncan accordingly:

> *I am sorry to find by a letter from Count Woronzow [Vorontsov], that there has been a misunderstanding between Admiral Peyton and Vice Admiral Hanickoff respecting a salute. We must do what we can to rectify it, but as Admiral Peyton has abided literally by the naval instructions, I do not immediately see what can be done.*

This matter of the number of guns to be fired as a return salute remained a delicate issue, with Spencer soon after receiving a further complaint from Khanykov when Charles Buckner, commander-in-chief at the Nore and a vice admiral, also fired fewer guns in return. This time, Spencer provided a workable solution:

> *To satisfy Vice Admiral Hanickoff that it was a difference in ranks and not any disrespect to the Imperial flag that occasioned the difference in salute, I have imagined the expedient of ordering the Russian squadron when they return to anchor at the Nore, when, if he salutes, Admiral Buckner may return an equivalent number of guns without transgressing the rules.*

The presence of the Russian Fleet, once the quality of its seamanship had improved, was invaluable, given that the British Navy was overstretched and undermanned, with many of its own ships, through extensive sea time, needing drydocking for essential repairs. According to one of Duncan's biographers, the North Sea Squadron was certainly in dire need of whatever could be provided by Russia:

> *The ships of the North Sea fleet, even tried by the standard of that day, might well have driven an Admiral to despair. In the commencement they*

> *numbered only four sail of the line. When their number increased their quality remained worse than indifferent: converted Indiamen, captured prizes, anything that was to be found, had to do duty in the North Sea. The better ships were all wanted for the more distant commands, such as the Mediterranean.*

Certainly, the Board of Admiralty wished to supply Duncan with more and better ships, a point made by Admiral Sir Charles Middleton, a member of the Board of Admiralty, informing Duncan in August, at the time of the Russian squadron arriving in the Downs:

> *My own wish is to have your force very strong, but I plainly perceive from the many irons we have in the fire that I shall be overruled. The same cause obliges us to employ your frigates on many extra services, and which I have charged the secretary to acquaint you with as often as it happens; but, necessary as this information is for your guidance, I am afraid it is often forgot.*

At Texel, a large portion of the enemy Dutch fleet was known to be stationed, with a further tranche of ships thought to be assembled and ready to sail from the port of Flushing [Vlissingen]. However, and unbeknown to Duncan and Khanykov, the Dutch squadron based in the Texel had sailed just a few days prior to the Russians having arrived in the Downs. Indeed, Khanykov's squadron must have come close to meeting with the Dutch while making passage to the Downs, with the possibility of both falling into battle. Instead, it was not until 17 August that the Dutch were finally discovered at sea, a British naval lugger, *Spider*, sailing to the Texel, sending a report to the Admiralty of having seen the Dutch 'under easy sail' 10 miles to the south east of Camperdown on the Dutch coast. On the following day a further sighting was made, this time by three British ships of war, *Lion, Nassau,* and *Glatton,* with it reported that the Dutch were on a bearing of seven leagues to the south-south-east of Goree. Both reports arrived at the Admiralty on or around 20 August. With the Dutch now at sea, a clear danger existed to convoys sailing out of the Baltic, as well as 'so rich an object as the East India fleet.'

At that time, and demonstrating the value to Britain of Khanykov's squadron, was that of Duncan only being able to muster just one ship of seventy-four guns (*Venerable*), three of fifty guns (*Calcutta, Jupiter,* and *Leopard*), and two frigates (*Circe* and *Qader*), with the Russians having a much greater force. However, it was Duncan's smaller force that was first to meet with the Dutch, this off Bremerhaven. Immediately, Duncan realised he was at a considerable disadvantage, for the Dutch force was larger than had been reported because, unbeknown to him, the ships in Flushing had also sailed and had joined the Texel squadron, giving the Dutch a combined force of five battleships, eight frigates and several small vessels amounting to twenty-one ships in total. Immediately, the Dutch formed into line of battle, endeavouring over a period of five hours to come up with Duncan's ships. Wisely, given that his ships were outgunned, Duncan hauled the wind, and carefully avoided the Dutch until the hoped-for arrival of Khanykov, detaching one of his cutters to inform the Russian admiral of the developing situation. Should matters have continued as they were, a battle might well have resulted had it not been for a change in the weather, the outbreak of a violent storm forcing the Dutch to return to the protected waters of the Texel.

Unaware that a Russian squadron of considerable strength would soon be reinforcing Duncan's smaller number of ships, and still hoping to take advantage of their numerical superiority, the Dutch again sailed on the twenty-first intent upon battle. Such might have occurred if, during the night, while off Cape Egmont, a second fierce storm broke out, the Dutch again choosing to return to the Texel. Almost certainly, if they had remained at sea, they would have been confronted not just by Duncan's ships but also Khanykov's much larger force. Likely as not, and proving just how close the enemy squadrons came to each other, signals heard that night by the Dutch, and claimed by one Dutch officer to be 'shots fired by the English squadron', were Khanykov's ships signalling their arrival. For the Dutch, it was only on the following day they realised the Russians were present, the same Dutch officer writing of 'the combined English and Russian fleet...composed of about 30 sail, 20 of which were line of battle ships.' According to a Russian officer, Khanykov's squadron had made the Dutch coast in just a few hours, discovering the enemy near the mouth of the Texel, adding, 'we instantly pressed all the sail we could, but before it was possible for us to come up with them, they effected their escape into that Harbour.' For the previously quoted Dutch officer, and despite not having gained the desired battle in which victory appeared to him to have been an absolute certainty, he believed his navy had gained most from the affair, for in bringing about a junction of the Texel and Flushing warships, this combined force would soon 'humble England's pride, and avenge the honour of the United Netherlands.'

While Duncan's squadron returned to port at the end of August, Khanykov's maintained the blockade, carefully observing the Dutch warships for any sign that they were about to sail. From a distance, their top masts and sails could be observed but much more information could be gained by close-in shore reconnaissance, with *Arkhangel Mikhail* on several occasions entering the outer roadstead from which was discovered to be present 'eighteen Ships of War', of which 'eight or nine' were 'of the Line'.

Despite the number of British and Russian ships available for deployment in the North Sea, the numbers were still inadequate for maintaining a constantly effective blockade of the Texel, especially as any ship on blockade duty had to be relieved after three or four weeks to revictual and take on water. With the Russian squadron having returned to the Downs, and some of their ships replenishing at the Nore, the Dutch appeared ready for another break-out during the first week of October. Immediately, Khanykov was ordered to sail, although some of his ships were severely undermanned by disease, with 500 Russian seamen having been transferred to the naval hospital at Deal but with many more also suffering scurvy and typhus but not transferred to the hospital. On this occasion, through the timely arrival of the Russian squadron, depleted as it was in numbers of fit and able seamen, the Dutch made no effort to sail.

During the opening months of 1796, following a continuing period of extremely violent weather, observation of the Dutch squadron was given over to a single Russian frigate and a cutter, the latter there to carry communications back to England. On 23 February, it was reported that a Dutch squadron of six two-decked ships, eight frigates and three smaller vessels were at sea, detected 40 leagues north of Yarmouth by the British sixteen-gun sloop *Espiegel*. It was the intention of this force, which was under the command of Vice Admiral Adriaan Braak, to retake the Cape Colony, which had been captured by the British the previous year. From the Nore, Duncan was immediately ordered to sail, taking five sail of the line alongside the Russian sixty-six-gun *Philippe*. More Russian ships might have been available if several were not at that time in the hands of the dockyard at Chatham undergoing repairs to their rigging and sails following storm damage. The storms encountered had been especially severe and led to the loss of several merchantmen and military transports, but no Russian ship. Spencer, who always expressed amazement at anything the Russian squadron achieved, seemed surprised that all the Russian ships had survived, for upon learning of the state of the weather at sea, he feared it would reduce 'Her Imperial Majesty's squadron to a very unpleasant state.' As for *Philippe* and the other ships in pursuit of Braak, they were unable to make contact, Braak taking the northern route into the Atlantic rather than sailing south through the Dover Strait. Meanwhile, within the Texel roadstead there remained a force of six or seven ships of the line together with numerous frigates, a seagoing force over which a continued watch had to be maintained.

Even if more ships of the Russian squadron had been able to put to sea in February, their fighting efficiency would have been limited. Typhus and scurvy continued to rage, the hospital ship *Union*, moored off Sheerness, receiving, between 3 September 1795 and 28 January 1796, 479 typhus sufferers from Khanykov's squadron. Archibald Menzies, a surgeon sent on board *Union* to help combat the disease, witnessed a truly appalling sight upon his arrival on 24 November:

> *The lower and middle gun decks were divided into large apartments, or wards, by cross partitions, with free communication between each; they were extremely crowded, and the sick of every description lay in cradles, promiscuously arranged, to the number of two hundred; of which about one hundred and fifty were in different stages of a malignant fever, extremely contagious, as appeared evident from its rapid progress, and fatal effects, amongst the attendants on the sick, and the ship's company.*

Throughout the rest of 1796, and with the remaining Dutch ships making no attempt to sail, the blockade was maintained. Russian warships, once released from the dockyard at Chatham and with their crews now in better health, continued to cruise off the Dutch coast, relieved in turn by other Russian ships for the purpose of revictualling. One major change occurred in August when Russian ships, including *Graf Orlov*, *Philippe*, *Parmen* and *Helena*, were ordered back to Russia, with a new contingent of ships passing through the Straits to replace them.

The need to end the constant squandering of warships on a continuous blockade of the Texel resulted in the hatching of a plan to undertake a combined land and sea attack in which the gun batteries covering the sea approaches to the roadstead were to be taken and fireships used to destroy or cause confusion among the sheltering Dutch ships. In doing so, it was supposed that the Dutch, to avoid the fireships, would come out and attack the ships of the blockading squadrons or sail deeper into the Zuider Zee, leaving the roadstead in the hands of the Anglo-Russian forces. Continued winds blowing onshore made it impossible for any landings to be made, with the entire project, which was to have been carried out during the final week of October, consequently abandoned. In the event of the Dutch breaking out of Texel to attack the blockading fleet, the Russian squadron would have played a significant role, providing the additional strength that would have prevented any of the Dutch ships escaping while helping to ensure overall victory. Consequently, with the failure of this plan to go ahead, the need to maintain a steady watch on the Texel had to be maintained, and was to be continued into the following year.

In addition to maintaining a watch upon the Dutch warships, Russian ships were also giving protection to merchant convoys and individual ships passing along Britain's east coast while smaller ships of the Russian squadron searched out and captured a few Dutch and other enemy merchant ships. In the North Sea, Chichagov, in capturing several merchant ships, used tactics that might have been taken straight out of the pages of a C.S. Forester *Hornblower* novel. His ship, *Retvizan*, unlike other warships of the period, had no raised forecastle or poop deck and, as such, gave appearance, especially if seen from a distance, of being much like a merchantman. Using this to advantage, and covering over her lower gun deck with painted canvas to add to the illusion of *Retvizan* being a merchant ship, Chichagov was able to close with unsuspecting enemy merchantmen without them taking flight and more easily escaping capture. His most spectacular success came during the winter of 1795.

While sailing close to the Dutch shoreline, *Retvizan* was approached by a heavily laden armed Dutch merchantman attempting to gain the safety of the Texel roadstead. The captain of that ship had assumed *Retvizan* to be a fellow merchantman bound for Texel and had come up to her so that the two, if attacked, could combine their fire-power in protecting each other. Once she was close to *Retvizan*, a single shot was fired with the whole *Retvizan*'s lower battery simultaneously displayed. Faced with the possibility of being raked by a crippling broadside at close range, the merchantman had no choice but to surrender.

An interesting corollary to the taking of that ship was Chichagov receiving, after several years, prize money to the value of £2,500. Within the Royal Navy prize money was a primary means of motivating both crews and officers, as all involved in the capture of a ship would, once the captured ship was brought into a friendly harbour and an adjudication made as to its value, be eligible for a share of its value. Admittedly proceeds were not divided evenly, senior officers received a considerably higher proportion than that allotted to the lower deck and petty officers. Within the Russian Navy, prize money was rarely paid, and when it was paid, was much less generous. According to Chichagov, his father, Admiral Vasiliy Chichagov, in capturing or destroying much of the Swedish Fleet during the Swedish War, received in prize money only £300. As to whether others, particularly the seamen of the lower deck, received their share of prize money from the capture of the Dutch merchantman, Chichagov says nothing, but most probably they did not, the money likely to have been subsumed into the Russian treasury.

Another capture made by Chichagov while captaining *Retvizan* was a trove of three vessels taken off Texel in early July 1796. This was to prove of particular value as a pilot on board one of these ships, when questioned, provided detail of Dutch naval affairs, indicating that in Texel at that time there were nine sail of the line, two frigates, two brig cutters, and one schooner. While these numbers were already known, what did prove useful was the pilot indicating them to be all badly manned, with seaman only volunteering to serve, 'but such as are in a starving condition.' Instead, crews could only be raised if they were compelled to serve by forcible impressment. Shipwrights called upon to undertake any refit work on these ships were refusing to comply, believing that they would receive no pay for any work performed.

Chichagov was not the only Russian to capture enemy shipping, but as a self-publicist he purposely brought attention to his various achievements while others were less forthright. On 2 December, several British newspapers reported *Graf Orlov* having taken the sixteen-gun Dutch sloop *Van Trump*, a useful capture as *Van Trump* had proved herself extremely valuable to the Dutch, for while at sea over the previous week she had captured and sent into Texel several British coasters. Equally as valuable was the taking of *Augustine*, a French privateer of ten guns, by the Russian sloop *Dispatch*. Once again this was off Texel, with *Dispatch* also retaking *Nelly*, an English merchantman, which *Augustine* had previously taken as a prize.

Only one Russian ship during this period was lost, *Arkhangel Mikhail* running aground on hidden rocks in the Gulf of Finland on 15/26 October 1796. She was returning to Kronstadt having been temporarily recalled by Catherine, with the frigate losing her rudder and her hold filling with over 7 feet of water. While the crew managed to remove the ship from the rocks and take her into a nearby bay, she hit more rocks and took on even more water. Fortunately, the entire crew managed to get ashore. A court-martial held at Tallinn in February of the following year, which lasted five weeks, found Captain Brown, the commander of *Arkhangel Mikhail*, alongside the ship's officers, to not be responsible for the loss of the ship and all were honourably acquitted.

# CHAPTER 8

# THE ANGLO-RUSSIAN EXPEDITION OF 1799

Paul, who became emperor in November 1796, immediately set about reversing his mother's policy of fighting expansionist wars, choosing a more peaceful foreign policy that relied upon diplomacy rather than intervention. In June of the following year, and for this reason, he ordered a return to Kronstadt of the Russian squadron operating in the North Sea. This recall might well have allowed the Dutch Batavian fleet to freely sail as most ships belonging to Duncan's North Sea Squadron were no longer blockading the Texel, their crews having mutinied and taken their ships to the Nore, where they remained for several weeks. Joining a loose collection of other warships that had also mutinied, they remained orderly but non-compliant to Admiralty instructions before returning to sea in July. This left Duncan with just two ships of the line and two frigates to hold back the nine battleships and several smaller ships taking refuge in the roadstead or within the Zuider Zee. However, the situation was saved by Rear Admiral Makarov who, on the instructions of Vorontsov, the Russian ambassador, and contravening Paul's instructions, returned to the Dutch coast at this crucial moment in time. In thanks for this, Makarov was presented by Britain's King George III with a gold sword richly decorated with diamonds and inscribed 'Texel, June 12, 1797'. Paul, for his part, was much less pleased. Later claiming it was the Russian ships under Makarov that had 'saved the greatest fleet in the world', Paul nevertheless punished Vorontsov by confiscating his estates in Finland.

It was following the departure of the Russian Fleet that the Battle of Camperdown was fought, with Duncan's North Sea Squadron inflicting a major defeat upon the Batavian Navy. During the first week of October 1797, with Duncan's squadron back to full strength, a force of fifteen Dutch ships of the line had left Texel in the hope of meeting with smaller units of the enemy that could be overwhelmed. Instead, on 11 October, they were brought into battle by a comparable-sized force under Duncan, with the British capturing nine of their battleships. Nevertheless, six Dutch ships of the line together with several frigates managed to escape to Texel, so enforcing a continuing blockade. Russian ships were again involved for Paul, in fear of the growing strength of France, had reversed his earlier decision, ordering ships of his imperial navy to return.

Makarov, promoted in September 1797 to the rank of vice admiral, was first to sail, leading a squadron of five ships of the line and two smaller ships into British coastal waters during the early summer of 1798. From Arkhangelsk on 3 July, five more ships of the line, two frigates and some smaller vessels were also sent into British waters, these commanded by George Tate, a vice admiral since the beginning of the year. In October, five more ships of the line and a frigate were dispatched from Kronstadt under the command of Rear Admiral Pyotr Kondratievich Kartsov. But in passing through the Skagerrak on 15 November a severe storm was encountered that inflicted considerable damage on

**Russian warships dispatched to the North Sea, 1798.**

| | Guns |
|---|---|
| ***From Kronstadt sailing under Vice Admiral Mikhail Makarov*** | |
| *Elisaveta* (Elizabeth) | 74 |
| *Iaroslav* (Yaroslavl) | 74 |
| *Retvizan* | 64 |
| *Europa* (Europe) | 64 |
| *Boleslav* (Boleslav) | 64 |
| *Narva* (Narva) frigate | 44 |
| *Dispatch* brig-sloop | 18 |
| ***From Arkhangelsk sailing under Vice Admiral Tate*** | |
| *Vsevolod* (named after Vsevolod I, Grand Prince) | 74 |
| *Severny-Oryol* (Northern Eagle) | 74 |
| *Isidor* (Isidor) | 74 |
| *Pobeda* (Victory) | 66 |
| *Aziia* (Asia) | 66 |
| *Schastlivyi* (Happy) frigate | 44 |
| *Pospeshnyi* (Hasty) frigate | 38 |
| ***From Kronstadt sailing under Rear Admiral Pyotr K. Kartsov*** | |
| *Aleksei* (Aleksei) | 74 |
| *Sviatoi Pyotr* (Saint Peter) | 74 |
| *Prints Gustav* (Prince Gustav) | 74 |
| *Sofiia Magdalina* (Sofiia Magdalina) | 74 |
| *Iziaslav* (Iziaslav) | 66 |
| *Riga* | 38 |
| ***From Arkhangelsk sailing under Vice Admiral Baratynsky*** | |
| *Moskva* (Moscow) | 74 |
| *Tikhvinskaya Bogoroditsa* (Tikhvin Mother of God) frigate | 44 |
| *Sviatoi Feodosii Totemskii* (St Feodosiy Totemskiy) frigate | 44 |

Kartsov's ships, with his flagship, *Prints Gustav*, springing her timbers and completely lost. Kartsov was among the few who survived, transferring his flag to the sixty-six-gun *Iziaslav*, with his remaining ships forced to enter the dockyard at Chrstiansand where emergency repairs were carried out. The squadron eventually entered Yarmouth Roads on 8 November. Finally, but not until August of the following year, a further ship of the line and two frigates under Vice Admiral Baratynsky arrived from Arkhangelsk.

While still hoping to achieve a peaceful outcome to the war, Paul went further, giving his support to an Anglo-Russian invasion of the Texel that had as its object something much more ambitious than the earlier planned but not carried out attack on the roadstead. Again, the intention was to destroy or capture ships of the Batavian Navy, primarily those that had escaped Duncan during the Battle of Camperdown. To this was added the reinstatement of the exiled Dutch King Willem V in the belief that he would be supported by a wide element of his people and so bring an end to the Batavian Republic and its alliance with revolutionary France. Russia, on receiving subsidy payments by Britain, would make available over 17,000 troops while Britain in turn would provide 13,000 troops alongside funds for the procurement of transport craft and escort vessels. To convoy the troops across the Baltic numerous ageing warships lying idle in Kronstadt were converted into transports, a task overseen by Captain Home Popham, a British naval envoy, with Popham informing Spencer at the Admiralty that:

> *His Imperial Majesty [has] agreed to give ten sail ships, and on Tuesday last the vice president of the Admiralty put six [of the line] ships, three large frigates, two small ones and two store ships under my direction to be fitted out as transports...I have not left one idle man in Kronstadt.*

Those ships, once converted would carry nearly 7,000 men, while from Britain came thirty-one ships, a mix of converted warships and merchantmen, to take from Tallinn just over 13,000 troops and 108 horses. To protect their way out of the Baltic, a Russian squadron consisting of seven ships of the line under Admiral Khanykov left Tallinn for the Sound where, should the Danes attempt to obstruct their passage in some way, they were to land troops and take possession of Copenhagen. However, the Danes offered no opposition and all of the troop ships successfully passing through the Sound and into the North Sea where Admiral Duncan, working in conjunction with eight line of battle ships and two fifth rates under Makarov, added further protection.

First assembling in the Downs, the invasion fleet, on 27 August, began landing troops at Callantsoog, 18km south of the port of Den Helder, with the flanks of the landing area covered by ships of both the British and Russian squadrons. While the landings were successful, British troops and volunteer Russian seamen landed from 180 transport ships, a substantial counter-attack by forces loyal to the Batavian Republic, forced a hasty evacuation. On 30 August *Europa*, *Iaroslav* and *Retvizan*, alongside several British warships entered the strait between Texel and the mainland, to which there was no opposition from the Batavian Navy, despite eight ships of the line, three frigates and a brig in readiness to sail. Instead, those ships remained moored in the shallower waters of the Zuider Zee, many of their crews, through loyalty to Willem V, refusing to fight and throwing cannons and other weapons overboard. Faced with this situation and confronted by the powerful Anglo-Dutch squadron, commander Vice Admiral Samuel Storey, following a council of war with his senior officers, chose to surrender, with Makarov, the senior Russian commander, taking possession of several Dutch warships including Storey's flagship *Washington*. Paul later gifted all these vessels to George III.

Further and much larger landings were made during the first two weeks of September, including troops convoyed from Tallin that were, while at sea, under the charge of Chichagov, now a rear admiral. In total, 35,000 troops were brought ashore, their ultimate but unrealised objective the capture of Amsterdam. Although meeting with initial success, this force was finally to be defeated on 6 October, with the British commander-in-chief, the Duke of York, compelled to conclude a truce that saw the entire Anglo-Russian force departing the country by the end of November.

The overall failure of the Anglo-Russian expedition, with its only success the taking of twelve Batavian warships, did little to encourage Paul to continue the alliance against France. Adding to this was his increasing realisation that within British naval and military circles there was considerable prejudice against Russia with the Duke of York, himself a less than competent military commander, blaming the ultimate failure of the expedition upon the Russians. As for British naval officers, some were openly boasting that the Russian ships had fallen short of the efficiency of British ships, to which was added the more than questionable observation that, during their time in the North Sea, the Russian squadron had achieved little. More specifically, and coming to the attention of Paul, was the behaviour of seamen and junior officers on *Diadem*, a British warship converted into a transport for evacuating Russian troops out of Holland. Seemingly, the Russians on board were frequently abused with *Diadem*'s captain, John Dawson, through taking no action, effectively inciting the crew to continue those insults.

# PART THREE

# New friends and new enemies

Penetration by the French into the Balkans together with occupation of the Ionian Islands opened the possibility of the French entering the Black Sea and posing a direct threat to Russia. This new revolutionary government was now something to be feared, showing an interest in dominating eastern European trade combined with foreign policy aggression that had previously not existed under more decadent aristocratic governments of the past. When it was also learnt in St Petersburg that the French Directory in 1798 was concentrating in their Mediterranean ports a great number of transports and battleships for an expedition, it was feared that it was destined for the Black Sea. To counter such a possibility, Paul, in May of that year, ordered Vice Admiral Mordvinov 'to be in full readiness in all ports.' Consequently Ushakov, commander of the Black Sea Fleet, was instructed to patrol between Sevastopol and Odessa and 'that as soon as [he] received news that a French military squadron is attempting to enter the Black Sea then, in having found it, to immediately enter into a decisive battle.' The Ottomans also felt threatened, but for them it became a reality when Egypt, an Ottoman client state, fell to the French under Bonaparte, with Malta also occupied by the French. In a hitherto unimaginable turn of events, the implacable enemies, the court at St Petersburg and the Ottoman Porte, formed an alliance that was to be first evidenced by warships of the Imperial Russian Navy entering the Bosporus to fight alongside ships of the Ottoman Navy. Into this alliance was also drawn Britain's Mediterranean Fleet following Nelson's victory at Abū Qīr Bay, but in this there were problems from the outset, for both Ushakov and Nelson were unable to form a working relationship, something that became even clearer when the two admirals met face-to-face during September 1799.

# CHAPTER 9

# PROBLEMS WITH AN IRRITABLE ENGLISH ADMIRAL

There were two meetings between Ushakov and Nelson during September 1799, both held in the Bay of Palermo. The first on Nelson's flagship, the eighty-gun *Foudroyant*, and the second on Ushakov's eighty-four-gun *Sviatoi Pavel*. That the two detested each other was already clear from their correspondence. Not to each other, for in letters they exchanged there was nothing but politeness. But in writing to their closest associates, each mounted a cascade of damning complaints as to the behaviour and actions of the other. For Nelson, hostility towards Ushakov was almost overwhelming. At the very least he seemed unable to accept that Ushakov, a full admiral, was two ranks senior to him with Nelson at that time a vice admiral. Indeed, Nelson believed he had the right as a British naval commander to order any officer of a friendly or allied nation, irrespective of their rank, to obey his instructions. Not surprisingly, Ushakov came to resent such an assumption, choosing to make his own decisions based on his own assessment of any given situation.

While neither of the meetings was minuted, a few clues exist as to what transpired. Nelson, following those meetings, unflatteringly described Ushakov as possessing 'a polished outside, but a bear close to his skin.' This was possibly because Ushakov, following an initial exchange of polite words, had been direct and to the point, accusing Nelson of trying to push him away from where his ships and those of an Ottoman squadron sailing with him might be of most value in fighting the French. Nelson expressed his annoyance, accusing the Russian admiral of having concentrated his efforts upon acquiring the Ionian Islands, especially Corfu, rather than supporting a blockade of Alexandria that Nelson had put into effect. As in any argument, Nelson may well have thumped his fist on the table around which they were seated to emphasise his resolve that the Adriatic was of little importance to the war that he, Nelson, was fighting in the Mediterranean. What Nelson doubtless failed to mention but had told many others was his wish to reserve the Ionian Islands for himself, viewing them as strategically important to Britain, and his disappointment that Russia had got there first.

Making matters even worse, and during one of those meetings, Ushakov let slip that he had been instructed by his emperor to set sail for Malta to 'force the French enemy to surrender the fortress.' Not only did Nelson see this as an unwarranted intrusion into an area of water he had already reserved for himself, and to which the Ionian Islands were to have been added, but he may have also taken this as a disparaging remark. For while Ushakov, using a combination of shipborne artillery and a direct land assault, had taken in four months the island of Corfu and its heavily fortified main town, Nelson had been struggling to free Malta and capture the French-held citadel of Valletta for the previous eleven months.

Either to Ushakov during the meeting, or maybe just later in writing, Nelson said that Ushakov was 'jealous' of Nelson's successes, referring to the battle recently fought in Abū Qīr Bay, and the Russian admiral lacking 'natural sense'. This, Nelson declared, was why Ushakov wanted 'to get to Malta', caring 'for nothing else.' Not surprisingly, Soviet and Russian historians are quick to defend Ushakov, now, quite literally, the patron saint of the Russian Navy. In doing so, they provide their own retort, with one of Ushakov's defenders, Alexander Vaylov, indicating it to be Nelson who exuded jealousy, resentful of Ushakov's success in the Ionian Sea. In Vaylov's opinion, Nelson was expecting to be confronted by 'a submissive instrument who under his influence, would act in the interests of England'. Instead, he 'found in him a smart independent Russian admiral'. In a fictionalised account of that same meeting, another Russian writer, feeling free to take matters further, describes a crabby Nelson, throwing barbed remarks in Nelson's direction and concluding, in common with Vaylov but using inventive phrasing, that 'the English scythe' had found 'a Russian stone'.

Stepping back in time, it was during the summer of 1798 that Nelson and Ushakov, alongside Vice Admiral Abdülkadir Beg of the Ottoman Navy, were required by their respective governments to co-operate in opposing the French in the eastern Mediterranean. Whereas during much of the eighteenth century the Russian and Ottoman Empires had been openly hostile towards each other, Bonaparte, in one stroke, had changed all this. His invasion of Egypt, alongside the taking of Malta, was seen by Paul and Selim III, the ruling Ottoman sultan, as a direct threat. For the Ottomans it was a possible precursor for attack on Istanbul, with Malta the ideal midway supply base for sustaining a French military operation. If carried out, such an assault on the Ottoman capital would force Selim into an alliance with the French, an alliance that Paul feared would threaten Russia's interests in and around the Black Sea. In the words of Alexander Bezborodko, imperial chancellor of Russia, 'I am sure that they [the French] are preparing an expedition to the Black Sea in order to force the Turks to act against us in every way.' It was this new and increased fear of the French that now drew these two former enemies into an alliance that at any previous time would have been impossible. Again, in Bezborodko's words, 'it would take such monsters as the French to produce a thing that I did not expect in my life time, that is our alliance with the Porte, and the passage of our fleet through the [Bosporus] channel.'

The first move in the forming of this alliance was a naval convention agreed between Russia and the Porte signed on 20 August 1798. Fourteen days later, on 4 September, but recorded by Ushakov in the Old Style as 24 August, his six Russian ships of the line, eight frigates and three brigs entered the Bosporus. The rapid arrival of the Russian squadron resulted from Paul having already instructed Ushakov to put to sea in expectation of a possible French entry into the Black Sea. Furthermore, it was a well-trained unit of ships, as different from Khanykov's squadron that had entered the North Sea from the Baltic as chalk is to cheese. While serfs and peasants served on the lower deck, these ships had a much greater number of skilled seamen: Greek seafarers who were more than willing to enlist in the Russian Navy. These ships were already frequently at sea, Ushakov having placed, since his appointment in 1790 as overall commander of the Black Sea Feet, much emphasis on combat readiness. Timely attention had also been given to replenishment of stores, ordnance, and technical equipment. To ensure that the sailing of those ships into the Bosporus did not compromise Russia's naval strength in the Black Sea, a reserve squadron at Sevastapol was also in the process of being formed, a squadron designed to defend the Crimea if it came under attack, but also, if necessary, to strengthen Ushakov's squadron in the Mediterranean.

Once in Turkish waters, the Russian squadron under Ushakov joined an Ottoman squadron under Abdülkadir, both units together sailing to the French-occupied Ionian Islands. Although Russian historiography makes am assumption that Ushakov had general command of this combined force, this was not formally determined, with each of the two squadrons subject to the command of their own flags. However, and it is from

**Russian warships dispatched to the Bosporus, 1798.**

| **Ships of the line** | **Guns** |
|---|---|
| *Sviatoi Pavel* (St Paul) | 82 |
| *Svyataya Troitsa* (Holy Trinity) | 76 |
| *Zakharii I Elisavet* (Zachary and Elisaveta) | 74 |
| *Sviatoi Pyotr* (St Peter) | 74 |
| *Epiphania Gospoda* (Epiphany of the Lord) | 72 |
| *Mariia Magdelina* (Mary Magdeline) | 68 |
| **Frigates** | |
| *Grigorii Velikiia Armenii* (Gregory the Great of Armenia) | 50 |
| *Sviatoi Mikhail* (St Michael) | 48 |
| *Sviatoi Nikolai* (St Nicholas) | 46 |
| *Kazanskaya Bogoroditsa* (Our Lady of Kazan) | 46 |
| *Aleksandr Nevskii* (Alexander Nevsky) | 46 |
| *Soshestvie Sviatogo Dukha* (The Descent of the Holy Spirit) | 44 |
| *Navarkhiia Voznesenie Gospodn*e (Ascension of the Lord) | 66 |
| *Schastlivyi* (Happy) | 36 |

this that the confusion arose, Selim III gave instruction to Abdülkadir that he should 'respect the Russian admiral as a teacher', so effectively placing Ushakov in the lead position. Instructions given to Ushakov by Paul had sanctioned him to work alongside Nelson, and whose squadron, following the Abū Qīr Bay victory, was correctly regarded as an essential asset in overcoming the French. To this, however, Paul did add that such co-operation should only be 'when circumstances require'.

The terms of the naval convention as agreed between Russia and the Porte were communicated to Nelson in October by Earl St Vincent, commander-in-chief of the British Mediterranean Fleet. St Vincent was Nelson's overall superior, but with Nelson commanding the detached squadron that had pursued Bonaparte's expeditionary force across the Mediterranean before gaining victory at Abū Qīr Bay. Following the battle, Nelson had remained in the eastern Mediterranean to ensure that no additional French seaborne forces entered the region. As for the Admiralty communique sent to St Vincent, this informed him:

> *That a Treaty has recently been concluded between the Porte and Russia, by which His Imperial Majesty [Tsar Paul I] was engaged to furnish a number of ships for the purpose of being employed against the common enemy, part of which has actually arrived in Constantinople [Istanbul] and joined the Turkish squadron.*

To this was added the need to maintain 'good intelligence' with the Russians and to avoid giving 'the smallest cause for suspicion, jealousy or offence.'

Nelson, who received a copy of this communique while in Naples, was dismissive of its content, indicating to St Vincent that he had no desire to work alongside any Russian naval force, believing their presence would be an encumbrance to his own plans. Elaborating on this, Nelson declared that 'Malta, Corfu and those islands are my object after Egypt', and wished that the Russian squadron 'be kept to the East'. In this respect, and as subsequently demonstrated in a series of later letters, Nelson was concerned that Great Britain should not lose the advantage of his squadron being in the eastern Mediterranean. At the same time, to Ushakov he was respectful, even unctuous, writing to the Russian admiral in mid-November from *Vanguard*, his flagship until June 1799, which was lying off Naples, the capital of the Two Sicilies:

> *I greatly embrace the opportunity of paying my respects, and of assuring you how happy I feel that we are so near each other, and working together for the general cause of our sovereigns. I should be proud when opportunity offers, of paying my respects in person.*

To ensure that the Russians did not gain any advantage from the arrival of Ushakov's squadron, or so he hoped, Nelson began a series of actions that would secure the eastern Mediterranean from not just the French, the real enemy, but Russia as perceived by him as an additional enemy. To 2nd Earl Spencer, First Lord of the Admiralty, Nelson wrote on 9 October:

> *Respecting my movement, my intention is to go off Malta...there to leave a proper force...then to proceed to Zante, Cephalonia, and Corfu to see what can be done.*

Off Malta, Alexander Ball, commanding the seventy-four-gun third-rate *Alexander*, would soon be leading a blockading force, while Thomas Troubridge, commander of the seventy-four-gun third-rate *Culloden*, so Nelson expected, would soon be able to establish a blockade of the Ionian Islands. Malta and the Ionian Islands were all held by the French. For Troubridge to distribute, Nelson issued a letter addressed to the inhabitants of Corfu, Cephalonia, Ionia, Zante, and Kythira, which carried the promise that his only wish was 'to deliver good men from tyranny and oppression'.

By keeping 'them [the Russian squadron] to the east', the phrase Nelson used in writing to Spencer, he was referring to the blockade of Alexandria where a British squadron under Samuel Hood had already been established to prevent supplies and reinforcements reaching Bonaparte's expeditionary force. It was here, Nelson claimed, the Russian squadron would be of most value, while keeping Ushakov away from areas where Nelson wanted a free hand to operate as he wished. Effectively, Nelson was attempting to completely seal off the greater part of the eastern Mediterranean for his own purpose, attempting to take overall command and expecting everyone else to fall into place. Ushakov recognised this to be an attempt to deliberately sideline him for what he supposed was for the purpose of Nelson, and only Nelson, gaining the glory that would result from victories achieved.

Because of the many years of hostility between Russia and the Ottomans, Ushakov, before entering the Bosporus, had first sought consent and an understanding that his ships would, upon completion of the campaign against France, be permitted a return passage into the Black Sea. With this agreed, Ushakov anchored off Büyükdere, close to the Russian consulate, with details of his arrival sent by Ushakov to Paul:

> *And having received a notice of consent, the desire and demand of the Sublime Porte with the assurance of the Minister, I entered the Strait of Constantinople with every opportunity and anchored against Büyükdere. By all appearances, the Sublime Porte, and all the people of Constantinople were incomparably delighted by [our] arrival.*

On 8 September a conference held at Bebek in the modern-day district of Beşiktaş was called to consider the strategy to be taken against the French. The conference was attended by Ushakov, Vasily Tomara and John Spencer Smith, the Russian and British plenipotentiaries to the Ottoman Porte, as well as various Ottoman naval and government officials. Particular attention was given to protecting areas viewed as vulnerable to further

French incursions, with it agreed that two-thirds of the warships available to Ushakov and the Ottoman squadron should initially sail into the Ionian Sea to investigate more closely the actual strength of the enemy. From reports received, it was understood that the French had recently increased the size of their occupation forces in this region that could be for the purpose of occupying further Ottoman territory, possibly the Peloponnese or islands belonging to the Greek archipelago. The remaining third of those vessels belonging to this combined force were detached to the seas off Rhodes and Crete, these islands also perceived as potential if unlikely targets for a French attack. In addition, these detached ships would undertake convoy protection duties for troop transports and supply ships passing between the Anatolian coast and Alexandria. Placed in command of these detached units was Captain Second Rank Alexander Andreyevich Sorokin, a much experienced and decorated officer who had fought in Catherine's earlier wars and who departed the Dardanelles on 7 October 1798.

At the Bebek conference, the importance of Nelson's squadron was far from forgotten, but with no direct contact having been made with Nelson, it could only be assumed that he would continue the blockade of Alexandria, with a request sent to him that he might provide information as to his own intentions. Immediately, a stream of letters from the various parties involved in the conference were sent out to Nelson, including two from Ushakov, both written on 11 October, the first one praising Nelson and his 'famous and glorious victory at the River Nile' before explaining that he had been ordered by his sovereign to act in concert with the enemies of France. Turning to decisions taken by those attending the conference, Ushakov explained how the ships of the joint Russo-Ottoman squadron were to be deployed while asking Nelson to inform him of news he had 'about the actions and intention of the enemy' and 'the dispositions of his ships'. As for the second of Ushakov's two letters to Nelson, this was of a more practical nature, containing the secret identification signals to be used should any British warship meet with ships of the Russian squadron and a request that Nelson give information on the signals he would be using 'for mutual identification of each other'.

Having learnt that Ushakov and the Ottoman squadron would be concentrating their main force in and around the Ionian and Adriatic, Nelson set about attempting to gain a reversal of that decision. His first move was to write to British Plenipotentiary Smith in Istanbul, urging 'the immediate necessity, if not already sailed, of sending the Turks and Russians to Egypt', so that they might give their full support to the blockade of Alexandria. This proved ineffectual, with the combined Russo-Ottoman squadron, at the time of Nelson writing this letter, having already sailed. Recognising this as a possibility or, if the two squadrons had not sailed, his request being ignored, Nelson developed an alternative strategy, one that went a good deal further than merely keeping Ushakov away from Malta and the Ionian Islands. This was an attempt to completely undermine the naval compact through telling all who would listen that the Russians had only one purpose for being in the Mediterranean: that of strengthening their position for a future war against the Ottomans and that Istanbul was their ultimate objective. To Ambassador Smith he wrote, 'If they [the Russians] establish themselves in the Mediterranean,' referring tacitly to Corfu and Malta, 'it will be a thorn in the side of the Porte.' Presumably, Nelson was hoping that Smith, who fully empathised with Nelson's Russophobia, would share this information with officials of the imperial Dîvân, the ruling body of the Ottoman Empire.

Smith had every reason to support Nelson in this endeavour, being on the payroll of the British mercantile Levant company that was looking to supplant Russia as an Ottoman trading partner, becoming after resigning his ambassadorial position the company's representative in Istanbul. The Russian ambassador certainly affirmed this, making it clear that Smith's overriding interest was that of securing advantages for British merchants over those of Russia, stating on one occasion, 'the English minister at the Porte [Smith] serves the Levant Company, which supports them, much more diligently than the King [George III].'

It must be assumed, given the number of times that Nelson was to repeat the accusation, that he genuinely believed Russia to be untrustworthy, and more so than any of the other parties in this seagoing alliance. Even later, when Nelson had long left the eastern Mediterranean, he still chose to reiterate his view that Russia was Britain's chief rival in those waters. To Alexander Ball, who was then the *de facto* governor of Malta, he wrote in August 1804 that his view on 'Russia has long been formed, and to this moment I see everything she does works to the same end – the possession of all European Turkey.' A month earlier, he had written in a similar vein to Hugh Elliott, British ambassador to Naples, declaring that 'Russia will take care of the Ionian Republic, the Morea, and, in the end, Constantinople. The views of Russia are perfectly clear.'

As for the foundation of such a belief, and the reason for him holding it so strongly, this is something to which Soviet and Russian historians very much ascribe to Pitt the Younger's failed attempt to take Britain into a war against Russia in 1791. Yevgeny Tarle, a leading Soviet historian and academician, writing during the late 1940s and whose works in Russia are highly regarded, wrote of it in the following terms:

> *A man of the generation of William Pitt the Younger, Nelson from the first moment Ushakov appeared in the Mediterranean, did not trust Russian plans and tried to fend them off as far as possible, while appearing outwardly friendly. He grew up, acquired political views, sympathies, and antipathies in precisely those years when Pitt the Younger sharply turned the helm of British politics against Russia.*

While this might explain Nelson's distrust of Russia, it does not explain his seeming attachment to the Sublime Porte, and his concern at how the Ottomans might unduly suffer at the hands of the Russians. In letters that he wrote of his suspicions and hatred of Russians, he would by contrast write of the 'upright Turk' and the 'good Turk'. One possible explanation lies in the adulation that Nelson, a man sometimes lampooned for his self-glorification of his own character, received in Istanbul following the Abū Qīr Bay victory. Constantine in a biography of William Hamilton, the British ambassador to the Court of the Two Sicilies and whose wife, Emma, fell into bed with the naval hero, describes Nelson as shamefully arrogant, obsessively conceited, and uncouth. In this respect, Nelson was highly vulnerable to falling under the influence of anyone who bestowed upon him great honours and so possibly explaining his attitude to 'the good Turk', while rejecting Russia as an enemy of 'the good Turk'. In Istanbul, not only did Nelson become aware of his name being fêted across the city following his victory over the French, but the sultan personally ordered 'a fine fur and a superior çelenk' that he had delivered to Nelson. Both were of considerable value, the çelenk (pronounced chelenk), a plume of more than 300 diamonds, was at the time valued at around £1,000, and the robe, which was lined with sable fur of the best quality, of similar value. By comparison, Nelson viewed the presentations he received from England as inadequate, expecting from the king a viscountcy rather than the baronetcy that was bestowed upon him. Similarly fêted by the king and queen of the Two Sicilies, Ferdinand IV and Maria Carolina, receiving also from them expensive gifts that included the dukedom of Bronte with its annual income of £3,000, he similarly fell under their charm, taking actions on their behalf that no other British naval officer would have contemplated.

With the Russo-Ottoman squadron having left the Dardanelles on course for the Adriatic, then known as the Gulf of Venice, it became for Nelson a race as to whose ships would first make their presence felt in this region. On 11 November, instructions were given to Troubridge to sail for Zante and Cephalonia, two of the largest Ionian Islands, where he was to use his best endeavours to take them into his possession. Before Troubridge sailed however, Nelson learnt that Ushakov had won this race, having already captured both these islands, and had moved to Corfu, which he would also eventually capture. A frustrated Nelson once again wrote to St Vincent, expressing his annoyance that 'the Russians seem to be more intent on taking ports in the Mediterranean than destroying Bonaparte in Egypt.'

Unfortunately for Nelson, he appears to have had a complete misunderstanding of the geo-political reality of the region in which he was now dabbling. In viewing Russian aims to be ones that were designed to give them an advantage in any future war fought against the Ottomans, he failed to see that possession by the French of those islands and a lengthy swathe of the nearby littoral, was a direct threat to both Russia and the Ottoman Empire. Should France use its possession of the strategically important Ionian Islands as a springboard for seizing the Balkan Peninsula, France would then present an immediate threat to Russia's recently acquired Black Sea coastline. In addition, continued French possession of the Ionian Islands would allow them to interfere with all shipping movements across the Mediterranean, serving as a constant thorn to all countries in the alliance against France. These were the important reasons that had brought the combined Russo-Ottoman squadron into the Adriatic, with Ushakov aware that the Ionian Islands could also be used to strengthen the French position on the Italian Peninsula, which he viewed as an additional threat to the Ottomans. It was a point he expressed to Tomara in March 1799:

> *There is only one danger for the Sublime Porte, that the French will take possession of all Naples, especially Puglia [region] and with [Puglia*

> *taken] the cities and fortresses of Brindisi and Otranto [will be in French hands], from where they can spread their lordship everywhere.*

Unable or unwilling to accept this, Nelson took it upon himself to convince the commander of the Ottoman squadron working alongside Ushakov that Egypt and not removal of the French from the Adriatic was where they would be best placed. Before making direct contact with Abdülkadir to sow this message, alongside the notion that the Russians were not to be trusted, Nelson instructed Troubridge, should he be able to contact the Ottoman commander, 'to judge whether he is of sufficient rank [with which] to hold a confidential conversation'. Acquiring, in time, an affirmative from Troubridge, Nelson proceeded to write a confidential letter to Abdülkadir, indicating his hope that 'the united Turkish and Russian squadron would have gone to Egypt' and telling Abdülkadir that Egypt was 'the first object of the Ottoman arms' and that Corfu was 'a secondary consideration'.

To continue his scheme of destroying the naval compact as agreed between Russia and the Ottomans, Nelson, on the same day of writing to Abdülkadir, wrote to Smith, telling him of an earlier conversation he had held with Kelim Effendi, a senior Ottoman diplomat. Kelim had been sent to meet with Nelson and present him with the diamond-studded çelenk chosen for him by the sultan following his victory at Abū Qīr Bay. In that letter Nelson reported that the two spoke of 'the conduct likely to be pursued by the Russian court towards the unsuspicious (I fear) and upright Turk.' Furthermore, Nelson went on to add, 'our [Nelson and Kelim's] ideas have exactly been the same about the Russians.' Seemingly, Nelson assumed, both he and Kelim were in complete agreement as to the British admiral's next pronouncement that 'a strong squadron should have been sent to Egypt to have relived my dear friend Captain Hood, but Corfu suited Russia better'.

The letter sent to Smith also reaffirmed Nelson's belief that it was he and he alone who had the right to besiege and capture Malta and the Ionian Islands, expecting Ushakov to concentrate his ships on the blockade of Alexandria. 'Surely my dear Sir,' Nelson wrote in that letter and referring to Smith:

> *I had the right to expect that a united fleet of Turks and Russians would have taken care of things east of Candia [Crete]. I never wished to have them west of it. All those islands would have been ours long ago. Captain Troubridge was absolutely under sail when I heard with sorrow, that the Russians were there.*

That Nelson further stated in his letter to Smith that the Ionian Islands 'would have been ours long ago' makes little sense, given Ushakov's speed in the taking of those islands, relying on making direct attacks on their fortifications rather than a long drawn-out sea blockade.

While the two admirals still exchanged polite messages, Ushakov was becoming increasingly angered both by Nelson's interference in decisions taken at the Bebek conference and his apparent assumption that he should be the one in command, taking decisions about strategy to be pursued when he had no obvious right to do so, being junior in rank. In a letter written to Tomara on 16 March, Ushakov complained:

> *They [the English] show little friendship to us...Corfu has always been desirable to them and they intend themselves for it, and under various and vain appearance they want to alienate us without need.*

At the time of writing this letter, Ushakov was on the verge of capturing Corfu, but once this was achieved, he saw a further problem arising, claiming 'their envy of us', referring to Nelson and other British naval officers, 'will increase'. In this Ushakov appears to have been correct, for upon taking Corfu, Nelson certainly intensified his efforts to remove Ushakov from the Adriatic and to give his attention instead to the blockade of Alexandria, but also adding that more of Ushakov's ships, and those of Abdülkadir's squadron, be released for the protection of Crete. To Tomara, Ushakov wrote of this being of no value, for to do so would take his ships to an 'empty place' where they would be of no benefit and away from where there 'is necessary need'. And that place of necessary need, as far as Ushakov was concerned, was countering an increased French threat in and around the coast of Italy, and which would soon lead to a French occupation of Naples. Ushakov hoped that Tomara would not agree to any requests made by Nelson, stating it to be his intention to:

> *Observe the Gulf of Venice [Adriatic] and the coast of Italy to Messina, as...this place is now the most important in order to secure the shores of the sublime Porte by occupying the Venetian Gulf.*

In another letter written to fellow naval commander Count Grigory Grigorievich Kushelev, Ushakov confided that while 'the English Vice Admiral Nelson blocks Malta and Alexandria, and with himself and his ships in Palermo, there are no ships in the Gulf of Venice.'

# CHAPTER 10

# CORFU AND MALTA

The capturing of Corfu by Ushakov is a topic frequently returned to by Russian historians, seen as an outstanding achievement by an admiral much venerated in Russia – glorified in 2001 by the Russian Orthodox Church as both a saint and patron of the Russian Navy. Furthermore, his rapid taking of Corfu and the other Ionian Islands is compared with Nelson's blockade of Malta that saw the French holding out in Valletta for more than two years. Prior to the capture of Corfu, Ushakov had used a combination of land and naval forces available to him to remove French occupying forces from surrounding islands of the Ionian group, of which Corfu was the most northerly and most populous, and used by the French as their main base in the north-eastern Mediterranean. The islands, formerly part of the Republic of Venice, were acquired by France under the terms of the Treaty of Campo Formio (17 October 1797) following General Bonaparte's victorious campaign in Italy. As for the native population of these islands, they were unwilling to accept their new overlords with the French asserting themselves as conquerors rather than liberators of the oppressed. Throwing aside the rhetoric of 'liberté, fraternité and égalité', they instead plundered and took without restraint from both those of high and low status, imposed excessively high taxes, and diminished the importance of any who had once held office. Even the island's merchants and ship owners, alongside the island's bourgeoisie in general, in other words those who might otherwise have given support to the French by ending the hold Venice had once enjoyed over the islands, turned against the occupiers. Instead they, alongside most of the islanders, craved the day that would bring an end to their suffering.

Of the seven main islands of the Ionian group, Kythera, one of the more southerly islands was the first to be taken by Ushakov's squadron. An advanced force of two frigates, *Grigorii Velikiia Armenii* and *Schastlivyi*, under the command of Captain Lieutenant I.A. Shostak, were ordered by Ushakov to the island, approaching Kythera on the morning of 9 October. Upon the first of the two frigates firing warning shots, French troops occupying a small fortress overlooking the Gulf of St Nicholas, abandoned their position with some taking refuge in a hilltop fortress at Kapsali, the island's main stronghold.

Seeing only two frigates, the French commander initially gave no thought to surrender, but matters changed that evening on the arrival of the combined Russo-Ottoman Fleet that had at its disposal 300 Ottoman soldiers. From those ships cannons were brought ashore, and with much effort two batteries were created within range of the fortress. Ushakov, in a report to Paul, writing of these guns having to be carried on the shoulders of his men and taken across 'very high rocky mountains, ravines, and solid sharp stones' that might otherwise have been considered impossible other than for 'the ardent zeal of the landing party and those working in the deliveries'.

At dawn on 12 October, the bombardment of the fortress began from batteries and frigates that came close to the shore. The fortress responded 'with equal liveliness', indicating the enemy's intention to resist. An artillery duel broke out. At this time, the landing party from the ships was fully prepared for the assault. 'The landing troops from ships and frigates,' wrote Ushakov, 'with undaunted courage and zeal, performed their duties diligently, prepared and impatiently wanted to storm the fortress.' Meanwhile, destruction and losses occurred in the fortress from Russian artillery fire. The effectiveness of this and the readiness of the troops for a decisive assault forced the French command to stop resisting and at noon the French tricolour was lowered and two white flags raised to announce the garrison's surrender. In total the French numbered just over seventy, with Ushakov agreeing to their repatriation to France.

Two weeks later, Ushakov took the island of Zante. Covering landings here was cannon fire from frigates commanded by Shostak. The French soon abandoned their shore batteries, retreating to a fortress that overlooked the main town of the island, Zakynthos. Prior to Shostak's arrival, a letter had been sent to the inhabitants of the island inviting them to help in their liberation, with many offering their support. In writing to the emperor, Ushakov explained that the islanders were:

> *Waiting for us, already prepared, and in great numbers...not even allowing our soldiers and Turks to cross the water, but persistently and with great zeal, relentlessly carrying them to the shore in their arms.*

Realising their position was hopeless, Lieutenant Lucas, the French commander, surrendered the fortress the following morning. Because of the anger of the islanders towards the way they had been treated, Ushakov's men had to provide the French with an armed escort to protect them from the vengeance of the people, taking them on board the Russian ships as prisoners. In turn, Lefkada, where a considerable force was landed and the French-held fortress was bombarded for several days, was also taken, alongside Paxos, Ithaca and Kefalonia.

The subduing of Corfu, the capital of the islands, was to prove much more difficult as it was protected by a powerful complex of fortifications of which those on the eastern side defended the city of Corfu. Here were two massive fortresses, the Old Fortress and the New Fortress, both constructed of solid stone and both able to defend the other with high-up covering fire. The Old Fortress, dating back to the Byzantine period but much improved under the Venetians, lay on top of a rocky promontory and was surrounded by a double rampart with a 22m-wide deep, dry moat. Separating the fortress from the city, and effectively turning it into an island, was the *Contrafossa*, a canal built by the Venetians that effectively changed the fortress into an island within an island. The New Fortress, built on two levels, occupied St Mark's Hill, and was built by the Venetians between 1576 and 1645. It was connected to the Old Fortress by a coastal wall on one side and bastions on the other. Also giving protection to the town were the bastions St Abraham and St Salvatore, these so placed that if one was taken, it would come under fire from the other. In total, the defences around the town of Corfu housed more than 600 guns and a garrison of 3,000 soldiers. Adding to the defence of Corfu, and within cannon shot, lay the island of Vido, a high mountain dominating Corfu and fortified by the French with three batteries to act as a forward outpost. The water area between Corfu and Vido served as an anchorage for several warships. Here lay the seventy-four-gun *Généreux*, the fifty-four-gun *Leander* (which had been captured from the British Navy in August 1798), the twenty-gun corvette *Brune*, the brig *Expedition*, the bomb-vessel *La Frima*, and six galleys.

Upon learning that Russian and Ottoman squadrons had liberated several of the islands, the Corfiots initiated an uprising against the French, but it was brutally suppressed. Nevertheless, upon the arrival on 24 October of the third rate *Epiphania Gospoda,* commanded by Captain I.A. Selivachev, the ship was joyfully received by the islanders. Leading a mixed force of Russian and Ottoman vessels, Selivachev immediately established a blockade to prevent the supply of provisions and the landing of enemy reinforcements. In doing so, several merchant ships and an eighteen-gun xebek were captured, but with a much tighter blockade being possible two weeks later upon the arrival of Ushakov with four ships and two frigates. Throughout the blockade there was increasing friction between Ushakov and Abdülkadir with Ushakov informing Paul that everything achieved was by ships of his own squadron as those of the Ottoman squadron 'wherever I sent them will go for two hours and then return back'. Instead of performing anything useful, Ushakov claimed, 'When I tell them where to cruise and to not come back to the fleet, they leave, stop at anchor and doze the whole time without caution.' This was strongly disputed by Abdülkadir, and it does appear that the Ottoman squadron did play a more significant role than Ushakov would have, most certainly they were in the front line when direct fighting was underway with the French.

One early action taken by Ushakov was the landing of ships' guns and a force of seamen to set up a battery on the north side of the island armed with three unicorns (one a 53-pounder), two mortars and four small field guns to shell the French-held fortresses from a distance. Shortly after, a second battery was established to the south close to the Holy Chapel of Saint Panteleimon, which could fire in all directions, including across the strait should the French ships moored between Corfu and Vido attempt an escape. Once the island was taken, Ushakov viewed these ships as a valuable addition to the combined squadron. Already *Généreux* had made several tries at leaving her moorings, each foiled by Ushakov's blockading ships, with one such attempt described by Ushakov in a report written in late-December:

> *The 74-gun ship Généreux, has very strong artillery and, due to being sheathed in copper, great ease of movement. Taking advantage of this,*

> *before my arrival with the squadron, Généreux in fair winds several times weighed anchor and, without separating far from the fortress and the island of Vido, approached our squadron. From a long distance she gave battle, first with the ship Zakharii I Elisavet along the southern side of the strait, and then along the northern side of the strait, twice against the ship Epiphania Gospoda, but she was always driven away with some damage. Of our ships, the Epiphania Gospoda, was pierced by a cannonball. There was no more damage and no one was killed.*

To this, Ushakov described a second account of *Généreux* attempting a breakout:

> *On the 12th of last November, the said French ship, with a favourable wind, weighed anchor, approached our squadron on the southern side of the fortress to the ship Svyataya Troitsa and had a battle with her from a long distance. At that time the ship Zakharii I Elisavet happened to be under the lee and also tried to approach her [Généreux], but the French ship, having set all sails, went to the wind and returned to the fortress, and from there, at a very long distance, approached my ship Sviatoi Pavel, which had prepared a spring [a line run from amidships to anchor chain to allow the ship when at anchor to face the desired direction], and we had a small battle between ourselves. The distance was so great that the large guns could not reach it otherwise than with overhead shots. From the Sviatoi Pavel, artillery was noticeably more efficient and in a very superior number. The French ship, feeling this superiority, immediately tacked and went under the fortress...her stern gallery was broken, the boom was shot down, with which the flag sank to the bottom. It is also known that several holes were made in the side and eight people were killed.*

Eventually, *Généreux* did escape. With her sails painted black she stealthily put out to sea on the night of 26 January, sailing successfully to Ancona.

As well as the Saint Panteleimon battery, further batteries, with the help of armed residents, and using guns taken from Russian and Ottoman warships, were also put in position. To remove these, Chabot led a detachment of 600 men and two cannons in an attack on those batteries to the south, capturing seventeen Russian soldiers and three guns. A second attack that same day, involving a mixed force of infantry and cavalry numbering more than 1,000, was mounted on Russian batteries to the north defended by more than 400 Russians and Ottomans. The ensuing battle lasted from noon until evening, with the French coming close to success before being pushed back by a vicious bayonet charge that left the French with 100 dead and many wounded, while the Ottoman and Russians lost thirty-one killed and 372 wounded. Subsequent attacks were also made by the French on this same battery, but on each occasion were repulsed.

It was the island of Vido that Ushakov saw as key to the defence of Corfu, but he was unable to mount a full assault until he had been substantially reinforced. In December, Rear Admiral Pavel Pustoshkin arrived with reinforcements from the Black Sea, and the ships previously detached to Rhodes and Crete under Sorokin now also joined Ushakov. With these additions, the combined fleet under Ushakov totalled twelve ships of the line, eleven frigates, and several smaller vessels. Much more significant for the launching of a direct assault was that by the end of February, Ushakov had been reinforced by 4,000 Ottoman troops. The intervening winter, however, proved to be one of great hardship, for although the French ceased any further attacks on the batteries overlooking the forts, these had to be constantly manned, with Ushakov's men having to endure winter weather alongside hunger due to the failure of the Porte to issue the necessary supplies that had been agreed in the Bebek conference. This shortage of materials not only included victuals but ammunition. Shells had to be carefully conserved with few to spare for firing on the enemy.

A formal assault on Vido, following the arrival of a favourable wind, began at 7 a.m. on 29 February 1799. Ushakov had previously conducted a series of training exercises to ensure that there would be smooth interaction between the ships and landing parties with a special table of signalling flags developed. Upon the ships of the combined squadrons closing in on Vido, and using spring anchors, they turned their sides against the French shore batteries to unleash a cannonade of ball and grapeshot that took a considerable toll on the defenders. Those manning the shore batteries lasted no longer than four hours before abandoning their position, allowing for the landing of troops who soon took control of the entire island. In his report to Paul, Ushakov wrote:

> *By the bravery of the victorious troops of your imperial majesty, assisted by the Turks, who having united with ours with the same bravery, rushed into all places and conquered the enemy everywhere.*

*Leander* and the corvette *Brune* also came under fire with both ships attempting to defend those fleeing on small boats to the safety of the two fortresses on Corfu, with about 150 of the 800 French on Vido managing to escape. Brought under fire by the seventy-four-gun *Sviatoi Piotr* and the frigate *Navarkhiia Voznesenie Gospodne*, a separate detachment of two ships under Captain First Rank Senyavin, *Leander* was several times holed under water and forced to beach. Of the role of the Ottoman ships during the initial attack on Vido, Ushakov was far from complimentary, informing Abdülkadir of his displeasure:

> *Although during an attack on the island some [Ottoman ships] were sent to the northern and southern part of the strait between ours, they were always at anchor, never entered the battle against the enemy ships, and even during the storming of the island of Vido they were at a distance from it, except for one frigate.*

Yet such is disputed by maps of the action drawn up by the Ottomans and held in the Topkapi Palace Archives (Topkapı Sarayı Arşivi) and which show ships of the Ottoman squadron joining the Russian ships in the bombardment.

On the following day, the captured batteries on Vido, the Russian batteries on Corfu, and the Russian and Turkish warships opened a continuous cannonade on the French fortifications on Corfu, leading to the capture of the outlying forts, leaving only the Old and New Fortresses in the hands of the French. On the morning of the nineteenth, a letter was sent to Ushakov from General Chabot requesting a ceasefire preliminary to a surrender agreement. 'I in agreement with the commander of the Turkish squadron, Kadir Bey,' Ushakov explained, 'set a deadline of 24 hours and in that time an agreement was made.' The French, in surrendering, would hand over the two fortresses alongside all artillery pieces, supplies and ships. In turn, the surrendering French would be taken on Russian-hired transport ships to Toulon on the understanding that the entire French garrison leaving the fortresses of Corfu would not fight 'against the Russian emperor the sublime port of the Ottoman Empire, England and the kingdom of Naples and the allied powers' for eighteen months, and those released who were already in captivity 'will not fight during the entire duration of the war'.

That the British fifty-four-gun *Leander*, a French prize, had been taken by Ushakov was to cause further vexation between Ushakov and Nelson. Ushakov would like to have retained the ship for the use of his own squadron, but Paul ordered she be returned to the British Navy. Present at Abū Qīr Bay, *Leander* had been returning to England with dispatches from Nelson when she had encountered the much more powerful *Genereux* off Crete. Following an intensive exchange of cannon fire, with both ships sustaining heavy losses, *Leander* was forced to surrender. Sent into Corfu, she was subsequently repaired and given a French crew, but she retained her original name.

St Vincent, on being informed by London of Paul's decision to return *Leander*, sent a note to Nelson informing him that Commander Adam Drummond was to be appointed *Leander*'s temporary captain. Immediately, Nelson sent Drummond and three junior officers to meet Ushakov at Messina and present him with a letter, requesting that the transfer of the ship be made straight away. It was also required by Nelson that Ushakov provide *Leander* with a temporary crew to sail her to Mahon and that all 'the articles necessary for that purpose' be provided. Unfortunately, Ushakov had received no reciprocal instructions from Paul with Nelson merely stating that the orders had originated from the Admiralty in London and presumed that 'the Courts of Petersburg and London [had] decided the matter'. In other words, Nelson provided no clear evidence of Paul having made such an agreement. As a result, the Russian admiral denied Drummond the right to take command of the ship, but assured Nelson that as soon as he received instruction from his superior, he would 'not fail to act in accordance with it and will carry out everything that is prescribed'. Nelson took this as nothing less than a personal rebuff, angrily sending a copy of Ukashov's letter to

Andrei Yakovlevich Italinsky, the Russian minister to the Court of Naples, together with a few scathing words:

> *Whenever the Admiral chooses to send the Leander to Mahon, she will be received, but after even my word not being taken by his Excellency, I cannot again subject myself to a refusal of giving up the Leander, agreeable to the intentions of the emperor, although the form of order on this occasion is not arrived.*

Ushakov was equally annoyed over the matter, considering that he was being pushed on something upon which he had no right to act, until he had received a specific instruction from St Petersburg and not on orders given to him by a lower ranking officer of a foreign navy. In other words, he was being required to flaunt standard protocol – although Nelson's previous letters attempting to manoeuvre the Russian squadron away from the Adriatic was doubtless a contributing factor. To Tomara in Istanbul, he expressed his annoyance in a letter dated 22 August:

> *I am surprised at such shameless demands for the illegal rights to the whole world. The French took that ship in battle. I took it from the French in a fierce battle, it was placed in the defence of the isle of Vido and being under the protection of fortresses and batteries, fought to the last extreme, until she was defeated and began to sink, then she was taken ashore and put aground. My ship [Sviatoi Pavel] which was opposite her [Leander] was also damaged, and therefore her capture did not come cheap to me. Therefore, by all rights she [Leander] belongs to me.*

Eventually, upon Ushakov receiving instruction from St Petersburg, *Leander* was released into British hands and recommissioned in the Mediterranean under Commander Adam Drummond.

The ships of Ukashov's squadron, while successful in blockading Corfu and observing the fortress during the winter period, regardless of the weather, were in an extremely poor shape, a situation not helped by the distance from any secure naval base where repairs could be undertaken. Ushakov lamented:

> *I don't know and can't find examples in all of ancient history that any fleet could be at a distance without any weakening and in such an extreme as we are now.*

These were the same ships of which Ushakov was to write in August 1798 to Rear Admiral Kushelev (see Chapter 2), drawing his attention to their hasty construction, and the showing of considerable deterioration even before leaving the Black Sea. Nor was the condition of those ships helped by the rapid setting up of an impromptu naval base at

Corfu, for even if those in the worst condition were brought ashore and keeled over for the cleaning and repairing of their hulls, the necessary materials were lacking. Ushakov wrote:

> *The frigates Navarkhiia, Kazanskaya, Soshestvie and Sviatoi Nikolai must be keeled, but here [Corfu] for keeling there is no tar, no flammable sulphur, no nails, no iron, no hemp, no timber for the beams, in a word, there is nothing...In all our current state, the sails on many ships are dilapidated; the greater part of the rigging is in poor condition and requires replacement, and there is nothing here; equally all kinds of minor necessary supplies: no candles, no paper, in a word, there is extreme shortage of everything... Now how to leave here with these ships and frigates, if the circumstances require it, I do not know. I foresee nothing except danger.*

Around the time of Ushakov's successful taking of Corfu, several months before his meeting with Nelson, the Russian admiral's anger against Nelson was clearly intensifying. He was embittered by Nelson's constant interference with all the combined Russo-Ottoman squadrons were attempting to achieve. In part, Ushakov ascribes this to instructions that he felt Nelson must have received from London. Several letters written by Ushakov at this time, including one dated 16 March to Vasily Tomara, the official Russian representative to the Sublime Porte, are demonstrative of his anger:

> *They [the English] show little friendship to us...Corfu has always been desirable to them and they intend themselves for it, and under various and vain appearance they want to alienate us without need.*

In May 1799, following a request from Field Marshal Alexander Suvorov at the head of an allied Russian-Austrian army in northern Italy, Ushakov sent Pustoshkin with three battleships, four frigates and five small sailing vessels to the northern Adriatic to establish a blockade of French ships in Ancona that were threatening the safety of Austrian shipping in the northern Adriatic. Having no troops to land, Pustoshkin blockaded the town, which was occupied by 3,000 French and Cisalpine troops. In October, the Austrians arrived with the necessary reinforcements, but in claiming the chief command, completely evicted the Russian admiral, negotiating a capitulation that surrendered the town to the Austrians alongside a refusal to allow the Russians to even enter. Also, around the time that Pustoshkin was ordered to Ancona, Ushakov sent under the command of Captain Second Rank A.A. Sorokin a detachment of ships, four frigates, two small sailing vessels and four Turkish gunboats, to the Otranto area. Here, on 3 May 1799, Brindisi was taken and seventeen days later, Sorokin landed a force of 600 men at Manfredonia which, on reaching the coast of the Tyrrhenian Sea, took the city of Naples. In August 1799, while with his squadron in Messina, Ushakov received a letter from Suvorov in which he asked him to urgently send a group of ships to Genoa to blockade the port to prevent the supply of reinforcements and supplies to the French Army by sea. To assist the Russian troops on the coast of the Gulf of Genoa, Ushakov allocated two ships of the line and two frigates under the command of Pustoshkin. These ships continued to support Suvorov's army until the end of its stay in northern Italy and were successful in capturing several enemy transporters and supply vessel, among them a number lying close to the enemy-held shore in November, with the details of this exploit provided in a letter to Ushakov dated 8 December and reproduced below:

***Vice Admiral Pustoshkin account to Admiral Ushakov of a sea battle fought by him off Genoa.***

*On the 14th of this November [New Style 25 November], cruising with ships near the coast of Genoa, at Cape Meliá, we saw several small ships heading for Genoa right near the coast, and therefore I sent a notice to the trabakul [a small Mediterranean coaster sometimes also referred to as a trabàccolo]. Konstantin, under the command of Lt. Pogonya, adding to his unit, ten grenadiers, a non-commissioned officer, and with them 2nd Lt. Skorobogatov, who had volunteered at this time. Also sent was an Austrian corsair felucca [a small single-masted lateen rigged sailing boat] 'Lyubeppina', which had 2-pounder guns, and was controlled by skipper Nikola Merkovich who had come to me on the same day. Having dispatched both vessels to Cape Meliá in order to cause damage to the enemy small ships that night right off the coast, and as far as possible capture them. I then kept with these ships along the coast at a moderate distance from it...*

*At dawn on the 15th [26 November], being opposite Cape Oneglia, we saw near the shore an enemy transport consisting of up to 20 feluccas, a tartane [small coastal trader], a brigantine, small ships, which were lying in a fairway on the port tack, while our trabakul was to leave with us with a small 2-master ship on the bow stern.*

*We and the ships laid down on the starboard tack to block this transport to Genoa, and at 7 o'clock all these enemy ships...came close to the shore and stood under the batteries fortified in these places. So as not to miss this opportunity and to take advantage of a convenient fresh wind...we went down to the ships one after the other and having come to the closest distance, opened a lively and strong cannonade on the decks on these places and on the ships [we received return fire] from six batteries from the French. Then, having brought our ships on a left tack, they lay away from the shore to win the wind, and then a second time in the same order, having approached to a close distance, they carried out a cannonade which caused visible damage to these hostile places and ships, and more than 10 ships were sunk, including one large three-masted new transport. The enemy troops, consisting of cavalry and infantry, which were on the banks of these places and visible on ships, turned in disorder to flee towards the mountains and to other adjacent places. Cavalry and infantry were following at speed along the coast, from which it was possible to conclude that significant damage had been caused to these places.*

*Having moved with the ships two miles away from the enemy batteries, we anchored at 28 fathoms with the intention of sending armed launches and cutters to the shore at night to take several ships, but the wind which had increased in the evening did not allow us to do this, and with the ships, having weighed anchor, lay in the sea on the left tack towards Corsica. On our ships, damage was done only to the rigging and sails. Three [seamen] were wounded on our ships, Simeone and Anna. Thank God, no one was killed.*

*The enemy batteries had guns of 24 and 36-pounder calibre.*

*Having gone a little downwind at 9 o'clock, a trebuchet also came up to us, and the commander Lt. Pogonya and 2nd Lt. Skorobagatov, reported to me that they, together with the trabakul and the Austrian corsair, on the night of the 15th [26 November], having approached the towns of Santo Stefano and Riva Ligure, saw three small enemy vessels right under the shore, at which they fired their cannons, and they also fired, but then turned to flee going straight to the shore, and the people then ran away.*

*One vessel, which had 2-pound cannons loaded with flour, was taken as a prize, and a second sunk...but the wind having strengthened on the night of the 16th [27 November] did not allow them to have any more of it, the trabakul, they were forced to leave at sea, removing two guns.*

Having launched active military operations against the French in the areas of Ancona and Naples, Ushakov brought his main forces closer to the shores of Italy in preparation for a campaign against Rome. For this he allocated 120 grenadiers and 200 seamen taken from his ships as well as 2,500 troops from the King of Naples. However, before preparations for this expedition were complete, Nelson, who was obsessed with the thought of Ushakov upstaging him, ordered Troubridge to take Rome ahead of the Russians. For this, Troubridge was instructed to attack the French garrison at Civitavecchia, the main port of Rome, before making a claim on the 'eternal city', all this running counter to instructions given to Nelson by his superiors in London that required him to maintain 'good intelligence' with Ushakov and avoid giving the Russians any 'cause for suspicion, jealousy or offence'. Instead, Nelson informed Troubridge that his move against Rome 'must be kept secret' from Ushakov as otherwise 'we shall give jealousy to the Russians'.

That Ushakov might have been able to learn of Troubridge proceeding to Civitavecchia if not all was kept secret was because Ushakov and his squadron of warships was in Palermo and Ushakov was about to board *Foudroyant* for the first of those two prickly meetings with Nelson. Also having arrived at Palermo, and for the purpose of reinforcing Ushakov's maritime force, was a further detachment of Russian ships under Vice Admiral

Kartsov: *Aziia* (66), *Isidor* (74) and *Pobeda* (66), and the frigate *Pospeshnyi* (36). The inevitable fraternisation between British and Russian officers would have seen any known future assignments being a hot topic of conversation, so explaining why Nelson required Troubridge to keep the assault on Civitavecchia an absolute secret from his own junior officers. Incidentally, Kartsov, who had now been promoted to the rank of vice admiral, was the same Kartsov who had been shipwrecked in the Skagerrak and forced to abandon his flagship *Prince Gustav*. Having been assigned briefly to the North Sea, he was instructed to support Ushakov in the Mediterranean.

Arriving ahead of the Russians, Civitavecchia and Rome were duly taken by Troubridge, the French offered by Troubridge highly favourable terms on agreement that they would capitulate to him before the arrival of the Russians. Ushakov, on learning of this treacherous behaviour, was outraged and did not cancel his own march on Rome. A detachment of Russian seamen commanded by Lieutenant Balabin entered the city, but only after its capitulation to Troubridge. Of this, Balabin sent the following report to Ushakov:

> *Yesterday, with our small corps, we entered the city of Rome, the light with which the residents greeted us brings the greatest honour and glory to the Russians. From the very gates of St John to the soldiers' quarters, both sides of the street were dotted with inhabitants of both sexes. Our troops could only pass with difficulty. 'Viva Paulo Primo, viva Muscovite!' were proclamations heard everywhere.*

In December 1799, and as indicated to Nelson during the two meetings held in Palermo, Ushakov's squadron, along with transports carrying 2,000 Russian soldiers, approached Malta to unite their forces with the British Fleet. According to Russian documents, Nelson proceeded to prolong the blockade operations, leaving the Russian Fleet 'idling' in Maltese coastal waters, while ordering that no Russian troops nor their commandant, Major General Prince Pyotr Volkonsky, be allowed to land on any of the Maltese islands. This placed Ushakov in an extremely difficult situation and one that would appear to have been deliberately manipulated by Nelson, for Ushakov could not remain cruising off Malta indefinitely. His ships were not carrying sufficient victuals for those manning them, much less the 2,000 troops that were forbidden to land. Faced with no other alternative, Ushakov abandoned Malta and returned instead to Corfu.

If the refusal to permit the Russians to land on Malta was not sufficient, two other matters added fuel to Ushakov's anger. Soon after returning to Corfu in January 1800, he learnt that Nelson was giving support to a group of disgruntled nobles on the island of Zante. They were unhappy with a series of liberal reforms that Ushakov had introduced that had undermined their former authority in favour of the island's merchants and bourgeoisie. In gifting Nelson a sword and diamond studded cane they accompanied these with a pompous address that thanked Nelson for liberating the islands. While the actions of those aristocrats might have been ignored by Ushakov, it was unforgiveable in his eyes that Nelson, who had played no part in liberating any of the Ionian Islands, had accepted not just the gift but also the title of 'liberator'. Indeed, Nelson even went one stage further, throwing out veiled hints that he would continue to act as the island's liberator.

Adding to this was that Ushakov learnt of the presence on Corfu of Major General William Anne Villettes, a British officer who was there to recruit an army of Albanian irregulars. Apart from any lack of consultation between the two supposed allies, the British plan, despite its apparent harmlessness, ran counter to Russian interests. The recruitment of this planned 2,000 first class Albanians into British service would be diverting those same men from Russian service. That Corfu would also be the main assembly point for those recruited would have transformed the island into something akin to a British military centre, allowing British agents practically unlimited opportunities to expand their connections and intrigues against Russia. On finding Villettes on the island, Ushakov exhibited fury and categorically demanded that the recruitment be stopped. In turn, this provoked a sharp reaction in British diplomatic circles, with Lord Thomas Elgin, the British ambassador to the Porte since December 1798, accusing Russia of aggressive plans, going so far as to insist that the British Fleet in the Mediterranean be strengthened since only this 'can ensure the degree of influence that we want to achieve'.

The rage against the British felt by Ushakov was as nothing compared with the court of St Petersburgh. Every agreement made with Britain over matters relating to Malta was now being reneged upon. Clearly the British government was showing every intention of keeping Russia away from the island for the sole purpose of annexing it for the exclusive use of the British Navy and British commerce. Or at least, rightly or wrongly, that is how it appeared to Paul and those who were advising him. No less insidiously, as far as Paul was concerned, another supposed ally, Austria, had also acted behind Russia's back in having secretly accepted the capitulation of the French garrison in Ancona and thereby nullifying the successes there of Russian military detachments. As for Malta, with every intention of later asserting his own authority over the island, Paul took the immediate decision to recall Ushakov, aware that his ships, long at sea and hastily built, were now in a considerable state of disrepair. In July 1800, Ushakov's squadron left Corfu and after a long, almost two-month voyage arrived in the Bosporus. Istanbul greeted the Russian squadron with honours, the sultan as a token of gratitude awarding Ushakov a diamond çelenk and five bronze cannons. Entering the dockyard at Istanbul, Ushakov's ships underwent repairs and took on provisions. This, and adverse winds, delayed the squadron in the Strait and it was only on 6 November that Ushakov finally dropped anchor in the Sevastopol roadstead.

# CHAPTER 11

# WAR WITH ENGLAND NARROWLY AVERTED

Paul I, Emperor of all Russias, was a man quick to anger and often appearing to act irrationally. Ask most Russians today and they will pass him off as historically one of the nation's worst rulers. But those who created that image of him as an abysmal potentate were the ones who had most reason to dislike him. They were the ones who he dismissed from office, men who were incompetent, corrupt or unable to accept his vision for the future of Russia. Those who stood in his way, or questioned his decisions, were swept away, imprisoned, or exiled, because Paul demanded total obedience. His rages and temper tantrums, and there is plenty of evidence that he did have rages and temper tantrums, were neatly turned against him. His opponents let it be known that these were an outward sign of Paul suffering a mental disorder, that he was unfit to rule. In plain language, they alleged him to be mad.

Among those who were happy to push such an idea was Pavel Chichagov. He was one who claimed himself later to be part of the conspiracy that resulted on the night of 24 March 1801 in Paul's murder. But Chichagov was not one of those who burst their way into Paul's sleeping chamber, battered him and throttled him with a scarf. Another who was not present, but who often wrote harshly of the emperor, was Charles Lord Whitworth. He was the British ambassador to Russia and had been subjected to Paul's outbursts of rage. Paul eventually banished him from Russia. Yet that anger, as directed at Whitworth, was not totally inexcusable. In letters Whitworth believed to have been intercepted, he had been less than judicious in his comments, writing of the emperor that he 'is literally not in his senses [and] since he has come to the throne his disorder has gradually increased.' In another, Whitworth wrote, 'the more he is courted, the more difficult it is to manage him.' And that's the nub of it. Those who wished to profit from the emperor, and Whitworth wished benefits that could profit his masters in London, wanted Paul to give them what they wanted. And this Paul would not do unless it was directly to the benefit of Russia.

In conversations that Whitworth is known to have had with the main conspirators, including one on the day prior to his return to England, he would have learnt that Paul was making overtures to Bonaparte, First Consul of France since the 18th Brumaire (9/10 March 1799) coup. From this, and information gleaned elsewhere, Whitworth would have known that the alliance between Russia and Great Britain was a dead duck, soon to be repudiated by the emperor. But even worse, the two men, Bonaparte and the Russian emperor, were in cahoots to divide the world between them. For Paul it had become increasingly clear that Britain, while ideologically opposed to the revolution in France, was now using the war to gain even greater prosperity through a concentration upon the gaining of further territories that could be colonised. It was Russian forces that were helping Britain achieve this, but Britain pushed Russia aside whenever the spoils of war were shared out.

Not surprisingly, in France there was no jubilation upon hearing the news of Paul's assassination, for immediately it was realised that it would bring benefits to Britain. *Le Moniteur*, an official French government publication, certainly pointed an accusing finger at Britain, stating not unreasonably:

> *It is for history to develop the mystery which surrounds this tragic death, and to declare which Cabinet in the world was most deeply interested in bringing about such a catastrophe.*

Was Britain, or at the very least Whitworth, directly involved or was it just a fortuitous turn of events? Although the trail has long gone cold, there is evidence that Whitworth backed the plotters with British gold, and encouraged the assassins to carry out the task. Immediately before his dismissal from Russia, Whitworth spent vast amounts of secret service money for undeclared purposes, as much as 24,000 roubles (roughly £320,000 in today's money) failing to provide adequate answers as to the use of this money when questioned by Parliament. One comment he made, on being pressed by parliamentary audit commissioners, was to remain vague, indicating that part of it was used to accomplish an 'object for which the cash subsidy was given'.

To this can be added his connections with the assassins that included his mistress, Ol'ga Alexandrovna Zherebtsov, and her two brothers, while it was at her house that the plot was discussed, sometimes with Whitworth present. Ol'ga Zherebtsov herself certainly had knowledge of the plot, openly stating while in Berlin that Paul was to be removed and upon hearing the news of the murder immediately travelled to London to meet with Whitworth. In a letter to Vorontsov in London, she acknowledges it to have been English gold that had financed the conspiracy. While open to interpretation either way, unless Zherebtsov's unsubstantiated statement is fully accepted, Whitworth certainly expressed much pleasure in hearing of Paul's assassination, writing to Foreign Secretary Lord William Grenville, 'I shall, so long as I live, celebrate as a festival the day on which I learned of the death of that arch-fiend Paul.'

In having instructed Ushakov in the autumn of 1801 to return his squadron to the Black Sea, Paul, while accepting Ushakov's ships needed repairs, had a further reason. Bluntly he told Ushakov it was also because of 'the behaviour already given to you [Ushakov]' by Nelson. While a statement that might have pleased Ushakov, with Nelson's behaviour certainly irritating Paul, it was Malta that was really at the heart of Paul's thinking. Malta was central to Paul's belief that Russia was being used in the war against France only for the benefit of Great Britain. It was Malta to which Paul had become especially attached and had become the pivot of his foreign policy. Although his thoughts were less directed to the commercial value of Malta rather than the value of the Order of St John, a religious order of fighting monks that had once ruled Malta but had been ousted by Bonaparte. To this Order Paul had been elected grand master and in this position he had determined to return the Order, with himself as grand master, to Malta and use it as a platform to fight revolutionaries and revolutionary ideas. The fact that the Order had long been the guardian of aristocratic traditions, with only Catholic nobility of impeccable origin once accepted but now, on Paul's obvious insistence and since January 1799, also including Russian Orthodox nobles, corresponded closely to the emperor's plans. He was confident that by patronising the Order he could attract the sympathies of the European feudal reaction. This is something Bonaparte had previously identified and counts as one reason he chose to occupy Malta. By 1800, Paul had come to believe that Britain had no intention of honouring the treaty of April 1798 in which it had been agreed, if only verbally, that upon the French surrendering the Maltese islands, they would be jointly garrisoned by Britain and Russia. Validating such a belief was Herbert Dundas, Britain's secretary of state for war, who six weeks before the taking of Valletta confirmed Nelson's earlier instruction that no Russian troops be allowed on the island and, upon the actual fall of the island, further ordered that only the British flag should be raised, a move that symbolically announced Britain's undivided domination over Malta. Upon this being challenged by Paul, the reply from London was that the agreement was neither obligatory nor binding, indicating it had lost all legality upon Paul recalling Ushakov to Sevastopol.

Much else that was also annoying Paul added to his determination that he turn against Britain and form an alliance with France. The failed invasion of the Netherlands featured high in his thinking and was certainly the initial cause of the breakdown. It was Paul's belief that his troops had been used against the best trained of the enemy forces, sustaining as a result a much higher loss than their British counterparts. Subsequently, a misunderstanding also arose over subsidy payments promised by Britain for Russia's participation in the campaign, it being claimed by Paul that Britain was deliberately underestimating the amount due to Russia by a shortfall of £0.5m. Not helping matters was that Paul heard from conversations with his naval officers of the insults directed towards them by some British naval officers with his attention especially drawn to the behaviour of the seamen and junior officers on board *Diadem.* The effect on Paul's mind may be easily imagined, and not a result of, as indicated by Whitworth in one of his letters, that he was 'literally not in his senses'.

The first clear sign that Paul no longer wished to continue his alliance with Great Britain came in the form of a memorandum of March 1800 written by Count Fyodor Rostopchin, president of the college of foreign affairs. This set out a new policy establishing Russia to be best served by forming a partnership with France, while in November 1800, a treaty giving France access to Russia's highly prized naval stores was announced. Further discussions, unknown to Britain, saw France and Russia considering a proposal for the two nations combining in a move against India, Britain's major source of wealth. The plan would have entailed the movement of 70,000 troops, with the French contingent first entering the Black Sea by way of the Danube. Having reached the Black Sea, the Russian Fleet would then take responsibility for transporting this force to the Caucasus where it would proceed by land towards the borders of India. However, only one part of this plan was initiated with Paul moving a force of 22,000 Cossacks into Central Asia.

Without doubt, Paul was moving Russia towards war with Great Britain. Secure on land, Russia's major point of weakness if war broke out was at sea. In acting against Russia, Britain would certainly sail a powerful fleet into the Baltic to unleash havoc on Paul's navy, either at sea or by bombarding Russia's various ports and harbours. In May 1800, as the first step to fighting this war, Paul ordered ships under the command of Makarov still in British waters, some under repair at Chatham following the attack on Den Helder, to return to the Baltic:

> *We command you to return with all the squadrons under your command, as well as the land forces, to your ports, and we order that this be carried out with all possible urgency; those ships and other vessels that are still under repair shall not be allowed to delay [their return].*

The flash point that ensured the inevitability of war was a request from Denmark that Paul might form a second neutrality league similar to the one that Catherine had created some twenty years earlier. This request resulted from the Danish government suffering the indignity of seeing merchant ships under the Danish flag stopped at sea by British warships and privateers to ensure they were not carrying warlike materials into ports deemed as enemy ports and under blockade by the British Navy. As with the league formed by Catherine, any participating state would have to agree to protect, and by force if necessary, the merchant ships of all league members. Only if a port was subject to an effective naval blockade would it be accepted that neutral ships should not enter. If only proclaimed on paper, the blockade was to be ignored, neutral ships deemed to have a right of entry that would be enforced by the navies of Russia, Denmark and any other nation subscribing to the league. On learning of the Danish request, and in mid-August before Paul had even given his response, a British squadron of seven warships presented themselves off Denmark for the purpose of cowering the Danes into accepting Britain's self-proclaimed right of searching ships at sea bound for any port, whether that port was under actual or paper blockade. Threatened with Copenhagen being cannonaded by British warships, and not at that time having received a reply from Paul, the Danish government agreed to back down. For the British government this for the moment proved sufficient and the naval force standing off Copenhagen was withdrawn. A few days later, on 4 September, the long-awaited message from Paul was received in Denmark. Not only did it indicate the Russian emperor to be favourable to establishing a new armed league of neutrality, but also that Paul intended to include Sweden and Prussia in what is sometimes labelled as the Northern League.

To Paul, the arrival of British warships off Copenhagen was tantamount to a declaration of war, for not only would their continuous or future presence impede the movement of Danish shipping, it would also interfere with Russia's maritime trade conducted beyond the Baltic. It was also expected that the British squadron, once Copenhagen had been bombarded, would attempt a similar bombardment of Kronstadt and Tallinn. While such a scenario was avoided during the summer of 1800, there was every likelihood that the British Navy, in even greater number, would return the following year. It was for this reason that Makarov, who had been given command of the Tallinn section of the fleet, was ordered on 5 September to make all necessary preparations to frustrate the British approaching any of the Russian Baltic ports, receiving on the following day an important set of instructions from Kushelev:

> *Should they [the British Fleet] enter our sea...to carry out hostile incursions on our shores, you must be ready to repel them by bringing the [imperial] fleet out of the harbour as quickly as possible, arranging it as you deem advantageous.*

To this was added:

> *If the English fleet goes to Kronstadt, then immediately you must weigh anchor and sail to cut off his retreat and pursue him, positioning him between your guns and those of the Kronstadt [coastal artillery] detachment.*

Regarding coastal artillery, Makarov was ordered to build additional shore batteries for which, if there were not sufficient readily available guns, additional ones could be supplied from ships remaining in harbour.

In October, having now agreed to Denmark's request, Paul placed an embargo on British ships in Russian ports, sequestrating 200 craft and sending their British crews into the Russian interior. This was a move that Paul assumed would greatly increase the likelihood of a British naval attack on Russia's Baltic coastline, but on the appearance of British warships, it was intended by Paul to use the sequestrated ships as a bargaining chip, discouraging any attack by burning some of the vessels within sight of the British. Given that Tallinn would inevitably be their first target, Paul wrote in December 1800 to Makarov:

> *If [the British] approach the port of Reval [Tallinn], then we command you, having brought out all the English ships in the harbour in to the roadstead, to burn them before his eyes [those of the British]. In the deliberations of the port, to have all due cautions and immediately after the burning of ships, send by courier to notify the commandant of Narva [in Eastern Estonia] and Admiral Khanykov [at Kronstadt], who are ordered to do the same with the English ships [in those harbours].*

For Denmark there was an expectation that Paul would also send ships for the protection of Copenhagen, and this might well have been his intention had not the British Navy struck so fast, arriving off Copenhagen before the waters of the eastern Baltic had thawed and the Russian Fleet able to sail. Commanded by Admiral Sir Hyde Parker, with Nelson as his second-in-command, the British had assembled in quick time a powerful force of thirty capital ships that would first threaten and then, if necessary, bombard Copenhagen until the Danish government agreed to withdraw from the Northern League. Having achieved this, the British would sail into the Baltic and, as Paul rightly assumed, attack various Russian ports, including Tallinn and Kronstadt.

While Copenhagen did, on 2 April, suffer the hellfire of bombardment that forced Denmark to end her obligations to the league, it all proved quite unnecessary. Unbeknown to all those involved in the attack, Paul was no more. Ten days earlier, on the night of 23 March, Paul had been assassinated and replaced by his son Alexander. The new emperor soon proved more favourable to Britain, agreeing to open a negotiated end to the differences separating Britain and Russia. While Whitworth before his expulsion from St Petersburg may have supplied some of the finances to back the coup, those who had enacted the plot, and the reason for it being carried out, was the threatened approach of the British Fleet. Merchants feared the likely destruction of Kronstadt and Tallinn, for both were not just naval bases but also important commercial ports. For those merchants, and others disenchanted with Paul, re-establishing peace with England was a priority.

For Nelson, now in command of the British Fleet in the Baltic, a more dramatic turnaround of events is difficult to imagine. No longer would Russia be talking to Bonaparte, no longer would Malta be an issue, no longer would Russia continue to support the making of a new armed neutrality league, and no longer would India be threatened by a joint Franco-Russian campaign. All this was to become clear over the next few months with Alexander agreeing early on to withdraw from the Northern League and giving his approval to the searching of neutral vessels on the understanding that Britain would abandon the upholding of paper blockades. No wonder was it that *Le Moniteur* came to suggest that Britain was in some way involved in the emperor's death.

While it was certainly true that the Russian Fleet did not sail due to the eastern Baltic being icebound, a fact confirmed by Nelson in various communiques sent to London, doubt must exist as to whether the Russian Fleet had, even if the ice had cleared in time, the capability of sailing out of Kronstadt to meet the British Fleet in battle. Trapped within Kronstadt were forty-seven ships, of which barely fifteen were fit for sea, lacking rigging, ropes and pulley blocks, all this equipment in either a rotting state or entirely missing. As for the cannons, gun carriages and anchors of most of those ships, these had been left ashore, exposed to all weathers, and piled on top of each other. Again, sickness had taken its toll with more than 2,000 of those who would have manned those ships dying in barracks that winter. Tellingly, Chichagov was to write, 'the English did not lose as much in their last battles as we did in waiting for them.'

To have stood a chance against Nelson, the fleet in Kronstadt would not only have had to have been much better prepared, but would have required inspired leadership. This inspired leadership was missing. During the Swedish War, British officers had played a significant role in directing the Russian Fleet, but these had now been released from service while others had been transferred to the rowing fleet. As for officers returning from recent assignments in the North Sea, while serving well, they had only witnessed the ordinariness that result from a continuous blockade of the Dutch coastline.

Nothing could have been done in such a short time to save the fleet if it had been ordered to sea. What would have been needed was a man of Ushakov's ability, but appointed several years earlier and using the same approach to naval warfare as he had done while commanding in the Black Sea: constant training of the men in the use of ordnance and boarding of enemy warships in conjunction with practising battle tactics as used by Ushakov in the war fought against the Ottomans. But of course, Ushakov was many miles to the south and had only just returned from the Mediterranean.

Prior to his death and in the expectation that a British fleet would attempt to bombard Tallinn and Kronstadt, Paul had set about strengthening the defences of Kronstadt and St Petersburg, appointing Chichagov alongside Makarov to oversee this work. It was, to say the least, an unenviable task as the existing defences had long fallen into decay and urgently needed new gun batteries. But these would take several years of intensive work. As to why these defences were in such a poor state, Chichagov places the blame on the man against whom he believed was also responsible for the poor state of the navy, Kushelev. In a letter to Peter Ludwig von der Pahlen, the military governor of St Petersburg and one of Paul's most favoured courtiers, Chichagov explained that Kronstadt had no existing defences that could withstand attack, the ordnance was old and neglected, and that nothing could be done immediately. To Vorontsov he wrote, 'with all the intrepidity of the universe and the skill and patriotism of all humanity,' would not prevent the defenders being 'enveloped and mutilated in the bosom of this edifice'. While all of this was probably correct, Chichagov later used the situation to demonstrate the fear Paul's sudden outbursts of rage engendered. Claiming that in wishing to inform the emperor of just how weak the defences were, he tells of being advised by Pahlen not to do so.

According to Chichagov, Pahlen was fearful of Paul's reaction and that Chichagov would find himself incarcerated. 'For God's sake, my dear Admiral, come to your senses,' he reportedly told Chichagov. 'Yes, you can only say yes and very good, otherwise you risk attracting new displeasures. I feel your intentions.' As for the truthfulness of Chichagov's statement, this is impossible to verify and might well have been invented to cover Chichagov's own shortcomings or simply a further attempt to smear Paul's reputation. In a similar situation, but some 145 or so years later, Konstantin Rokossovsky, a leading Soviet military general, had no hesitation in standing up to Stalin in bringing to attention matters that were wrong, knowing that he risked being returned to the Gulag Peninsula. In other words he, unlike Chichagov, put his country before his own safety. For Chichagov, the worst that could happen was dismissal and a short term of imprisonment. For Rokossovsky, it was torture and death.

Seemingly the defences of Tallinn were in no better state, forcing elements of the fleet based there as soon as they could break through the ice to sail to Kronstadt and join the rest of the fleet. A later Russian naval officer in describing the situation at Tallinn added that the Tallinn squadron, which had sailed to Kronstadt on hearing that Nelson was approaching, had deliberately 'hid' itself from Nelson, knowing that if they had been forced to fight, they would have been annihilated.

Nelson, learning there were no remaining warships in Tallinn, decided it was now completely safe for his squadron of eleven battleships to enter the port, insisting it was for the purpose of proving that Russia and Great Britain were now once again in friendship, adding:

> *I ordered that there be no bombs in the squadron, and by this I want to show even more clearly that I have no other intention than the desire to express the deep respect that I have for the person of His Imperial Majesty.*

But such an explanation did not satisfy Major General Alexander Dmitriyevich Balashov, the military governor, who viewed it as an 'audacious' and only undertaken because the Russian Fleet at Kronstadt was still locked in ice. Instead, Balashov refused the request, allowing only one unarmed boat to enter. From Pahlen, who was also governor of the Baltic provinces, Nelson was further informed that the new emperor considered it 'entirely opposed to the spirit of the instructions' of the British government and that negotiations for a settlement with Britain would only be considered once Nelson had withdrawn his ships from Russian waters. Consequently, Nelson, having arrived off Tallinn on 12 May, in a show of anger was to lead his ships away from the harbour and into the Gulf of Finland just five days later.

However, during those five days, Nelson took the opportunity of viewing the defences surrounding the harbour at Tallinn, confirming them to be in a very weakened state. In his opinion, should the Russian Fleet have remained hostile, 'it might have been attacked with success by firing the wooden mole' against which it was 'always moored during the winter months'. In addition, he informed Lieutenant Colonel Sir William Stewart, the military commander attached to Nelson, 'a position seemed also to present itself for a three decker to be sited across the mouth of the harbour, by which ship the whole dock might have been raked from end to end.'

# PART FOUR

# Bringing the fleet into better condition

The purpose for which Russia's imperial navy existed was a matter of debate during the reign of Paul and into the early years of Alexander I's reign. Should Russia possess a large and powerful navy that could perform on the world stage, or should it be one that existed to ensure Russian control of the seas that surrounded its immediate shoreline? Paul, who had great ambitions for Russia as a sea power, favoured, in common with Catherine, the navy having a wider reach in the world. Alexander pulled back from such thinking, choosing to reduce money available to the navy and giving great attention instead to the army.

# CHAPTER 12

# NEW THINKING AND REDIRECTION

Due to the shortness of Paul's reign, a period of a little over four years, it is not possible to say exactly where he would have taken the navy if he had ruled for longer, but there are numerous clues as to him being a keen supporter of Russia possessing a strong navy, something to which he had given much thought in the years that preceded his accession to the imperial throne. On the fourth day after his coronation, he was occupying himself with arrangements for reviewing the Baltic Fleet, asking Makarov which ships he could inspect and which could accompany him out to sea. During the second year of his reign Paul secured for the navy a budget of 15 million roubles, whereas Catherine, by the end of her reign, following a series of incremental rises over the preceding years, was spending annually upon the navy no more than 5 million roubles. In addition, Paul created the Northern League with a commitment that included Russian ships acting as escorts to merchant shipping belonging not just to Russia but also those of Sweden and Denmark. For Britain, as demonstrated, this was seen as a provocative act and one that had every possibility of a seaborne confrontation between Russia and Britain, something Paul appeared to willingly accept, but in doing so might have caused his navy considerable damage. Only the speed with which Britain reacted and the dramatic ending to Paul's life prevented the two countries engaging in such a conflict.

However, it is Paul's Mediterranean ambitions that provides greater clarity as to his direction of travel regarding the navy. Upon the return of Ushakov's squadron to Sevastopol during the autumn of 1801, an instruction was issued from St Petersburg that those ships, alongside other ships of the Black Sea Fleet, should hoist and continue to fly the flag of the Order of St John, a sign that Paul was planning a later onslaught on Malta. This desire to possess Malta, with Britain conversely excluded from the island, was one that Catherine would have approved, given that she at the time of the American Revolutionary War had also sought to establish ties with the Order of St John, straddling as Malta does the eastern and western Mediterranean, and easily accessible to Russian ships entering the Mediterranean from the Dardanelles. In St Petersburg, the possession of Malta was seriously debated, with much thought given to the possibility of it being re-peopled by faithful Russian subjects and the value of Valletta as a naval base of sufficient size to accommodate a new imperial fleet centred on the Mediterranean alongside an extensive mercantile fleet. In voyaging from Kronstadt to Malta, so claimed in a discussion paper written by one St Petersburg merchant, this would have the effect of changing 'the Russian freshwater men into sailors'. Malta as a warm water port would also allow the Russian Fleet to remain at sea, with no winter to 'check their operations or suspend [them from] acquiring skill in naval tactics.' As for Russia's mercantile community, the acquisition of Malta would not only provide it with the markets already open to Malta, but possession of the island would create 'a new spirit [of] commerce, and the hitherto unpractised art of sailing.' In this vein, the writer added:

*Malta can merely boast an extent of twenty miles by twelve, and a population of 60,000 souls; yet this extent is sufficient to be a depot, a secure invincible depot for the Russian articles much wanted in South Europe, of Siberian oil, of salted fish, of flax and hemp, and of corn and timber. All the commodities which the Island requires; Petersburg or the Black Sea could cheaply and plentifully afford.*

In fact, the list of mercantile advantages seemed almost endless, especially if aided by the presence of Russian warships to protect and convoy merchant shipping whenever required and which:

*Would oblige the Turkish Empire to permit the Russia articles of fish, hemp and flax, timber, and iron to be exported to Malta direct, or to the Mediterranean seas: a plan which would direct the trade of Europe into its ancient Channel, which would enable the nations of the Levant, to receive the useful articles from Russa at easy prices and in the most incredible abundance.*

And the list continued, finishing with the possibility that through possession of Malta Russia would become 'a second China, a warehouse of exportable commodities for all the neighbouring world'. At the same time Paul showed every intention of returning warships to the Ionian Islands, now the Septinsular Republic, having ordered that, on Ushakov's departure, he should leave under the command of Captain Second Rank Voinovich, a small garrison in the fortress of Corfu in addition to two battalions of Russian grenadiers sent to form a guard for Ferdinand IV of Naples.

The assassination of Paul brought to the fore a whole new coterie of naval administrators, a faction of individuals who had felt slighted by Paul and in different ways had supported the plot to remove him. Of significance was that many of the new ingroup associated with the navy wished to reduce the imperial navy's ability to act as an independent force operating in more distant waters, becoming instead subservient to the needs of the army. In doing so, this dovetailed into a new direction for Russian foreign policy. Instead, as under Catherine, the direction had been one of territorial acquisition, the new policy was that of securing existing boundaries through maintaining a status quo in areas beyond those borders rather than the extension of existing borders. As such, it reduced the need for an expanded blue water navy, as territories beyond

Russia's immediate borders would no longer be in contention, requiring the navy to act in the capacity of a border defence force. In terms of managing and reducing possible future threats from other major powers, the new government of Alexander stood for the removal of both French and English forces from Egypt and for the neutralisation of Malta through a wish that Malta should be returned to the Order of St John rather than acquired by either Britain or France. Only regarding the Ionian Islands was an exception made, Alexander prepared to defend Russian predominance over the islands as won by Ushakov.

Among the most ardent and influential supporters of this new direction for the navy were Semyon Vorontsov (the Russian ambassador in London), his brother Alexander Romanovich, and Pavel Chichagov. Of the Mediterranean expeditions favoured by Catherine, Alexander Vorontsov, who would become Alexander's imperial chancellor, noted that they had 'cost the state a lot, brought some brilliance, but no benefit'. As for Catherine's foreign policy, he considered that internal difficulties had been created by her constant wars, and that Russia under Alexander needed 'nothing more than the multiplication of its people, of whom there is a great shortage...and war costs people.' Referring more specifically to the navy, Alexander Vorontsov opined that 'Russia cannot be among the leading maritime powers...there is no reason for it, no benefit and none can be foreseen.' Instead, he suggested that Russia required only a navy capable of defending Russia's coastline and harbours, a force that could be called on by the army and be subservient to the army, not a force designed to be independent of the army and venture deeper into the oceans of the world. 'Our direct power and strength should be in the ground forces,' and as for maritime defences:

> *It is enough if our naval forces are organised on only two themes: protecting our harbours and coasts in the Black Sea, having forces there that are commensurate with the Turkish, and a sufficient fleet in the Baltic Sea to dominate it. Sending our squadrons into the Mediterranean Sea and other long-distance expeditions costs the state considerable sums, does little to shine and does no good.*

Chichagov, who was to rise to the pinnacle of naval administration through appointment by Alexander to a newly created post of minister of naval forces, was the most influential, able to persuade Alexander to permit this wholesale redirection of the navy. Even before Chichagov was offered ministerial authority, the young emperor had turned to him for advice on all matters regarding naval affairs, the two having weekly meetings held in private. As for why Chichagov, who it will be remembered had already had a successful naval career in the North Sea, should now wish to see a diminished role for the navy, this would seem to relate to him being much more of an army man. Before joining the navy, he served in the Guards and during the time of Napoleon's invasion of Russia he would command the Army of the Danube. Appointed naval forces minister, he resigned the post after a period of only five years, and when he did return to public office a few years later, he rejected the opportunity of returning to the navy, preferring instead to take the post of commander-in-chief of the Third Western Army. While not conclusive as evidence, it does serve as a further indication of where Chichagov's true loyalties lay, rejecting the value of the navy as a means of securing Russia's wealth through a navy that could help develop an overseas trading network fashioned on the British mercantile system.

In Chichagov's view previous sovereigns except Peter the Great and Catherine towards the end of her reign had seen the navy as 'an object of curiosity, of amusement or of vanity'. For Russia, he confirmed that in his opinion a sizeable fleet was unnecessary, arguing that the navy was not 'in the spirit of the people', nor could it be looked upon 'as a necessary condition for the welfare or security of the empire'. In other countries, the navies created had a clear sense of purpose, but in Russia, the navy was simply 'a burdensome luxury of imitation' that was 'dependent on the goodwill of the sovereign'. In Russia, Chichagov continued:

> *Maritime strength has never been calculated on a foundation of holding the whole machine together. We know that our navy is not made for the defence of the empire because it hides when the enemy appears. It is certainly not for the glory of the country because so many times it has been its shame. It is not for wealth because the money spent on it annually is a pure loss.*

As with Alexander Vorontsov, Chichagov insisted that the purpose of the navy should be redirected from such projects and should act with clear purpose as 'one of the arms of the national force', serving alongside and meeting the needs of the army.

Firmly establishing this new policy was a special committee that had nominally been given the task of considering ways to 'bring the fleet into better condition'. However, no free discussion of various possibilities was embarked upon by the committee, for the fate of the navy had been sealed even before its first meeting. Basically, the membership of this committee had been carefully weighted, those chosen to join the committee handpicked by Alexander Vorontsov and Chichagov, with Alexander Vorontsov its chair and Chichagov its secretary. For, even if discussion within the committee did veer away from the direction pre-ordained by Vorontsov and Chichagov, the latter, as secretary, in continuing to report to the emperor, could slant those reports in ways that favoured the doctrine of the navy becoming subservient to the army. Once Alexander had been fully converted to the new idea, Chichagov was charged with drawing up the detail, focussing first on the number of ships of the line that Russia should possess, ensuring only that these numbers were commensurate in size with the fleets of the neighbouring powers in the Baltic and Black Sea – namely the Ottoman Empire and Sweden. These numbers, Chichagov later recalled from memory, 'were for 8 or 10 three-deck vessels, 30 of different sizes, 74 and 64 and frigates and other vessels, in proportion for the Baltic Sea, and half the number for the Black Sea'. It was a number far below the size of the fleet under Catherine.

Once these figures had been adopted by the committee, they were passed to the emperor, who offered no opposition, awarding Chichagov the Order of St Aleksandr Nevsky, the empire's second highest decoration. Soon after, with Chichagov appointed minister of naval forces, and Alexander Vorontsov the new imperial chancellor, work began on refashioning the navy into a force that would concentrate only on protecting Russia's position in the Baltic and Black Seas. Greater emphasis was now given to the needs of the in-shore squadron and rowing fleet, with many of the larger sailing ships discarded, either through age or the need for extensive repairs. Ships, once designed for the line of battle, now began to be armed *en flûte*, meaning that the armament they carried was reduced, allowing them to carry military stores and troops. Other ships, but in much reduced numbers, were assigned to the role of protecting these newly created transports in any mission by sea or in coastal waters undertaken by the army.

# CHAPTER 13

# UNDER TWO EMPERORS

While the two emperors, Paul and Alexander, had very different ideas as to which role the navy should be given, both were keen to ensure that it should operate with much greater efficiency. Although Catherine had brought improvements, especially in terms of its shore-based infrastructure and the expansion of its officer corps, she had made relatively few improvements to the navy's administration and had not been well served by those holding high administrative posts, men upon whom she had come to unduly rely. One especially prominent example was Count Ivan Grigoryevich Chernyshyov, who she appointed in 1768 as president of the Admiralty Collegiate. Responsible for all matters relating to the Baltic Fleet, Chernyshyov had been a somewhat bizarre choice, only appointed because he and his two brothers had backed Catherine in the coup placing her on the throne. Chernyshyov had no previous experience of naval affairs. Described as 'an amiable man of the world', he showed not 'the slightest interest in or capacity for the career which he had by chance embraced'. Under him, and during the later years of Catherine's reign, he had allowed the fleet to fall into decay, directing his energies to concealing this from the empress. Under the indolent administration of Chernyshyov provisioning and equipping the fleet had become the home of corrupt practices from which commanding officers derived enormous profit. Catherine bravely made up her mind to put up with it. 'I am robbed like everybody,' she said, 'and that is a good sign, because it shows that there is something to steal!'

The Black Sea Fleet, with its position of semi-independence from St Petersburg, was free of Chernyshyov's ineptitude and its officers were possibly a good deal less corrupt. Barre de Saint-Leu, a French naval officer familiar with Russia, writing in September 1796, offers a critique of the fleet's more senior officers:

> *Admiral Mordvinov [Vice Admiral Mordvinov] is Commander-in-Chief in the Black Sea. He is a sailor in spite of himself... Vice-Admiral Ushakov [naval commander] is an old woman, always making a fuss about nothing. Vice-Admiral Ribas [commander of the fleet] is in a military sense quite incompetent and one of the most cunning intriguers alive. Rear-Admiral Pouchtchine [naval intendant] is bold only in making foolish speeches.*

To this Barre did add that it would be quite possible to corrupt most of these officers, even Mordvinov himself, who he described as a 'decent fellow'.

For various reasons, but mainly because of having too close an attachment to Catherine, Paul dismissed many of the navy's top ranks, replacing them with new appointees. This had several unintended consequences. Within the higher echelons of the navy, competing factions had long existed with different aristocratic families and their protégés constantly striving to gain dominance. In his choice of new appointees, Paul accelerated this rivalry, choosing not to retain some who by right expected to hold their positions, while failing to appoint others who were expecting promotion. These now became the emperor's bitterest enemies, among which was Chichagov. His grievance against Paul was that he had rapidly raised a fellow captain, Grigori Grigorovich Kushelev, to the rank of vice admiral and then to full admiral in a mere two years, while offering Chichagov no promotion whatsoever. Furthermore, in November 1798, Paul appointed Kushelev to the Admiralty Collegiate as its vice president. This Chichagov saw as a further blow to his pride, reminding everyone of Kushelev's former inferiority of rank by calling him the 'one-time ensign'. However, if Kushelev's rapid promotion was not enough to fuel Chichagov's anger, accusations made by Kushelev to the emperor claiming Chichagov had little interest in the Russian Navy ignited his full fury. In speaking to the emperor, Kushelev had also suggested that following Chichagov's engagement to the daughter of a British naval officer, he would prefer a transfer into the British Navy. This resulted in the emperor having Chichagov imprisoned in the Peter and Paul fortress for eight days (21 June to 1 July 1799). For this Chichagov appears to have taken his revenge, admitting in a letter to Semyon Vorontsov in London that he had played a part in Paul's assassination. Unfortunately, he failed to provide any further detail. While Chichagov, in his version, blames Kushelev for his imprisonment, others tell a different story, indicating that Chichagov was imprisoned following a series of insults directed at the emperor, an action that in other navies might well have resulted in his total dismissal rather than allowing him a period of reflection. The Vorontsov brothers also held deep grudges against Paul and were possibly aware of the plot. Semyon Vorontsov had been removed by Paul from his ambassadorial position in London, while Alexander Vorontsov had felt himself ignored by Paul, failing to receive any official appointment despite having at one time been president of the collegiate for foreign trade.

Paul, upon his accession, chose to retain Chernyshyov as president of the Admiralty Collegiate, a decision even more bizarre than his original appointment made by Catherine. Paul also chose to promote him to the rank of navy field marshal. By then, Chernyshov had not only a history of incompetence but was in such a poor state of health that he rarely attended collegiate meetings, dying just a few months later.

During the short period he ruled as emperor, Paul pushed through a remarkable number of naval reforms, all improving the state of the navy. Doubtless, if his reign had not been cut short, he would have entirely reshaped the navy's administrative structure, with the possibility that newly built ships would have been of an improved quality, the officers of the Baltic Fleet much better trained and ships taken out to sea more often. Directing himself to the prevention of wastage, Paul established a board of control that was charged with regularly inspecting the magazines and verifying stores, so discouraging captains from private graft in supplies. In addition to those appointed to serve as administrators, the committee, which was independent of the Admiralty, had among its members merchants who could evaluate the quality of purchased stores. In tandem with the board of control, Paul also established a chief inspector of naval construction, a position that had at one time existed under Peter the Great, with the bureau attached to this office taking responsibility for inspecting the quality of work upon ships before they were launched. Among those carrying out this inspection work was Le Brune de St Catherine, a leading French constructor who first entered Paul's service in 1799. Le Brune had originally worked at the Toulon naval yard but having royalist sympathies had fled to Istanbul, where he saw construction of several ships, before his recruitment into Russian service, initially employed in the Admiralty yard. Other reforms inaugurated by Paul included a revision of the department of justice at the Admiralty Collegiate, organising it on a regular basis for the first time.

In recognising the need to ensure a plentiful supply of timber for the construction and repair of ships, Paul created a special department under the Admiralty charged with preserving and replanting forests that under Peter the Great had been assigned exclusively to provide timber for the repair and construction of naval warships. In more recent times, the forests had been exploited in ways other than for the service of the navy. Often, timber felled was distributed to government favourites or pillaged in some other way. At the same time, Paul introduced an embargo on the export of timber to help preserve existing timber supplies for the navy. His policy of reforestation was of particular importance, for with the cutting down of trees and failure to replace them, this had led to a steady loss of the woodlands previously used as a naval resource. In this Paul was influenced by a policy introduced in France during the seventeenth century by Jean-Baptiste Colbert, secretary of state for the navy under Louis XIV.

For the training of future naval officers and shipwrights, Paul established new schools of navigation, naval tactics, and construction, taking boys of 14 years or younger, with their studies to include not only mathematics, astronomy, navigation, the science of ship construction, naval tactics, artillery, and surveying, but also mechanics, hydrodynamics, and physics. The Marine Cadet Corps that had originally been centred on Kronstadt was under Paul moved to St Petersburg where the emperor could frequently visit and keep the cadets alert and studious. Through an allocation to that institution of a supplementary credit of 100,000 roubles, this ensured an improvement in the level of naval education by permitting the award of scholarships to the less affluent alongside providing financial support for poorer cadets undergoing training abroad. Another issue taken up by Paul was the reform of naval uniforms for officers, simplifying the dress code while checking a tendency to slovenliness. In Catherine's time a certain commander used to appear on the quarterdeck of his frigate in 'a dressing-gown and slippers, surmounted by a pink cravat and a nightcap'. In Paul's reign, a button sewed on crooked meant dismissal.

Paul, whose ambitions clearly outstretched what might sometimes have been possible, showed a great passion for naval affairs. Despite, prior to his accession, having never set foot on a warship, he was proud of having been given by Catherine the title of High Admiral, an honour he continued to boast after becoming emperor. However, Chichagov, whose dislike of Paul showed no bounds, was nothing but critical of Paul's efforts in the realms of naval affairs, failing to admit that the reforms Paul introduced were long overdue. Disparagingly he referred to Paul as 'the cruellest enemy of our fleet', labelling him the 'Gatchina Boatman' under whose 'degrading yoke' the Russian Navy 'groaned'. Gatchina was a reference to the palace where Paul, during the 1790s, had built a structure known as the Admiralty to accommodate sailboats and other vessels and where, on a lake, battles had been played out with an eight-gun yacht *Mirolyub* and a frigate *Imprenable* (French for 'impregnable') that was equipped with sixteen guns. While Chichagov belittled this as Paul playing with toys, there was more to it. These were war games conducted in the presence of Kushelev, the man who Chichagov equally despised, and were used to better understand the principles of combat and through later analysis how they might be better applied when facing an actual opponent. It was also at Gatchina, and in discussions with Kushelev, that Paul was developing a vision for the navy, intending on coming into power to reform the navy in terms of that vision rather than allow it to develop in an unplanned and poorly co-ordinated fashion that was very much the way the navy had developed in the later years of Catherine's reign. Given the extent to which Chichagov detested both Paul and Kushelev, it is likely that his desire to see a refashioning of the navy away from Paul's vision may well have been the seed for his wish to push the navy in a very different direction.

Following the assassination of Paul, and once firmly in a position, Chichagov, and others of the incoming coterie, carefully ensured the removal of the senior naval administrators who had been appointed by Paul. Referring to them as 'the source of all evil', Chichagov very much included Kushelev, ignoring the fact that he, alongside Paul, had done much to contribute to the betterment of the navy Apart from bringing about improvements in shipbuilding, Kushelev had drawn up a new Statute of the Navy, established a repository of nautical charts and foreign atlases and introduced new signalling arrangements that he authored in a manual distributed throughout the navy entitled *Discourse on Naval Signals Serving at the Disposal of Naval Fleets*. Not surprisingly the signalling manual was later ridiculed by Chichagov, despite its undoubted usefulness. Under Alexander, and at the behest of Chichagov, Kushelev was quickly dismissed from all positions he held. Another who would soon lose out was Mordvinov, Alexander's first appointee to his newly created post of minister of naval forces. The appointment of Mordvinov had been against advice given by Chichagov, primarily it must be suspected because Chichagov himself wanted this position for himself. Mordvinov had previously served under Paul as vice president of the Admiralty and also supported the new foreign policy direction that went against further acquisition of territory, complaining that the high level of recruitment into the military arm had 'turned so many farmers into warriors' and had undermined the national economy. However, as to the precise role of the navy, he held to a different course, believing that Russia, for the security of her borders, needed an independent navy with 'blue water' capabilities. But on Alexander accepting the recommendations of Chichagov as supported by the committee to 'bring the fleet into better condition', Mordvinov felt himself to be out-flanked and isolated. In consequence, and after only three months, he resigned his ministerial position, with Chichagov taking his place under the title of deputy minister of naval forces, but effectively holding the office of minister.

That Russia now had a ministry of naval forces (renamed ministry of the navy in 1810) resulted from Alexander having abolished the old collegiate system, introducing in September 1802 new administrative reforms influenced by government reforms adopted elsewhere in Europe. In doing so, he made no attempt to lessen his autocratic powers, continuing to hold sway over all decisions, whereas European ministries had acquired greater independence of authority. Under the new system in Russia, the navy became one of several ministries with other ministries overseeing foreign affairs, war, finance, the interior, justice, commerce and education. Each minister was given direct access to the emperor and expected to attend with all other ministers a weekly meeting. Within the ministry of naval forces, two distinct branches were created: a board of Admiralty and a navy department, both functioning by 1803. Serving as the navy's executive branch, the board of Admiralty was responsible for maintaining the fleet and directing its activities alongside apportionment of finances, the arming of ships, provision of supplies, and work upon constructing ships. The navy department was responsible for scientific and technical areas, primarily factories, hydraulic engineering plants, military barracks, fortifications and educational institutions alongside training, libraries, printing houses, museums, tool shops, inventions, and publication of a maritime magazine. For some of these functions, separate committees were formed, including a committee for medical matters consisting of selected naval surgeons.

The subdivision of the navy into separate branches was designed to reflect the system that had long operated in Great Britain where the board of Admiralty, in first acting as an advisory body to the government, was responsible for the preparation and disposition of the fleet as well as the appointment and promotion of officers. Separate from the board of Admiralty were three inferior boards, namely the navy, victualling, and sick and hurt boards. The Navy Board was responsible for all matters relating to ship repair and construction and the payment of wages and prize money, the victualling board for the supply of comestible products, and the sick and hurt board for medical services and the appointment of surgeons. For the supply of ordnance, this came under the charge of the ordnance board, a department of the army. The advantage of such a system was that it allowed the board of Admiralty to concentrate on operational matters uncluttered by extraneous issues best dealt with by experts of the navy department and its sub-committees. Given the authority Chichagov was able to claim upon the accession of Alexander, it seems most probable that he influenced the new arrangement, having familiarity with the British naval administrative system following his time of service in England. It was then that he had met his future wife, Elizabeth, the daughter of Charles Proby, the resident commissioner of Chatham dockyard. Frequently visiting the Proby family in the commissioner's house, which lay within the dockyard at Chatham,

Chichagov gained a minute understanding of the British system and how it might be used to Russia's advantage.

Holding ministerial office from December 1802 until 1807, it is difficult to assess Chichagov's actual achievements during this period. If one considers his writings, the impression received is that he began to transform the navy from a decaying military force into a first-class fighting machine designed to protect the shores of Russia. Others, however, suggest that he achieved little.

The problem is that within the naval departments was a good deal of rivalry, and Chichagov, being so favoured by the emperor and part of the emperor's inner circle, was intensely disliked by those on the fringes of naval administration. Creating even further confusion was that of Chichagov being a very prickly character, quick to take offence and more than capable of making enemies. According to one contemporary, who clearly thought little of Chichagov, he was:

> *A spoiled child of happiness, he knew everything from books and nothing from experiments, he always over commanded everyone and was never under anyone's command. He considered himself capable of everything, but not others for anything.'*

Elsewhere it is suggested 'that the only thing he managed to bring to completion was reconstruction of the St Petersburg Admiralty', but admittedly one of the finest buildings in that city. Employing Andrey Zakharov, chief architect of the department of the navy, it is the same building that still stands today as the symbol of St Petersburg and is the architectural centre of the city.

Some substance to the claim that Chichagov did in fact achieve little during his time in office as naval forces minister is supported by Chichagov in his own memoirs. He provides several examples of schemes he attempted to put in place, but all failed in some way. These failings he claimed resulted from circumstances beyond his control – although lack of forethought was the primary factor, one example being that of improving naval recruitment by taking into the navy 'cabin boys', youngsters aged between 10 and 12 who, in being given barrack accommodation, would undergo a regime like that on board ships. The expectation was that by adulthood they would have fully acquired the skills of seamanship. In the event, few entered the navy. Chichagov later claimed it was due to a 'lack of opportunity' rather than the real cause, a failure to ensure (as Chichagov should have done) a clear progressional pathway, with suitable inducements, to support the scheme.

Another failed project was a plan to build ships for the British Navy at Arkhangelsk with the necessary materials brought from the Russian interior and built on the spot by Russian workmen supervised by master shipwrights from England. The advantage claimed by Chichagov was that Russia would benefit from providing at a cost the 'natural products available in Russia' alongside the training of Russian shipwrights. That it failed, according to Chichagov, was its rejection by 'touchy' and 'ignorant' members of the committee of ministers. However, Chichagov neglects to remind readers of his memoir of a severe shortage of available timbers near Arkhangelsk, with any ships built for Britain sucking out of Russia much of the remaining timber nearby. This, in turn, would ensure that any future vessels built for the Russian Navy would require timbers sourced from greater distances, so adding to overall costs.

One further failed project was a school built on the banks of the Neva for the children of marine workers and designed in the form of a circular building with projecting galleries. Pupils in training would be under perpetual surveillance from a supervisor positioned in the central circular building, ensuring they worked diligently. The building though was never finished and subsequently converted into barrack accommodation before its destruction by fire a few years later.

The new administrative system, through being newly implemented, had many shortcomings, with each minister still retaining absolute control over their individual departments and rarely sharing issues arising within their department with other ministers even during the weekly council meetings. Chichagov was no exception, taking umbrage at the slightest threat to his position as head of the navy. Count Nikolai Petrovich Rumyantsev, shortly after his appointment as foreign minister in 1808, told the French ambassador that he dared not meddle in naval matters, and remarked:

> *The navy has a special leader. This leader is like the God of Israel, a God jealous of all other Gods, and, to top it all, a somewhat stubborn God.*

Chichagov and each of the other ministers were continually vying with each other to curry favour with the emperor through their right of speaking to him directly and in private. While Chichagov was one of Alexander's most favoured, he found that others bringing influence to bear upon the emperor led to decisions being taken that affected the navy, and with which Chichagov was not privy. When this occurred, Chichagov reacted angrily, expressing annoyance in hastily written letters to Alexander Vorontsov. Sometimes he would threaten to resign. One of the fieriest exchanges between him and the emperor occurred in early 1807 when, following instructions from Alexander, Chichagov informed Admiral Senyavin, commanding a squadron in the Adriatic, to undertake a particular operation against the Ottomans. Soon after he learned that Senyavin, over Chichagov's head, had received counter-orders from Andreas von Budberg, Alexander's advisor on foreign affairs. Chichagov's anger was made clear in a letter written to the emperor, with Chichagov receiving in return a severe reprimand that forced him to back down. When, on an earlier occasion, with Chichagov annoyed over another matter, walking out of a ministerial meeting with a threat to resign, Alexander had made a similar stern response, writing:

> *I thought that the daily experience of my respect towards you would have aroused some kind of gratitude in you, and that especially at this time, when you yourself know how many cares I have, you would not have*

> *tried to multiply them...Therefore, I reject your request, nor will I tolerate anything of this kind in the future.*

If Chichagov can be accorded with anything more than initiating a rebuilding of the Admiralty and retaining a tight hand over naval affairs, it is regarding a major reconstruction of the Tallinn naval base. This was a scheme originally sanctioned by Catherine in May 1792 and based on a plan produced by Admiral Vasily Chichagov, Pavel Chichagov's father. Upon the accession of Paul, all work on the project was abandoned. Central to this scheme was an enclosed harbour of sufficient depth and size to accommodate first-rate warships and which would have two entrances to allow ships to enter and leave regardless of wind direction. In addition, storehouses, maintenance shops and barbette fortifications were also to be built. Persuaded by Chichagov, Alexander, soon after his accession, appointed a committee to re-examine the value of Tallinn as a naval port, with a decision taken to complete, with just a few minor modifications, Admiral Chichagov's original design, with Chichagov the naval minister charged with its completion.

Chichagov's time in office came to an end in December 1807, but not because of some unreconcilable difference between him and the emperor. Instead, it resulted from his request to leave office because of his wife having a serious illness, possibly tuberculosis, and a wish to join her for a period of convalescence in the South of France. Reluctantly, Alexander agreed but chose to call it a temporary arrangement with Chichagov retaining the title of minister of naval forces alongside the 4,000-rouble annual salary that came with the post, together with an annual 6,000 roubles payment referred to as 'table money'. In his place, Alexander appointed Jean-Baptiste de Traversay, formerly and since 1802, commander-in-chief of the Black Sea Fleet. A highly regarded naval officer, Traversay had originally distinguished himself in the French Navy, but as a member of the nobility fled France at the time of the revolution, eventually accepting an invitation from Catherine to join her imperial navy.

A lack of funding resulted in the new minister finding it difficult to maintain a fully functioning maritime force, a difficulty that was only to be partially reversed during the months leading up to Napoleon's invasion of Russia. Traversay was demanding 22 million roubles, but granted only 17 million. Even after approval for this amount, Traversay, who lacked Chichagov's fearsome reputation, had to go cap in hand to Count Dmitry Guryev, minister of finance, to get the money released, arguing:

> *We must carry out the defence programme planned and approved by the Emperor. We must not make small savings that will prevent the defence programme planned and approved by the Emperor.*

While such an amount might just about have sufficed a few years earlier, inflation had done much to increase costs, especially material needed by the dockyards. At the beginning of the century, 16kg of oak could be purchased for 42 kopecks. By 1812, the price had doubled. During the war against Napoleon, known in Russia as the Patriotic War, the navy was entirely subservient to the needs of the army with the new funding used for the construction of gunboats that could be used to support military operations on land. Some sixty of these were completed at the Admiralty yard in Okhta in 1812, bringing the total number available to defend the empire to just over 300. These proved pivotal in the defence of the Russian coastline and river estuaries, but in particular defending Riga (see Chapter 14). As for the main ships of the fleet, and with the fear that Napoleon might capture Kronstadt and Arkhangelsk, Traversay worked tirelessly to evacuate them to Great Britain, where they were to operate alongside the British Navy until their return to Russia in 1814.

# PART FIVE

# At war with Napoleon

The Treaty of Amiens signed on 25 March 1802 brought about a fourteen-month period of peace to a war from which Russia had already withdrawn. Desperation for peace between Great Britain and France in their conflict had left many questions unsettled or passed over, with regrets emerging on both sides as to terms so quickly agreed. The return of hostilities was inevitable, with Britain declaring war on France on 18 May 1803. Initially, in this renewed conflict, Russia adopted a neutral stance, but Alexander's dislike of Napoleon and the threat he presented to the balance of power in Europe saw Russia, in April 1805, entering an alliance with Great Britain – the Third Coalition – against Napoleon and which would eventually include Austria, Sweden, Naples, and Sicily. For Russia, the naval side of the new alliance mainly took the form of collaborative action in the Mediterranean directed initially at protecting the Ionian Islands. Here, at Corfu, Russia had established a military and trading centre, with the islands having now gained a degree of independence through a constitution naming them the Septinsular Republic. To reinforce her position in the Adriatic, Russia had been relocating to Corfu several warships, including larger battleships from the Baltic Fleet. One early operation conducted by the Russian Navy was escorting to Naples in November 1805 an Anglo-Russian military force assembled at Malta. In a short space of time, this force had to be re-evacuated due to a considerably larger French army advancing towards southern Italy following their victories at Ulm (16-19 October 1805) and Austerlitz (2 December 1805). A third and final naval reinforcement from the Baltic arrived at Corfu in January 1806 under the command of Vice Admiral Dmitry Nikolayevich Senyavin, and through his seniority in rank, he assumed command of the Russian naval forces in the area. The arrival of Senyavin occurred soon after the British victory at Trafalgar (21 October 1805), with the British Mediterranean Fleet, following the death of Nelson, then under the command of Vice Admiral Cuthbert Collingwood (1st Baron Collingwood since Trafalgar). As with Nelson, Collingwood resented the presence of a Russian squadron in the Mediterranean, with relations between him and Senyavin only marginally better than between Nelson and Ushakov. Russian participation in what by then had become the Fourth Coalition ended abruptly during the summer of 1807 following Russia's defeat at the Battle of Friedland (17 June 1807). This forced Alexander to sign a treaty of friendship with France that required Russia to participate in the Continental System, the means devised by Napoleon to destroy Britain financially by denying her trade outlets through ports in Europe. For the Russian Empire, ceasing all forms of trade with Britain was to threaten economic disaster, leading Alexander within a short space of time to effectively withdraw from the agreement. Napoleon responded with his calamitous invasion of Russia.

# CHAPTER 14

# CORFU – A NAVAL BASE AS SAFE AS MOSCOW

Senyavin's squadron, which sailed into the Mediterranean from the Baltic in 1805, was there to protect the Ionian Islands which, since their capture from the French by Ushakov, had become a valued Russian asset – a military and trading centre viewed to be 'as safe as in Moscow'. While Alexander had discarded any claims that Russia had on Malta, refusing to commit to safeguarding its security alongside Great Britain, the Ionian Islands were part of an obligation previously agreed and where a Russian presence was seen as more essential. Following the final evacuation of the Ionian Islands by Russia in August 1801, French privateers operating out of Ancona had begun to roam freely in the waters of the Adriatic while French agents were fermenting discontent among the islanders. This posed a security risk not only to Russian interests in Corfu but if unchecked could lead to increased French activities in and around the Balkan peninsula and eventually threaten Russia in the Black Sea. Alexander agreed during the summer of 1802 to transfer to Corfu part of the Russian force that had remained at Naples to protect King Ferdinand, with the other part of that force returning to the Black Sea. Brought to Corfu on three transports and escorted by two frigates, 600 soldiers were dispersed around the various islands with one of the frigates providing security at sea by regularly cruising from island to island. Further reinforcements arrived in 1804, including a naval contingent of two ships of the line and two frigates from the Baltic under the command of Captain Commander Aleksey Samuilovich Greig, the son of Admiral Samuel Greig. The entry of Russia into the alliance against France required an even stronger Russian presence in the Adriatic, this provided by Senyavin's squadron, which arrived in January 1806.

In this respect, the continuing Russian naval presence in the Adriatic might be considered appropriate to the defence of Russia and in accordance with the direction in which Chichagov, as minister of naval forces, was now steering the navy. However, if this was so, his concept of defence was very much on the borderline of a much more extensive use of the navy and exactly where the peripheries of that defence lay. In September 1805, with Senyavin's squadron having just departed Kronstadt, Chichagov wrote to Semyon Vorontsov saying that Russia should be paying a greater role in Egypt, as 'we are closer to the gates of the Mediterranean'. As with those in St Petersburg, who had been formerly extolling the views of Russia taking possession of Malta, he was now seeing similar advantages for Russian ships operating in the eastern Mediterranean:

> *The advantages that will result for us by this arrangement will be incalculable. The experience that will serve to train officers and crews, the pleasure of playing a role worthy of a power that has never appeared insignificant when it decides to act, the confidence that will be inspired in all peoples, which it is useful to attach to our principles, the facility and encouragement that will result for our commerce from the Black Sea. etc., etc. You know better than I all that will follow.*

As for the advantages accruing to Russia by continued possession of Corfu, Aleksey Greig in a letter to Semyon Vorontsov was even more effusive:

> *This island is without doubt of the greatest importance for Russia, as much for the political influence it gives her as for the excellent school it provides for the navy. Here the squadrons of the Baltic and of the Black Sea can be united and coordinated. Here they appear so different that it is difficult to tell that they belong to the same sovereign. The port is excellent; one can nearly always be on a cruise and learn more in one year than in ten in Russia.*

From the outset it was clear that Senyavin, despite his mission being fully supported by the government in London, was less than welcomed by Vice Admiral Collingwood, making this clear in a letter written to Hugh Elliott, the British ambassador in Naples. In this, Collingwood hoped that Senyavin could be sidelined, seeing him as 'undoubtedly better at Corfu' rather than breaking out into the wider Mediterranean. Nelson, of course, had attempted to sideline Ushakov, but hoping at that time to keep him out of the Adriatic. Although Alexander consistently denied that he had wider objectives, Collingwood took the view that Russia was using Corfu as a springboard for a more general expansion of the Russian Empire, concerned that Sicily, then firmly within the British sphere of influence was a desirable Russian conquest. Sicily, for Collingwood, was essential for the supply of Malta, another island now firmly in British sights, and which lacked self-sufficiency in food production.

On departing the Baltic in late September 1805, Senyavin's squadron first put into Portsmouth to take on water and provisions with those taken sick transferred to the hospital at Haslar. Through Senyavin's ships not being in good repair, the stay at Portsmouth lasted several weeks, allowing time for the dockyard labour force to replace masts and spars that were rotting, guns that were found to be defective and fitting lightning conductors. The fact of all this work having to be undertaken only a few weeks after leaving Kronstadt demonstrates the overall poor state into which the Baltic Fleet had been allowed to fall. Nevertheless, under Senyavin and on its arrival in the Mediterranean, those same ships and the crews that manned them, while a product of the Baltic, would go on to achieve a great deal. Sailing out of Portsmouth on 16 November, Senyavin's ships continued their passage into the Mediterranean, anchoring off the British naval base at Gibraltar where further supplies were received before reaching Corfu.

During the passage into the Mediterranean, the officers and seamen of the squadron gained much evidence of just how dominant Britain was at sea. Senyavin for his part already had that evidence, having as a naval cadet during the 1770s received his initial training at the Portsmouth Royal Naval Academy before serving as a midshipman on a British warship, though even he might have been surprised by the advances made at Portsmouth, especially in the use of steam. As one of Senyavin's midshipmen, Vladimir Bronevskiy, noted, when comparing Portsmouth with the naval yard at Kronstadt, 'where we use sheer manpower, here they utilize machines, fire, water, and horses', adding that for him it was impossible to describe 'all the myriad mechanisms' employed at Portsmouth, designs that 'might surprise even the most learned mechanics'.

Further evidence of Britain's dominance at sea gleaned by those manning Senyavin's ships during the passage into the Mediterranean was news of the Trafalgar victory, brought to Portsmouth on 6 November but recorded by Bronevskiy in the Old Style as 25 October, and while Senyavin's squadron lay in the Spithead roadstead. Of this Bronevskiy writes:

> *From the earliest morning, pages were brought along the streets describing the battle and the death of Nelson; everyone's face wore a mixture of grief and triumph and everywhere exclamations were heard: 'long live Nelson.'*

On sailing out of Spithead, the squadron was given a reminder of this same victory when on 3 December they passed at sea the twelve most damaged vessels from the battle, these heading towards Portsmouth. Off southern Spain, a further reminder of Britain's maritime strength came when fifteen ships of the British Mediterranean Fleet under Collingwood were encountered, these engaged in the prevention of French warships, mainly from Brest and Rochefort, entering the Mediterranean to join eight Spanish ships of the line moored in Cartagena. Upon his arrival off Corfu Senyavin, as the senior naval officer, took command of a mixed fleet that, alongside the squadron he had led out of the Baltic, now consisted of nine ships of the line, six frigates, seven brigs, one schooner, twelve gunboats, two transports and a hospital ship. Also on the islands were 10,000 Russian soldiers and a 2,000-strong Albanian corps.

Whatever Senyavin attempted, Collingwood found fault, complaining in November 1806 to Viscount Howick, the First Lord of the Admiralty, of the Russian squadron being 'in the greatest degree inactive' and that 'they have no desire to accommodate us in anything'. According to Collingwood, 'they have, indeed, had a squadron at sea, but with little effect in giving annoyance to the enemy.' Given Collingwood's earlier expressed hope that Senyavin might be 'best at Corfu', such inactivity should have pleased him. But then, in the eyes of some British naval officers, whatever the Russian Navy did, it could

**1.** Catherine the Great, otherwise known as Emperess Catherine II.

**2.** The house in Inverkeithing where Samuel Greig was born.

**3.** The Admiralty, situated alongside the Neva in St Petersburg.

**4.** Carron Ironworks, Falkirk.

**5.** A Russian-built carronade.

**6.** The Lutheran Cathedral of the Virgin Mary in Tallinn where Samuel Greig was laid to rest.

*Above*: **7.** The tomb of Samuel Greig, designed by the Empress Catherine's own architect Giacomo Quarenghi.

*Right*: **8.** Semyon Vorontsov, the Russian ambassador to the Court of St James during most of the wartime period.

**9.** The Russian Imperial Fleet naval anchorage lying off Paldiski.

**10.** Portsmouth dockyard in England, with *Victory* in the foreground. (Ministry of Defence Crown Copyright, 2004)

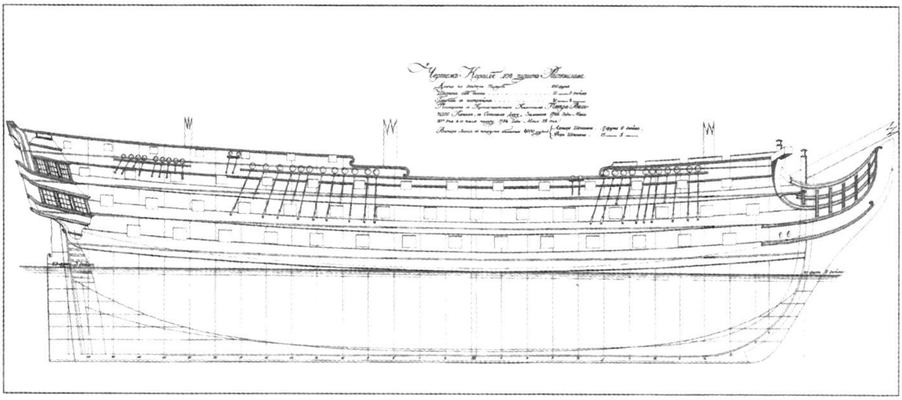

**11.** *Rotislav*, a 'Ches'ma' class battleship closely resembling *Victory.*

**12.** The River Medway looking towards the dockyard at Chatham.

**13.** Greig, Aleksey Samuilovich.

**14.** Fyodor Fyodorovich Ushakov.

*Right*: **15.** Horatio Nelson.

*Below*: **16.** The two massive fortresses defending the town of Corfu.

*Above*: **17.** Fortifications surrounding the Maltese city of Valletta.

*Left*: **18.** Emperor Paul I.

*Above*: **19.** Various Russian cannons on the quayside of Tallinn harbour.

*Right*: **20.** Alexander I.

*Left*: **21.** Dmitry Nikolayevich Senyavin.

*Below*: **22.** Dubrovnik.

**23.** Kilitbahir Kelesi.

**24.** Kale Sultanieh.

**25.** The naval Cathedral of Saint Nicholas in Kronstadt.

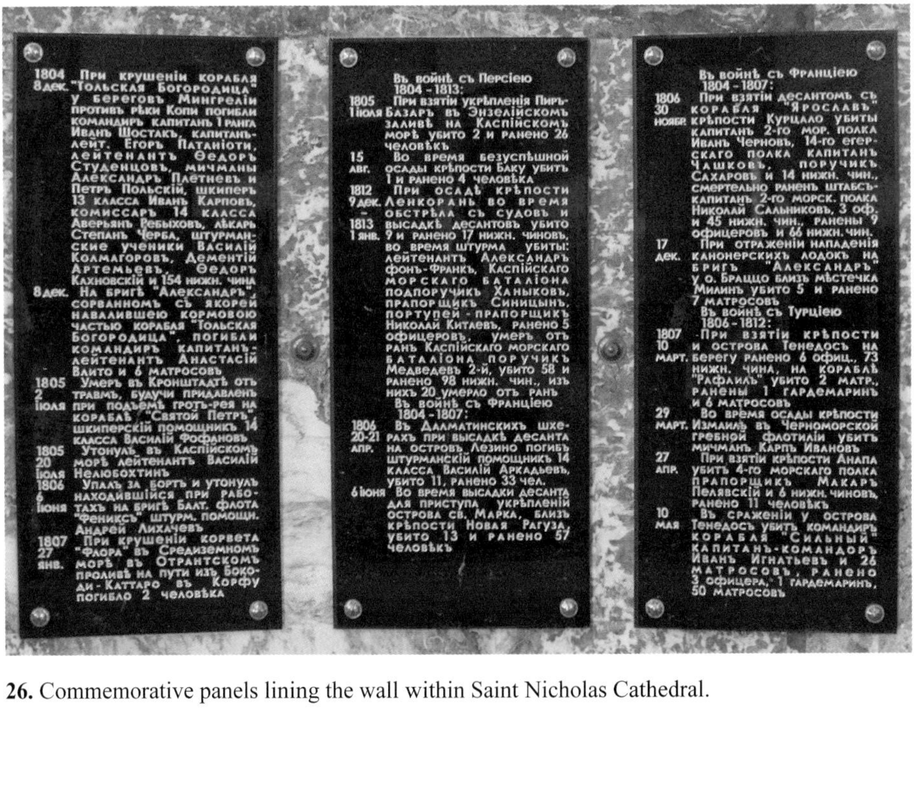


**26.** Commemorative panels lining the wall within Saint Nicholas Cathedral.

**27.** The burning in August 1808 of the seventy-four-gun *Vsevolod* outside the port of Paldiski.

**28.** Belem Tower, Lisbon.

**29.** Napoleon Dock, Antwerp.

**30.** Daugava River, Riga.

never be right. To Viscount Howick, Collingwood had nevertheless chosen his words more carefully than he might otherwise have done, for Howick was an appointment made by the newly formed 'ministry of all the talents', a Whig-dominated coalition much more favourable to Russia than the previous Tory administration led by the recently and by now deceased William Pitt. It was for this reason Collingwood doubtless added:

> *But these things, I hope, arise merely from the temper of individuals, and not from the disposition of the court. I shall endeavour, by a contrary proceeding, to conciliate them; and whenever they come into a British port, shew them every attention and give them every aid in my power.*

Senyavin, who had served as one of Ushakov's captains in the Mediterranean, commanding at that time the seventy-four-gun *Sviatoi Piotr*, while not necessarily aware of Collingwood's views might well have expected a certain coolness to be directed towards him upon his own arrival in the Mediterranean. Nevertheless, there was no immediate animosity or friction, with Senyavin first turning his attention to the Balkan Peninsula where, following the Battle of Austerlitz, several trading cities along the coast had been ceded by Austria to the French. A plan now being put forward, and one discussed in London between Stroganov, Semyon Vorontsov's successor as *chargé d'affaires* to the Court of St James, was that should Senyavin and the troops he had at his disposal prove successful in preventing the French taking possession or holding on to these possessions, that a series of Greek and Slavic states be created under the protection of Russia. Such a possibility moved only slightly away from the policy of Russia undertaking no further territorial expansion, as it would require, once any French forces had been defeated, only a limited military presence, with the Greek and Slavic states serving as an advanced ally. In this, the role of the navy would be that of transporting military personnel and equipment as and when required, and in keeping with the navy being subservient to the needs of the army.

Before the arrival of the French, Cattaro (Kotor) on the coastal region of modern-day Montenegro was taken by Senyavin. That his forces pre-empted the arrival of the French was because Senyavin's ships were dominant in the Ionian Sea, consequently forcing the French to take the mountainous and much more difficult land route. Ragusa (Dubrovnik) was the next target, but this was an independent neutral city not being ceded to France but likely to be taken by the French once their army moved south along the peninsula. Because of its neutrality, no attempt was made by the Russians to forcibly occupy Dubrovnik. Instead, a naval blockade and occupation of a few strategic positions was assumed. Directing these operations was Captain Henry Baillie commanding three battleships, and three smaller vessels. On 11 April, an attack was made on the French-occupied island of Korčula, with the surrender of its fortress described by Bronevskiy:

> *The Iaroslav [seventy-four-gun third rate], Ekspeditsion [sixteen-gun schooner], Letun [twelve-gun brig] and Azard [small xebec], having*

*anchored off the port of Kozola [Korčula], opened a heavy fire on the fortifications upon the signal of a pistol shot. In less than half an hour the guns on the walls were wrecked and the enemy defended himself with only musketry. When the Aziia [seventy-four-gun third rate] dropped anchor, a shore party consisting of two companies of a naval regiment and several sailors rowed on boats directly to the fort. The enemy commandant... hauled down the flag and departed with the garrison, laid down their arms and surrendered unconditionally.*

With little fighting, the French did indeed take possession of Dubrovnik, but with the Russians committed to removing them, bringing the town under bombardment both from the sea and cannons positioned in the mountains that overlooked the city. Again Bronevskiy:

*Two 48-funt [23.6kg] guns and two 24-funt [9.83kg] carronades were delivered up from the ships with extreme difficulty. Five hundred sailors dragged them over 10 verstas [10.67km] over rocks and into the steep mountains. The first battery was finished on the 10th [22 June] and the second on the 12th [24 June], from which point they began to operate well enough that each shot inflicted damage on the enemy. The city lay at the foot of the mountains, below a steep incline from which it was quite convenient to shoot. These batteries were soon reinforced by an additional three mortars.*

From both the sea and the batteries placed behind Dubrovnik, the city came under an intense bombardment of fire beginning from the sea on 18 June and continuing from both land and sea for nearly three weeks. However, the arrival of a 3,000-strong French military force capable of overwhelming the besiegers led Baillie to abandon his efforts, consequently leaving Dubrovnik safely in the hands of the French but still under naval blockade.

It was in 1807 and in support of the blockade mounted by Senyavin on areas held or under threat from the French that three battles were fought at sea, on 22 June, 16 September, and 16 December. The first had seen the fifty-gun frigate *Venera* and the twenty-four-gun frigate *Avtroil* (former Swedish frigate *Af trolle* captured in 1789) engage eleven French xebecs and gunboats close by the mouth of the Neretva River that lies 60km north of Dubrovnik. During the battle two French ships sank, three more surrendered and the remaining six escaped. The action fought on 16 September resulted from a French brig and ten gunboats attempting to break through to Dubrovnik, but the battleship *Azzia*, the frigate *Venus* and the sixteen-gun brig *Bonasorte* (formerly a French gunboat captured off Ancona in 1799) drove them back with their fire. Nevertheless, one gunboat managed to break through. Resulting from this engagement, *Venus* suffered damage to her mast and underwater to her hull. Finally, on the evening of 16 December, the twelve-gun brig *Aleksandr*, having dropped anchor near the Dalmatian coast off Brac, was attacked by a French tartane and three gunboats. Seen by the watch approaching *Aleksandr* from a nearby island with fifty soldiers ready to board, the alarm was raised and two of the gunboats sunk by cannonballs. In this engagement, which lasted about an hour, the French, mostly from grapeshot, lost 217 killed with *Aleksandr* suffering four killed and seven wounded. That one of the gunboats sunk was named 'Napoleon' and the Russian brig was named 'Aleksandr', additional sweetness was given to the victory.

The various actions taken by Senyavin's squadron effectively prevented French penetration deeper into the Balkans, but in doing so permitted the French ambassador in Istanbul, Colonel Horace Sébastiani, to persuade the Porte that Russia was preparing to use its newly strengthened position to mount a naval-military attack on Ottoman territory. Ultimately, Sébastiani suggested that Russia was working towards a revival of Catherine's 'Greek Project' that had been designed to re-establish the old Byzantine Empire by annexing into the Russian sphere of influence the Greek-speakers of the Ottoman Empire. In fear of this, and to put a stop to a further movement of ships and troops from the Black Sea, the Porte issued a prohibition on Russian warships passing through the Dardanelles. If maintained, this would not only prevent Russia resupplying the Ionian Islands but prevent ships of Senyavin's squadron entering the Black Sea for maintenance and repair, and so having either to rely upon British facilities or return to the Baltic. While Charles Arbuthnot, the British ambassador to the Porte, was as strident as Andrey Italinski, the Russian ambassador to the Porte, in attempting to persuade Selim III to reverse this decision, matters became worse when fighting broke out between the Ottomans and Russians in Moldavia and Wallachia, territories under the joint protection of both Russia and the Ottoman Empire.

Through fear that the position being adopted by the Porte would eventually result in a full-scale naval and military alliance with France, the British government ordered Collingwood to reinforce the number of ships he had in the region. For this purpose, Vice Admiral Sir John Duckworth was ordered to proceed with a squadron of ships to sail into the Golden Horn and 'demand the surrender of the Turkish fleet', and the Porte to enter a new alliance with Great Britain and Russia. If not agreed, all the Ottoman ships moored in the Golden Horn were to be destroyed and the city placed under bombardment. The expectation was that Duckworth would first await the arrival of Senyavin's ships before entering the Dardanelles, but instead he attempted a pre-emptive strike without the support of Senyavin. On anchoring in the Sea of Marmara, 8 miles south of Istanbul, on 24 February, Duckworth duly threatened to bombard Istanbul if his demands were not met, his instructions being that he should permit the Porte only thirty minutes to provide a response. Instead, he began negotiations that dragged on for several days, allowing the Porte, which was playing for time, to strengthen the shoreline defences of the Dardanelles. This left Duckworth worrying that his ships would now be trapped and unable to return, forcing him into making a hasty retreat during which his ships suffered a battering of artillery fire.

Senyavin, with eight ships of the line and a frigate, joined Duckworth in the north-east Aegean soon after, making the proposal that Duckworth should release to him a few ships for a bombardment of Istanbul. In rejecting this, Duckworth claimed that a force of fifty battleships would be required to successfully reach Istanbul, given the number of gun batteries now positioned on either side of the Dardanelles. According to Bronevskiy, the former midshipman in Senyavin's squadron but now commander of the *Hector* brig, Senyavin 'beseeched' Duckworth 'with all his ability for two days', although Senyavin gained the support of several British captains in the making of a second attempt, 'Duckworth resolutely and in writing refused'. As to why Duckworth had not waited for Senyavin's squadron, this clearly puzzled Senyavin, with Bronevskiy writing:

> *We first wondered what compelled that admiral, without waiting for our squadron, to sail on the enemy capital with this small force but our perplexity increased even more when, upon Senyavin's presentation, Duckworth announced on the 1st March [13 March] that he had another appointment and left us alone with just two ships and two bomb vessels to reinforce our fleet.*

The conclusion drawn, in answer to this question, both by those serving with Senyavin as well as later Russian historians, was that Duckworth, in expecting to gain success against the Ottomans, did not wish to share this success with Senyavin. Among Senyavin's officers much anger was directed at Duckworth; *Rafail*'s first officer, Lieutenant Pavel Ivanovich Panafidin, in one of a series letters written at the time, remarking that this was directed at Duckworth for not having waited for the arrival of Senyavin's ships before sailing into the Dardanelles, with such anger intensified by his refusal 'to act in concert' once Senyavin ships had arrived. In conclusion, Panafidin added, 'throughout [this] ongoing war with the French, they [the English] have clearly acted for themselves.' According to E.V. Tarle in 1966:

> *Senyavin's officers, not without irony, reacted to the deplorable end of the English exercise, started so hastily with the direct goal of taking all the glory for themselves in case of success, not sharing it with the Russians.*

Firsov made a similar point in 1997:

> *Senyavin received a letter from the commander of the British forces in the Mediterranean, Admiral Collingwood. He asked Senyavin to detach four ships to help the British in breaking through the Dardanelles. However, the English Admiral soon changed his mind, why share the laurels of the conquerors of Constantinople with the Russians?*

Driault, a French historian writing in 1900, took a slightly different approach, considering that Duckworth 'did not like to help the Russians in an enterprise which would not benefit England alone'.

Consequently, Duckworth led his ships out of the Aegean on 13 March, with Senyavin then establishing a blockade of the Dardanelles that would successfully prevent all shipping from the south, including those carrying essential supplies of grain from Egypt and the Levant, reaching Istanbul. On eventually discovering the nature of Duckworth's other appointment, the 'appointment' that took him so suddenly away from the Dardanelles, this simply intensified Russian anger, it being learnt that he had sailed to Egypt to support the landing of a British expeditionary force. Here, once again, Russia felt duped, as Senyavin's successful blockade of the Dardanelles which also prevented the movement of Ottoman warships out of the Dardanelles, effectively allowed the British landings to proceed unimpeded with no fear of an Ottoman Navy counter-attack. Again, this is picked up by Skritsky in a recent biography of Senyavin:

> *The British hoped that the Russian blockade would not release the Turkish fleet, and in the meantime, they would calmly take Alexandria.*

In St Petersburg the news of Duckworth's departure for Egypt was met with outrage, Alexander informing his foreign minister, Andreas Eberhard von Budberg, that the action was 'inexcusable' and that it put Senyavin 'in a difficult position'. To this he went on to add that 'nothing could be more contrary to the interests of the Court at St Petersburg' than 'the withdrawal of the British forces to Egypt'. If, instead, and as explained by Senyavin in a memorandum to Alexander in 1799, the near-6,000 troops it was later discovered Duckworth had landed in Alexandria had been taken instead to the Dardanelles, this would have been sufficient to silence the coastal batteries and would have allowed Senyavin, with the 2,000 troops that his own ships carried, to not just threaten a bombardment of Istanbul, but carry out a full-scale military landing.

# CHAPTER 15

# THE BATTLES OF DARDANELLES STRAIT AND ATHOS

For Senyavin, following Duckworth's departure, a blockade of the Strait had been established only because a direct attack on Istanbul by the limited forces now available to him would have been suicidal. Apart from the forts and gun batteries guarding the Strait, and which Senyavin's ships would need to silence, there was, lying in the Golden Horn and ready to pounce, a sizeable fleet of at least twelve ships of the line. Only the combined British and Russian squadrons and the land forces they carried between them would have been up to such a task. However, the blockade was only the first step in a series of moves designed by Senyavin to inflict even greater damage upon the Porte. The real object was to force the Ottoman Fleet into the open waters of the Aegean where Senyavin, in using the advanced battle tactics he had learnt from Ushakov, alongside his own refinements, could be used to advantage. In such a situation, even though he would be attacking an Ottoman fleet superior in both number of ships and quantity of ordnance carried, Senyavin was confident of victory. He just had to play his cards right, and if all fell his way, then Istanbul might also be within his grasp.

The immediate problem was that even if the citizens of Istanbul were desperately short of supplies, the fleet still might not sail should it be felt that it may have to fight a battle in which defeat was inevitable. After all, during Catherine's second Ottoman war, the Ottoman Fleet had suffered four defeats at the hands of Ushakov. To ensure that the enemy would leave the safety of the Strait required Senyavin to dispose of his ships in such a way as to be seen by the Porte as a real threat while making it appear that the Russian squadron was in some way clearly vulnerable. Only then would the Ottomans sail. It was as if Senyavin was playing a giant game of chess with the need to create a tactical target, through a series of opening moves that would first secure his own defence while at the same time serve as a decoy to distract the other player. Once the opening moves had been completed, his opponent would be lured into making an attack. And who was that other player? In this game it was Seydi Ali, the grand admiral or kapudan pasha, a former Algerian corsair. Once Seydi Ali made that attacking move, Senyavin would make his counter-move, one that had the possibility of checking his opponent and ultimately Ali's total defeat.

## Tenedos

For Senyavin, the opening move was taking possession of Tenedos, an island close to Türkiye's Asian shore 20 miles south of the Strait. Once taken, Tenedos, with its already existing fort, could serve as a defensible forward base that in tightening the blockade would increase the pressure on the Ottoman Fleet to sail and retake Tenedos. But would Seydi Ali do this? Possibly not. That is unless he was given to think that such a venture could be easily undertaken with no risk of encountering Senyavin's squadron. For this, Senyavin had to create an illusion to make it appear his ships had sailed from the island and were at such a distance they would be long delayed in returning. In other words, to give Seydi Ali the belief that he had sufficient time to sail out of the Strait, land a powerful force of troops on Tenedos, and safely return to the Strait and the security it offered.

This was Senyavin's game plan. In its implementation, his first move was to capture Tenedos. On 20 March, just one week after Duckworth's squadron had withdrawn, Senyavin landed 1,550 men on the island whose mission was to capture the Ottoman-held fortress defended by a 1,200-strong garrison. First the landing beach was cleared of sentinels by the guns of *Moshchnyi* (66) and *Venus* (50). Also giving support was *Rafail* (84), which came under fire from the fortress, but in replying with her powerful 36-pounder guns, the fort's defences were easily stifled. Soon, in finding themselves hard pressed, the island's Ottoman guards began to retreat, and even before the day had ended most of the island had been taken with only the fortress still holding out. Yet, for the Ottomans, the fort was only a limited place of safety. Targeted by several of Senyavin's ships, *Rafail* alone expending 2,760 rounds, it also came under fire from gun batteries placed on the surrounding hills that were able to fire directly into the fort. On the following day, and with no hope of relief, the Ottoman commander surrendered on the agreement that the garrison and 400 Turkish women and children would be transported to the Asiatic mainland.

With the Russian flag raised over the fortress, Senyavin had completed stage one of his game plan. Everything was going his way. Even the return of the surrendering Ottoman troops. By releasing them, they would provide the Porte with details of his land forces and that the total number he possessed could easily be matched and outnumbered by the massive forces that could easily be assembled in Istanbul. This would encourage the Porte to order the fleet to sea and land troops on Tenedos. To ensure that such a decision was even more likely, the Porte needed to be brought under further pressure – the pressure of the blockade and possible riots within the city if food became scarce. Using the island, the Russian squadron lay peacefully at anchor but always ready to intercept vessels, of whatever size, daring to approach the Dardanelles. Always at sea, Senyavin had two ships on patrol at the mouth of the Strait to report on any movement of shipping, but especially signs of the fleet being ready to sail. Off Smyrna (Izmir), a port city lying to the west, a secondary blockade was also begun. Here four ships patrolled the roadstead between Chios and Mytilene to prevent ships entering that port with supplies that could then be sent to Istanbul by land.

## Battle of the Dardanelles, May 1807

By the beginning of May, with Istanbul close to starvation and the people becoming increasingly restless, there was great urgency for Seydi Ali to break the blockade. On 19 May, just as the sun was beginning to set, it was reported to Senyavin that Ali had finally made his move. A fleet of eight ships of the line accompanied by several frigates and sloops was poised to sail. It was Ali's intention, Senyavin correctly assumed, to land troops on Tenedos, with these already assembled and waiting on the Asiatic shore opposite Tenedos. Once the Ottoman Fleet was at sea, these troops would board oared galleys that would, under the protection of Ali's fleet, carry them to Tenedos and run them onto the shore. It would be a speedy operation. Once the galleys had been safely beached and the troops disembarked, Ali would make a rapid return to the safety of the Dardanelles in the belief that the troops would successfully take the island. However, Senyavin also knew that the Ottoman Fleet would not leave the Dardanelles if there was any risk of encountering the Russian squadron. This required putting in place the final part of Senyavin's plan that was designed to draw the Ottoman Fleet into the trap he was about to set.

In his journal, Bronevskiy describes Senyavin's plan as '[intending] to bait the enemy into rushing the island and thereby luring him further from the strait'. Confident that the Tenedos fortress could hold out against the Ottoman forces, Senyavin ordered four of his ships (*Rafail*, *Retvizan*, *Sviatoia Elena* and *Arkhangel Selafail*) to sail under the command of Captain Commander Greig to the island of Lesbos. His remaining ships (*Arkhangel Uriil, Tvyordyi, Sil'nyi, Iaroslav, Moshchnyi, Skorii,* and *Venera*), Senyavin took to the island of Imbros. It was an arrangement meant to suggest to Ali that for some reason Senyavin was dividing his forces and Tenedos lay without any seaborne defence. However, it was Senyavin's intention, once Ali had sailed, to bring together at the mouth of the Strait those separated units to block Ali's return. As planned, it was the prevailing northerly wind that would ensure Senyavin's success, this necessary to delay Ali's return, giving Senyavin ample time to complete this manoeuvre.

However, as with most well laid schemes, not all went according to plan. It was the failure of that prevailing northerly wind that caused this scheme to 'gang agley'. Instead, of a wind from the north, a strong wind blew from the north-east, driving Senyavin back to Tenedos. Here, on 20 May, an attempt had been made by Ali, following his sailing out of the Strait, to land troops on the island, but this had failed with the Russian garrison successful in repelling troops brought over from the Asiatic shore. It was the morning after these failed landings that Senyavin returned to Tenedos where as soon as his ships dropped anchor, they were savaged by a squall from the north followed by the return of a north-easterly wind. Not realising that this same wind had also trapped Ali, Senyavin thought all had been lost. Then, soon after, Senyavin learnt not only of the unsuccessful landings but that Ali was anchored just a few miles from Tenedos close to the island of Mavro.

Two days later the wind changed again, shifting, unusually for that time of year, to a south-westerly, giving the Ottoman Fleet the chance of getting back to the Strait. But it also gave Senyavin an opportunity to attack, ordering his ships, and which now included the four detached units under Greig, to weigh anchor. His expectation, or more accurately his hope, was that the Ottoman Fleet would attempt to fight it out rather than run for home, thinking that they would most likely anchor and form a close battle line to receive the attack. This would have allowed Senyavin to use tactics previously adopted by Ushakov of mounting a concentrated attack upon the enemy flagships to bring confusion to the entire fleet while also breaking the enemy's line of battle, something Nelson had done at Trafalgar. Instead, Ali ordered his ships to haul anchor and to sail on the wind that would return them to the safety of the Dardanelles. This gave Senyavin no option other than to signal the raising of every possible sail and begin a sternward chase in the hope that his ships would catch the enemy while still in the open seas of the Aegean. Knowing that, even if they had chosen to fight, they would still, at some point, attempt a return to the Strait, Senyavin had pre-warned his ship commanders that their gunners be instructed to fire into the rigging and sails of the enemy, this slowing the pace of any retreat and allowing the pursuing Russian ships to draw level.

It was not until late evening with darkness descending, and the Ottoman Fleet then at the very mouth of the Strait, that any Russian ship came within firing distance of the enemy. This placed the Russian ships in an extremely precarious position, for in bringing the Ottoman Fleet into battle they were within range of the enemy shore batteries. Fortunately, the accuracy of this fire was not great, as according to Bronevskiy, their shots were 'striking friend and foe alike'. It was *Tvyordyi*, Senyavin's flagship, that was the most threatened, coming within range of at least one shore battery on the European side of the Strait. In demanding that his own ship pursue the enemy to the bitter end, *Tvyordyi* came so close to the shore that at one point she was hit by musket fire from those manning the Ottoman batteries. Fortunately for Senyavin, with darkness having fallen, and through extinguishing all lights on board, *Tvyordyi* became less of a target, and with boats lowered her crew successfully towed her away from the shoreline.

While this might be seen as a novelty factor in the fighting of this sea battle, an engagement fought within range of the enemy's shore batteries, another was that of some of the Ottoman ships failing to defend themselves when under attack. Instead, of firing on the Russian ships, several Ottoman commanders concentrated their crews entirely upon sailing their ships to safety, with no thought given to the manning of the guns. Finally, at 8 p.m., with both fleets entangled at the entrance to the Strait, the battle came to an end. It was at the very least a confused battle in which one ship set upon another, for that ship to escape and another then brought under fire. Bronevskiy, with just a few well-chosen words, gave this summary of events:

> *Our ships fell behind them, ran ahead of them, came alongside them, adding and removing sails to control their speeds, managed to pursue them and deliver broadsides against most of their vessels.*

In that desperate attempt to reach the safety of the Strait, three of the Ottoman battleships ran aground, with an attempt made on the following morning to tow two of them into the Strait and the third to be brought in under sail. On seeing this, Senyavin instructed *Retvizan, Skorii, Arkhangel Selafail, Iaroslav* and *Venera*, under the overall command of Greig, to capture them or bring about their destruction. Despite all three Ottoman ships being brought under fire by the Russian units, this was not until they had reached the protection of the Ottoman shore batteries, making their capture impossible. Nevertheless, and because of panic on board, all three Ottoman ships in running too close to the shore, ran aground and sustained considerable damage.

**Table 15.1: Battle of Dardanelles Strait (May 1807): The Russian squadron, ship by ship.**

| | |
|---|---|
| *Arkhangel Uriil* [Archangel Uriel] (88) | Captain Second Rank I.T. Bychensky. In closely engaging the Ottoman vice admiral's flagship, her rigging became entangled with the enemy's bowsprit. Fired a total of 406 shot (144 from her 36-poundres, 156 from her 24-pounders, fifty-eight from her 8-pounders and forty-eight from her unicorns). |
| *Rafail* [Raphael] (84) | Captain First Rank D.A. Lukin. Together with *Retvizan*, she was the first of Senyavin's ships to open fire on the retreating Ottoman Fleet, her officers criticised by Senyavin for not engaging the enemy close enough, firing at one Ottoman battleship 1,000 shot with little or no effect, and allowing the enemy ship to freely enter the Dardanelles. Equipped with carronades, these saw the expenditure of 45 shot. |
| *Tvyordy*i [Hard] (84) | Captain Second Rank D.I. Maleev. Flagship of Vice Admiral Senyavin. One of the few Russian ships that attacked at close range. In pursuing Seydi Ali's flagship, the 120-gun *Mesudiye,* the yards of the two ships nearly converged, but the intent of *Mesudiye* was to gain the Dardanelles rather than fight, giving *Tvyordyi* little return fire. With night falling and coming close to the enemy shoreline, *Tvyordyi* took casualties from muskets fired from the shore, forcing her to draw into the central channel. This allowed *Mesudiye* to escape deeper into the Strait due to greater manoeuvrability. In total *Tvyordyi* expended 928 shot, of which 300 were fired from her 36-pounder guns and 480 from her 24-pounders. *Tvyordyi* was the most damaged of all the Russian ships, with ten holes in her hull and forty-seven passing through her sails. |
| *Sviatoia Elena* [Saint Helena] (74) | Captain Second Rank I.T. Bychensky. Only engaged from a distance, firing a total of 430 shot (including 130 fired from her 36-pounders; 135 from her 18-pounders). Because of being at a distance from the enemy, she received only minimal damage, this to her masts and sails. |
| *Sil'nyi* [Strong] (74) | Captain Commodore Ignatyev. Her captain killed by a cannon ball while his ship was closing in on the enemy. Fired 719 shot. |

| | |
|---|---|
| *Arkhangel Selafail* [Archangel Selaphiel] (74) | Captain Second Rank P.M. Rozhnov. The first to overtake Seydi Ali's flagship, the 120-gun *Mesudiye,* which had become separated from the main Ottoman Fleet. Fired a broadside into the stern of *Mesudiye* before tacking to starboard to avoid her return fire. At one time *Arkhangel Selafail* engaged four opponents, firing three broadsides into the stern of one, but failed to press home her attack on any vessel. Fired 436 shot (including 168 from lower deck and 180 from her upper deck). Holed twelve times in the hull and suffered the most fatalities with twelve of her crew killed. |
| *Iaroslav* [Yaroslavl] (74) | Captain Second Rank F.K. Mitkov. Lost two masts and a broken halyard. Engaged several Ottoman ships but only from a distance. Fired in total 444 shot (133 from her 30-pounders, 176 from her 18-pounders, 115 from her 8-pounders and twenty from her unicorns). |
| *Moshchny*i [Powerful] (66) | Captain First Rank V. Krovier. Participation in the battle was negligible, failing to closely engage as evidenced by *Moshchnyi* only receiving four cannon ball hits to the hull. Any ship carrying out Senyavin's instructions to closely engage would have received a greater number of hits. |
| *Skorii* [Fast] (62) | Captain First Rank R.P. Shelting. Slow to engage, fired over 600 shots at a distance with little effect on the enemy. |
| *Retvizan* [Fairness and Justice] (62) | Captain Second Rank M.M. Rtishchev. Flag of Rear Admiral A.S. Greig. Along with *Rafail*, the first to open fire on the retreating Ottoman Fleet. A total of 249 shots fired (104 from the upper deck, 104 from the lower deck, 41 from the quarterdeck). |
| *Venera* [Venus] (50) | Captain Lieutenant Razvozov. The smallest ship of the squadron. In a forward position in company with *Arkhangel Selafail* attacked the stern of the separated and considerably larger 120-gun *Mesudiye*. Failed to engage sufficiently close to inflict any real damage on her opponent. |

For Senyavin the battle must be considered a victory, if only because the Ottomans suffered three seriously damaged battleships and the possible loss of 2,000 men, while Senyavin's squadron received only limited damage, mostly to masts and rigging, and the lesser number of 227 killed. More important, Tenedos was still safely held and the blockade could continue as before, inevitably forcing Ali to again sail out and support military landings to retake the island. Making this even more likely was the increasing impact the blockade was having on those living in Istanbul and with discontent continuing to rise. On 17 May, the government of Selim III was overthrown, an action not necessarily a result of the blockade, but the blockade very definitely serving as a factor that exacerbated the rise of internal dissent. Yet the outcome of the battle was not what Senyavin had been looking to achieve. He had hoped to inflict upon the Ottoman

Fleet a much greater level of destruction, one that would have neutralised it as a threat. In knowing that Ali must once again sail, he planned for a second battle, one that would in outcome be a total Russian victory.

Initially, though, Senyavin had to consider why that first engagement had failed to achieve a much greater level of success other than the forcing of three battleships to run aground. Approaching the enemy with all possible haste had certainly been the most appropriate tactic for the occasion. However, his commanders in general failed to adhere to one highly important instruction previously given: that of gunners firing exclusively at the enemy masts and to which he had added the need to close in on the enemy, firing only at point blank range and continuing to fire until the enemy ship was incapable of fighting back. Instead, the ships under Senyavin's command often fired from a distance and at random, even continuing to fire when the enemy became invisible through the smoke of battle and with no awareness of shots fired hitting their target (see Table 15.1). Another failing identified by Senyavin was that some of his captains, in bringing an enemy into combat, did not bring the fight to a conclusion, moving on to another opponent without disabling the one first encountered. The result was that in expending 16,149 cannonballs and 1,366 poods of gunpowder, not one single Ottoman ship had been sunk, forced to surrender, or seriously damaged. All might have been very different if Senyavin's instructions had been closely followed, not least the targeting of masts. This would have resulted in some Ottoman ships losing their masts, unable to reach the Strait, which would have left several stranded, if not all of Ali's ships, and open to destruction or capture.

To avoid repeating these same mistakes, Senyavin issued those same instructions but now in more detail together with a new set of signal codes designed to ensure he had better control over the movement of ships during battle. His instructions were comprehensive, making it clear as to how the enemy should be approached and what was expected of each of his commanders. Accordingly, once the enemy had entered open water and was sighted, Senyavin's ships were to form into tactical groups, each of two units. These groups would target one or other of the enemy's flagships, the paired ships of each tactical group attacking one of the flagships from either side. This would not only serve to overwhelm the enemy ship, but through first targeting flagships would disrupt the enemy's organisational command and control of the battle. One tactical group was to be held in reserve, the purpose of which was 'either to strengthen the attackers or to attack an enemy or enemy ships' when the need arose. Finally, it was also required by Senyavin that the ships under his command would fire exclusively at close range and engage in combat with enemy ships until 'the completion of victory'.

## Battle of Athos, 1 July 1807

On 19 June the Ottoman Fleet once again prepared to sail, leaving the Strait three days later with a force that would eventually consist of ten ships of the line made up of one ship of 120 guns, five eighty-fours and four seventy-fours alongside five frigates and several smaller ships. The intention as before was to lay siege to the fortress at Tenedos by landing troops assembled on the Asian shore near the island. Once more commanded by Seydi Ali, his ships first remained within close distance of the Strait, even at one time returning to gain temporary safety. To ensure that the Ottomans would sail further out and begin the landings on Tenedos, Senyavin repeated his ruse of leaving the island undefended from the sea by sailing to the west of Imbros. On 27 June, Seydi Ali made his move, sailing to Tenedos to cover the initial landing of 1,000 troops from seventy galleys. In turn, those same galleys, in returning several times to the Asian shore, would bring over to Tenedos a total of 4,000 troops. Despite stiff resistance from the Russian garrison, all were landed by the afternoon of the following day, with the fortress brought under bombardment from the sea.

Indeed, the island might well have fallen had it not been for the timely return of Senyavin's squadron early on the morning of the third day of the siege, 29 June. At 5 a.m. that morning the bombardment of the fort from the sea was once again underway, an Ottoman ship and frigate having manoeuvred into position to give the wake-up call. Soon after, two other ships standing at anchor also opened fire, with several others making an approach. Then, at eight o'clock, all of the Ottoman ships ceased firing, Senyavin's squadron having been spotted on the horizon, leading to Ali ordering a hasty retreat. In doing so, he abandoned the troops previously landed, feeling confident they would soon take the fort.

On his return to Tenedos, the first task Senyavin undertook was resupplying the fortress that was now running low on ammunition and would have to continue withstanding attacks from the Ottoman army that Ali had abandoned. To ensure, at the very least, that there was no possibility of the enemy force already on the island being reinforced, the flotilla of galleys used as transports, and which lay beached on the nearby mainland shore, were attacked and destroyed. As for the final task, that of bringing Ali's ships into battle, this much depended on Senyavin's guesswork as to where he might find them. At that time he knew only that Ali had sailed in a westerly direction, and in that direction the search began. Panafidin wrote in one of his letters:

> *On the morning of the 18th, with only 10 ships, leaving all the frigates for the blockade of the island, they set off in pursuit of the Turkish naval fleet. They sailed all day and could not discover the enemy fleet; general grief spread to our fleet through fear that the Turkish fleet had eluded us. All had a supposition: one said that they had gone to Egypt, another to Salonika, a third to Smyrna. But the two fleets were separated only by the island of Lemnos. At this time, they had anchored for the night near the fortress of Lemnos. Passing along the eastern side of the island, at dawn on June 19, we saw the Turkish fleet. There was joy throughout our fleet.*

At 7 a.m., Senyavin gave the signal to set all sails and attack while Ali, according to Bronevskiy, 'quickly and very adeptly formed the line of battle on a starboard tack.'

Initially, his line consisted of nine battleships as his tenth battleship was some distance to the north-east acting as a look-out and only joined the main force during the latter stages of the resulting battle. As for the five Ottoman frigates that were sailing alongside the battle fleet, Ali placed these into a second line behind and to leeward. As to his forward battle line, the arrangement chosen by Ali defied the convention of placing his three flagships to separately lead the rear, centre, and van columns. Instead, he placed them together and closely aligned within the centre, the three fully protected by ships immediately to their fore and rear. It was a placement that resulted from Ali correctly assessing that Senyavin would direct his initial attack upon the flagships. Against Ali's force of ten battleships, Senyavin also had ten ships of the line, but in terms of total ordnance the Ottoman Fleet was undoubtedly the more powerful. *Mesudiye* alone carried 120 guns and in total the Ottoman battleships carried 836 guns, to which could also be added 286 guns of the five frigates. Senyavin's squadron had a total of 684 guns.

The Russian attack was made in two columns, the left (*Moshchnyi*, *Iaroslav*, *Rafail*, *Sil'nyi*, *Arkhangel Selafail*, and *Arkhangel Uriil*) making for the enemy flagships at the centre, and the right column (*Tvyordyi* and *Skorii*) sailing for the van to encircle it, with Greig commanding the two ships of the tactical reserve (*Retvizan* and *Sviatoia Elena*) reinforcing the right column in their attack on the Ottoman van. On the approach of the two columns, the Ottomans opened distant fire, attempting to damage the sails and rigging of the Russian ships to deprive them of manoeuvrability. However, following Senyavin's more recent instruction, they would only open fire from the shortest distance. To ensure that none of his gunners would be tempted to fire during the approach, Captain Krovier of *Moshchnyi* put all 'who were at the guns and rigging' on the decks and away from the guns.

Forty-five minutes after giving the order to set sail and close the distance with the Ottoman Fleet, Senyavin ordered his ships to make ready for a close attack, the left column re-forming into pairs that would see each of the paired ships jointly attacking one or other of the enemy flagships. The first of the pairings to reach the enemy's centre column, and consequently coming under considerable fire, was the *Rafail* and *Sil'nyi* tactical group, their quarry being the mighty 120-gun *Mesudiye*. With their guns ready loaded and double-shotted, as were all the ships for the firing of their first salvo, *Rafail* fired into *Mesudiye*'s port side. It was possibly at that time that Ali sustained injury to both hands while fire also broke out on the ship but was soon brought under control. But *Rafail* was also in trouble during the approach and having received so much enemy fire into her sails, she was no longer responding to the helm. Instead, she began to float freely through the enemy line, drifting between *Mesudiye* and the eighty-four-gun *Sadd al-bahr*, flagship of Kapudan Bey Bekir Bey. This did provide her one advantage, allowing her to fire dangerous longitudinal salvoes at them before she came under their crossfire and her captain D.A. Lukin being killed. Panafidin provides an eye-witness account of the battering received by *Rafail*:

> *All enemy shots were aimed at us before we had time to come within range, all our topsails had already been broken by the cannonballs of the huge artillery of a 100-gun ship and many top sail sailors were killed. Having endured with the*

> *greatest composure, without firing a single cannon, until they came to pistol shot distance, the first volley at such a close range, and our cannons all loaded with two cannonballs silenced the Kapudan-Pasha's ship, and then the continuous fire forced her to deviate from the line. Our ship, covered with sails, all the topsails were lying...the braces broken, but undeterred by anything, we cut through the enemy's line under the stern of the Turkish admiral.*

*Sil'nyi* and the next four Russian ships followed through and took up line positions abreast of the three Ottoman flagships, their formation so closely packed that it was claimed the bowsprit of the rear ship lay on the stern of the front one.

Meanwhile, Senyavin took his right column to the head of the line with the intention of preventing those ships turning back to give assistance to the flagships in the centre column. The two reserve ships, *Rättvisan* and *Sviatoia Elena,* were initially to have been used to counter the Ottoman rearguard, but this became unnecessary as the rearguard had fallen back following a change of wind. Instead, Greig joined Senyavin in the attack on the Ottoman vanguard. Thus, Senyavin had fully implemented the planned strategy of concentrating a superior force on part of the enemy fleet with the fire power of nine Russian battleships concentrated upon six or seven Ottoman battleships.

Having realised Senyavin's intention, Ali attempted to fight off *Tvyordyi* by bringing into action the five frigates forming a second battle line. This merely complicated matters, as *Tvyordyi*'s more powerful guns soon drove the leading Ottoman frigate out of action with the eighty-four-gun Ottoman battleship *Besharet* immediately to the stern of the frigate receiving a longitudinal salvo at almost point-blank range. She began to drift. This stopped the movement of other ships, which threw the Ottoman battle line into confusion, increasing the gap between the centre and the van. *Rafail,* now back under control, ran along the Ottoman battle line to leeward to regain her position.

By 10 a.m., the enemy's battle order, having been caught in heavy cross-fire, was completely disrupted, the vanguard retreating on a wind from the south-east that took them towards the Bay of Athos while the ships at the centre attempted one by one to break out of their encirclement. As for the ships of the rearguard, they were still attempting to give aid to the beleaguered flagships, but Senyavin moved to intercept and forced them also to retreat. According to the logbooks of the ships that took part in the battle, Senyavin raised a signal at around 11.30 a.m. to break off the action to allow for pressing repairs to sails and rigging.

If the south-easterly wind had held, most of the Ottoman ships might well have been driven on to the promontory of Mount Athos or cornered in the bay between that headland and the island of Thasos. Fortunately for them, the wind dropped to be replaced by a light breeze from the north-west that put the Ottomans to windward. At 6 p.m., Greig was instructed to lead *Retvizan, Arkhangel Selafail, Sviatoia Elena, Sil'nyi* and *Arkhangel Urill* in a chase, not of the main Ottoman Fleet, but of two battleships (*Sed el Barra* and *Basharet Numa*), and two frigates (*Limno* and *El Beisuto*), which had become separated from the main force. In this Greig was successful, capturing near the Athos Peninsula one of the battleships, *Sedd al-bahr*, Bekir Bey's flagship with the admiral

**Table 15.2: Battle of Athos: The Russian squadron, ship by ship.**

| *Tactical groups on the right column of attack* | |
|---|---|
| *Arkhangel Uriil* (84) | Paired with *Arkhangel Selafail.* Attacked *Sadd al-bahr* (84), the Ottoman vice admiral's flagship. |
| *Arkhangel Selafail* (74) | Went into battle one-on-one against the eighty-four-gun *Sedd-ul-Bahri*. |
| *Rafail* (84) | The first to engage, attacking Seydi Ali's flagship *Mesudiye (120)*. In the approach she received considerable damage to her sails. She suffered the most casualties, twenty-two of her crew killed and forty-one wounded, her captain, Lukin, among those killed, decapitated by a cannon ball. |
| *Sil'nyi* (74) | Captain Lieutenant D.S. Shishmarev. Tactically paired to work alongside *Rafail*, she initially attacked *Mesudiye* but her logbook shows she did not fire at close range, keeping her distance while maintaining only a short period of fire. *Sil'nyi* ordered seven times by Senyavin to close-up. In the battle she sustained eight cannon holes in the waterline and stern and twenty-three above the waterline, with three crew members killed and forty-one wounded. |
| *Iaroslav* (74) | Tactically paired with *Moshchnyi*, a ship that she abandoned, with her captain criticised by Senyavin for completely falling away from the battle before re-engaging only when the enemy was in retreat. For this reason her captain, unlike those of Senyavin's other ships, received no reward from Alexander for the victory gained. |
| *Moshchnyi* (74) | Tactically paired with *Iaroslav*. On approach, although under distant fire, held back from offering return fire until within grapeshot range of the Ottoman vice admiral's flagship, *Anka-yi Bahri.* Recording this in his logbook, her captain, Krovier wrote: 'At this time the Turkish vice admiral's flagship opened fire on us with salvoes, and the commander seeing the unfavourable distance, ordered all the servants located at the guns and rigging on the decks to lie down as we came closer and closer to the enemy firing at us.' Remained closely mixed with the Ottoman Fleet during its retreat away from the battle. *Moshchnyi* recorded firing a total of 1,362 shots from her guns, including 330 from her 36-pounders. Of her crew, twenty-one were killed in the battle and forty-four wounded. Damage to the ship included several underwater holes, and damage to her masts, rigging and some of her cannons disabled with 1,159 holes shot through her sails. |

| *Tactical groups on the left column of attack* | |
|---|---|
| *Tvyordy*i (84) | Paired with *Skorii*. Led the attack on the van, firing first upon the lead frigate and a following battleship. This created confusion in the Ottoman line before attacking two following battleships and then, as she came up, *Sedd al-bahr*, the flagship of Bekir Bay, shooting away some of her sails before going on to support the much-damaged *Rafail*. |
| *Skorii* (62) | Tactically paired with *Tvyordyi*, she was part of the attack on the van, firing on the three lead ships and attacked in turn by several Ottoman ships, receiving considerable damage to her sails, masts and her rigging shot through. Remained closely mixed with the Ottoman Fleet during their retreat. Due to the closeness with which she engaged several Ottoman ships, including one of the three-deck flagships, her casualties were surprisingly light, recorded in her captain's log as one killed and nineteen wounded. |
| *Retviza*n (62) | Tactical reserve and flagship of Rear Admiral Greig. Gave full support to Senyavin's attack on the van. |
| *Sviatoi Elena* (74) | Tactical reserve. In attacking the van, it is clear *Sviatoi Elena*'s captain, Bychensky, did not fully obey Senyavin's instructions to fire at close range, keeping her distance and maintaining only short-term fire fights. Bychensky, admitted as much in his logbook, declaring that during the mid-point of battle, at 11 a.m., 'the enemy ship with which we were fighting moved away and therefore we stopped fighting...soon after that the place of the abandoned ship was taken by the enemy admiral's ship lying behind it, which, having drawn level with us, without drifting, began to fight.' Armed with 30-pounders, 18-pounders and unicorns, *Sv Elena* recorded a total 856 shots fired but with only limited effect on the enemy. |

still on board. Following the capture of *Sedd al-bahr*, it was discovered that she had on board several prisoners-of-war who had been forced to crew the ship. Eleven were from a Russian corvette, *Flora*, that had run aground in 1807 on the coast of Albania. An additional seven were British seamen.

To prevent the capture of the second battleship and two frigates, the crews on board were ordered to run them aground behind Ammouliani Island in the Bay of Mount Athos and set them ablaze (21 June). According to Panafidin:

> *First the red-hot cannons, which were loaded with cannonballs, began to fire alternatively. Then, like the eruption of a fire-breathing mountain,*

> *it flew into the air with a terrible crack amid thick smoke. The shock produced by the explosion was like an earthquake; the sea itself began to swirl and boil.*

Bronevskiy confirmed the shock of these explosions, writing that they 'were strong enough that the ships 20 verstas [21.34km] away could feel them'. No attempt was made to pursue the main element of the Ottoman Fleet, with Senyavin concerned for the fate of the besieged garrison holding out on Tenedos and the need to provide them with support.

In total, the Ottoman Fleet lost the two battleships and two frigates as described, although some writers suggest the Ottomans were forced to destroy a few additional vessels. This is contested by at least one Russian historian, Lebedev, who in considering data on the composition of the Ottoman Fleet for the period July to August 1807 concludes that there is little evidence of further losses. For their part, the Russians lost no ships, although a number suffered considerable damage to sails, masts and rigging, especially *Tvyordyi*, *Skorii*, *Rafail* and *Moshchnyi*, but all this was repairable with Senyavin's squadron soon fully operational. As for personnel losses, it is generally accepted by Russian historians that Senyavin's losses amounted to seventy-eight killed (one officer, one midshipman, seventy-six sailors) and 173 wounded (eight officers, four midshipmen, 161 sailors), although Bronevskiy gives the number wounded as 190. Ottoman losses are less clear, for while there is certainty that personnel losses were much greater, there is no available verification. Following the capture of *Sedd al-bah*, Russian sources indicate 230 of her crew were killed and 160 wounded. Undoubtedly, other ships of the Ottoman Fleet would have suffered similar losses, but whether it amounted to a frequently claimed figure of 2,000 is not known.

While the battle was clearly a Russian victory, allowing Senyavin to continue the blockade, with Seydi Ali failing to weaken in any way the Russian Fleet, the victory for Senyavin could have been greater. The failure to continue pursuing the retreating Ottoman Fleet was viewed by several of his officers as a mistake. While acknowledging that Senyavin had concerns over the fate of the Tenedos garrison, Panafidin weighed this against a pursuit of an enemy that 'would have been overtaken and captured one by one'. Effectively this would have resulted in the loss of a third of the entire Ottoman Fleet. Bronevskiy, in acknowledging that Senyavin's decision came as a surprise to some, fully defended his commander:

> *After the battle, the wind was weak, variable, and almost always foul when it blew at all between periods of dead calm every day. Consequently, after pursuing the enemy in such conditions, Tenedos would be lost and then the destruction of the enemy fleet would be less beneficial to us. Without a convenient port near the Dardanelles, there would be no means to replenish the men lost or to repair the damage suffered by the ships in the battle; we could only burn the Turkish ships and perhaps a few of our own and abandon the blockade of the strait or take up a new base at such*

> *a distance it would weaken our effectiveness and thereby compromise our primary objective; 'to deprive Constantinople of the supply of provisions by sea with the Russian Fleet present in the archipelago.*

Reference to the logbooks of several of the ships engaged in the action show that while *Skorii*, *Moshchnyi* and *Rafail* came within pistol shot of the enemy, there was no attempt to continue until 'the completion of victory', with the Ottoman ships engaged easily slipping away. As already noted, and following his analysis of the earlier battle, Senyavin had demanded of his captains that they open fire only when at close range and remain at a close distance. That this was being ignored becomes clear from logbook entries recording that during the three hours in which the battle was fought, Senyavin instructed one ship, *Sil'nyi,* on seven occasions to come closer to the enemy. Other offenders were *Sv. Elena* and *Iaroslav.* It was the culpability of the captains of those ships that allowed the enemy to calmly slip away from the battle, with at that time no ships destroyed or immobilised despite the Russian gunners making use of 2,360 poods of gunpowder to fire into the enemy 14,801 cannonballs (5,718 of which were from the 30- and 36-pounder guns). Senyavin, in his official report to Alexander, did not keep silent about the failings of many of his captains, writing that except for *Skorii* and *Sv. Moshchnyi*, others were no more than 'boxes of dust in the figure of a semicircle, and it seemed at a considerable distance' from the point of battle.

On returning to Tenedos, it was discovered that the Ottoman landing force was in possession of the entire island, with the single exception of the fortress. But with the return of Senyavin, and the realisation by the Ottomans that they were now completely cut off, a treaty of surrender was agreed whereby the entire Ottoman force, which numbered somewhere in the region of 5,000, was ferried across to the Asian shore, but without their cannons and small arms. Thus, in retaining Tenedos, Senyavin could maintain the blockade that continued to deny the supply of Istanbul from the south, with its effectiveness increased by several British warships later joining Senyavin.

# PART SIX

# How naval wars should not be fought

Despite the victory gained by Senyavin at Athos and the successful continuance of the blockade, events elsewhere were about to destroy all that had been achieved. The Russian Army, two weeks earlier on 14 June, had suffered at the hands of Napoleon a major defeat at Friedland. Following the battle, on the famous raft moored midstream on the River Neman at Tilsit, Alexander agreed with Napoleon that Russia and France would now work alongside each other against Britain. The terms included Russia ceasing all trade with Britain and committing to Napoleon's continental system, the means the French emperor had devised to destroy Great Britain by denying her an outlet for her merchandise throughout Europe. There were, however, some additional demands, and these heavily impacted on the navy, proving beyond doubt that Alexander had little interest in naval affairs, seemingly unaware of what his navy had achieved or might be capable of achieving. At Tilsit, Alexander agreed that Russia would demand of Great Britain that she bring an end to the war and surrender her colonial conquests. If this was refused, then Russia should declare war. It was a war Britain could only fight at sea with the most likely response that of once again sending a powerful fleet into the Baltic for a direct attack on the Russian Fleet. Making such a move an absolute certainty was Napoleon also insisting that Alexander declare war on Sweden, one of the few countries still trading with Britain. Elsewhere, Napoleon also placed on Alexander the requirement that he cede the Ionian Islands to France and abandon Tenedos to the Porte. Intended for the purpose of strengthening Napoleon's position in the east, it meant that in agreeing, Alexander wrecked everything that Senyavin, and before him Ushakov, had strived to achieve and for which many Russian seamen had risked their lives. In one final thoughtless decision, Alexander demanded that Senyavin, and the squadron he commanded, make an immediate return to Russia, despite there being no easy route back and Senyavin's ships so long at sea being badly in need of repair and maintenance.

# CHAPTER 16

# THE ADRIATIC: A SQUADRON STRANDED AND CAST ASIDE

By requiring Senyavin to return to Russia, the emperor had given Senyavin a truly impracticable task. To which port in Russia was Senyavin to return? Sevastopol in the Black Sea or Kronstadt in the Baltic? Sevastopol was the nearest, but this required passage through the Bosporus, an impenetrable pathway for such a small force while Russia remained at war with the Porte. The alternative, and it was the only alternative, was sailing to one of Russia's Baltic ports, a voyage that likely would be opposed by Britain, first by her all-powerful Mediterranean Fleet, and if in some way Senyavin successfully navigated the Mediterranean, he would then be confronted by either Britain's Channel Fleet or her North Sea Squadron. Of course, he could always seek sanctuary in Toulon or some other French port where his ships could be thoroughly repaired and made fully combat ready once again. Tempting as this may have been, it was something Senyavin himself chose to avoid, knowing that if he entered a French port his ships would most likely be absorbed into Napoleon's navy. He knew, as did any keen observer of maritime affairs, that Napoleon was desperate to augment his own navy in every possible way, as only through possession of a strong navy could he finally vanquish Great Britain and bring an end to a war he had long been fighting.

In this desire not to enter a French port, Senyavin would prove adamant, prepared even to disobey instructions from St Petersburg when told he must submit to any instructions given to him from Paris. This stubbornness would later be revealed to Alexander and would lead to Senyavin being refused any further employment at sea while Alexander remained emperor. But this was not until much later, and following a surprising series of events that began with Senyavin attempting to reach Tallinn before the Gulf of Finland froze for winter. With war between Britain and Russia not yet declared, there was just the faintest hope that Senyavin would be allowed to sail out of the Mediterranean unhindered by Britain's Mediterranean Fleet. Given that not all Senyavin's ships would be capable of making the voyage, it was accepted by Alexander that he should only take those in a suitable condition. This allowed Senyavin to abandon five of his ships – those regarded as beyond saving – which were sent to Venice.

Before attempting the voyage, Russian land forces previously occupying the Ionian Islands had to be transported to Trieste, a task undertaken by twenty transports escorted by several of Senyavin's warships. Once at Trieste, they were to march across Hungary and back into Russia. Consequently, this delayed Senyavin's departure, adding to the difficulties confronting him. No longer was it possible to reach the Gulf of Finland before the waters froze. Aware of the difficulty that Alexander had created for Senyavin, and wishing to keep Senyavin's ships out of the hands of the French, the British government went so far as to offer him assistance, suggesting that Senyavin might wish to over-winter in one of Britain's naval yards, be it newly acquired Malta or possibly Gibraltar or Portsmouth. In making this offer it was believed that Alexander's current leanings towards Napoleon was a short-term aberration and that nothing should be done to further alienate him. However, it was Alexander who rejected the offer, not wishing to see Senyavin's ships coming under the control of Britain, despite the British government pledging the safety of those vessels. In November British newspapers carried identically worded explanations as to what lay behind this unusual offer:

> *This situation of the Russian Fleet is a most happy circumstance for the English Government; and if the English ministry act in manner suitable to the delicacy of the case, they may avail themselves of this incidental advantage to obtain the most important results.*

Commander of the Mediterranean Fleet, Vice Admiral Collingwood, in a letter written in September to Rear Admiral Sir Alexander Ball, the now *de facto* governor of Malta, confirmed the fear that Britain had of not just of Senyavin's ships falling into Napoleon's hands but those of the entire Russian Fleet:

> *The Russians, I understand, have agreed to give their ships in the Mediterranean to France; and they will be employed immediately in the transport of troops. I hope this will not be undertaken under the Russian flag, or by the Russian people, because they would be identifying themselves with the enemy.*

By November, Senyavin had successfully reached the Strait of Gibraltar, with Collingwood making no attempt to interfere, unaware that Russia had now declared war on Britain. Quite the reverse, in fact. As noted by Collingwood, there was a demonstration of cordiality between them that had hitherto been lacking, with Collingwood informing Lord Mulgrave, the First Lord of the Admiralty:

> *Our correspondence with the Russian officers, to the last hour of their being with us, was perfectly friendly; they lamented the misfortune that had befallen their country with an air of having nothing to conceal; and when they left us, I believe they had no suspicion of any hostile intention of their court towards us.*

To solve the immediate problem of finding a haven that was neither British nor French, somewhere that would allow his ships to rest at anchor until the following spring, led Senyavin to Lisbon, but only after the squadron had suffered much from a storm encountered in the Bay of Biscay. With Lisbon around 400 miles from Biscay and, as far as Senyavin was aware, a neutral port, this would provide temporary respite and the chance to replace masts, spars, rigging and planking that was now missing from most of his ships. But what Senyavin did not know was that Portugal was in turmoil. The French had invaded and Lisbon, while not yet occupied, was preparing to receive General Jean-Andoche Junot, commander of the French forces. The first inkling that Senyavin received of entering not a neutral port but one subservient to France was that of his own ships being fired upon from the shore. This was because they were entering under false colours, those of the British Navy. While Portugal had been neutral, it had always shown friendship towards Great Britain, and by flying British flags Senyavin expected to be better received than if his ships had flown Russian flags. Realising his mistake, the British colours were hauled down and replaced by the Russian Navy saltire. This allowed Senyavin's squadron to safely enter the Tagus, but he was now where he did not wish to be, under the thumb of the French. Equally, it was a disaster for Great Britain, for in allowing Senyavin to sail unmolested they had simply gifted his ships to the French. London newspapers were quick to express their anger at what was seen as a major failing of the government and that Senyavin should not have been allowed to sail the length of the Mediterranean and into a port now in possession of the French. The *Morning Chronicle* expressed it:

> *There is another question, upon which, I believe, no two men can disagree; namely, the gross and culpable neglect, the want of vigilance and common prudence, in suffering, seven sail of Russian line of battleships to enter the Tagus, where they now remain at the disposal of France, in a harbour in which, I can venture to affirm, they can very seldom be blockaded.*

Lord Mulgrave, First Lord of the Admiralty in a new Tory administration, speaking to Parliament's upper chamber and responding to accusations that more could have been done to prevent this situation, made reference to a squadron under the command of Sir Sydney Smith, a rear admiral since November, that had been tasked with intercepting Senyavin before he reached Lisbon. But his squadron, it was claimed, had been delayed by unfavourable winds. In truth, even if Smith had been present off the Tagus when the first Russian division of ships entered, he had not yet been given orders to make an interception, only made aware on 9 December of hostilities existing between Russia and Great Britain, by which time Senyavin had been moored in the Tagus for nearly two weeks. Even on 30 November, while lying off the Tagus, Smith had permitted a Russian frigate to pass through the blockade and enter the port of Lisbon in the same way that he would have allowed Senyavin to enter Lisbon unmolested, given he had no instructions to do otherwise. The real reason for Smith's presence off Lisbon was to persuade Prince Regent João of Portugal to order the Portuguese Fleet, then moored in the Tagus, to escape the French and sail for Brazil, a task in which he proved successful. However, the arrival of Senyavin's fleet somewhat negated this British success, for in taking the Portuguese Fleet out of Napoleon's grasp (eight ships of the line, five frigates and four smaller warships), it was now replaced by another albeit smaller collection of ships, but ships with recent combat experience, a point underlined by the *Morning Chronicle*:

> *In point of naval security, England has gained nothing by the departure of the Portuguese ships, which has now been replaced by a Russian Fleet of equal force, and probably better manned and equipped.*

To prevent the French absorbing the Russian squadron into their own seaborne forces, the British placed the Tagus under blockade, the blockading squadron under the command of Vice Admiral Sir Charles Cotton. Mounting a direct attack upon the Tagus to either destroy or take possession of the Russian squadron was considered, but rejected because of the difficulty of navigating the Tagus and the strength of the shore defences in the hands of the French.

Despite the alliance with France, the relationship between Russian seamen and the French occupying force eventually came under great strain, a series of street brawls even resulted in the Russians being confined to their ships. This contrasted with the first arrival of Senyavin's ships in Lisbon, his officers initially invited to dine with their opposite numbers. But this ceased when the Russians refused to toast Napoleon. It was reported in several newspapers that members of the British community in Lisbon, for the purpose of escaping imprisonment by the French, were being sheltered on Russian ships. Greatly adding to the difficulties of both Senyavin and the French was that of Lisbon facing a severe food shortage through being closely blockaded by the British. Rioting within the city became a daily occurrence, with the Russian Fleet, despite having access to victuals accumulated within the storehouses of the departed Portuguese Fleet, also finding itself on short rations. Captain Duncan, a Scot by birth and who was serving in the Portuguese Navy, was one of those given refuge before being smuggled onto a British warship. Arriving in England towards the end of March, he provided a description of just how bad things were in Lisbon, indicating that the Russians were anxious to leave that uncomfortable station if they could do so safely. According to Duncan:

> *The Russians had suffered greatly from the want of necessaries of all kinds. Junot had forbidden any supplies being sent them; nor had they been enabled, for some time to procure from the stores of Portugal an ounce of fresh provisions of any kind. In the meantime, while the inhabitants of Lisbon were reduced to the necessity of making bread of pease, beans, and all other inferior sorts of grain, which, when mixed together, was scarcely eatable; and even of this kind the supply was scanty.*

Now everything changed once again. And with such rapidity.

At the Battle of Vimeiro, on 21 August 1808, Arthur Wellesley gained victory over Junot and gave Britain possession of Lisbon and a final say in the future of Senyavin's ships. At first it was agreed that the neutrality of Lisbon was to be recognised and that the Russian Fleet would 'not be disturbed' nor pursued when it did sail, 'until after the time fixed by the maritime law'. But this was soon overturned as it would have required British ships to continue the blockade. Furthermore, it raised the question of just how Senyavin, when he sailed, would be prevented from either returning to Russia or entering a French port, such as Brest or La Rochelle, while on his way to the Baltic. A battle might have ensued and a battle that would have more firmly committed Alexander towards Napoleon when the British government was still hopeful of inducing Russia back into friendship with Britain. Instead of that earlier and over-generous arrangement, this was replaced by the Cintra convention that required Senyavin's ships to be taken under escort into a British port but restored to Russia 'within six months after the conclusion of a peace between' Britain and Russia. While not as generous as the previous arrangement, it was offering clear encouragement to Alexander to break his alliance with France.

On 12 September, seven Russian ships of the line and a frigate left the Tagus, while *Rafail*, due to being in poor condition, was left in Lisbon and later broken up. Off Cascais, the Russian ships were joined by an escort of seven British battleships under the command of Rear Admiral Charles Tyler. Despite the Russian ships being technically prizes captured by British forces upon their occupation of Lisbon, they were treated as if they were allies and not enemies. Throughout the voyage, which would take them to Portsmouth, Senyavin's ships were permitted to fly Russian colours, the Admiralty having decreed that there should be no indication of superiority by the escorting ships. On 7 October, both Tyler's and Senyavin's ships before anchoring in Spithead lowered their colours, with neither firing the customary salute to the port admiral. In Portsmouth, such action was not universally applauded, described by one newspaper, 'as if the feelings of the Russians ought not to be wounded by seeing our colours hoisted on our ships and their own colours not hoisted on board theirs!' Although, of course, this is exactly what the government was attempting to achieve. As for the sight of those newly captured Russian ships arriving in such a fashion, the newspaper went on to assure its readers that it was a sight 'that galled the seamen and the people of Portsmouth grievously'.

## The Battle of Portsmouth

One little known event that took place in England, and within sight of the important naval town of Portsmouth, was the capture on the morning of 2 December 1807 by the British Navy of the fifty-gun Russian frigate *Spurknoy* (Captain Second Rank Khoverin) and store ship *Wilhelmina* (Captain Second Rank Pilhard). It was a one-sided affair as the two Russian ships were lying in the Spithead anchorage surrounded by British warships. The Russian ships had come to Portsmouth three months earlier to resupply Senyavin's fleet as there was an expectation that Senyavin in returning to Russia would overwinter at Portsmouth, a port frequently used by ships of the Russian Navy when sailing between the Mediterranean and Baltic. *Spurknoy* had on board a considerable sum of money (500 dollars and 170,000 ducats), plate (probably silver), and a cargo of copper, and *Wilhelmina* was deeply laden with clothing and naval stores.

Given that Russia by that time had declared friendship with France, alongside Alexander specifically instructing Senyavin not to enter any British port and the known intention that Russia would declare war on England, a declaration made on 26 October 1807, the anchoring of those two ships in the Spithead anchorage can be seen as one of the absurdities of the Russian naval war. It must be assumed that the decision to send those two ships to England resulted from poor communication between the ministry of naval affairs under Chichagov and the foreign ministry. The former, which was responsible for dispatching the two vessels, did so at a time when the latter was advising the emperor not to allow Senyavin to enter a British port. If the two departments had a functioning mechanism by which they talked to each other, then *Spurknoy* and *Wilhelmina* would not have been ordered to sail.

Once learnt that war between Russia and England had been declared, Khoverin, the senior Russian officer, prepared to sail, while at the same time an urgent message was sent to Portsmouth from the Admiralty in London ordering that the two ships should be seized. For this purpose, a force of 175 seamen was taken alongside the two vessels by longboats, but before an attempt at boarding was made, Khoverin was asked to surrender and to which, following a brief council of war with his junior officers, he agreed. Except for the officers, those on board the two ships were transferred to a prison ship in the harbour.

Viewed as a standard naval operation, those taking the ship were awarded prize money, with one newspaper estimating the amount received by Vice Admiral Sir George Montagu, the senior naval commander at Portsmouth, to be in the region of £6,000. Two weeks earlier the Russian sixteen-gun sloop *Diana* (Lieutenant Commander Golovnin) sailing to Kamchatka on a voyage of discovery had departed from Portsmouth bound for Japan. In later putting into Simonstown, she was here detained by the British Navy, but managed to escape and continue her voyage.

# CHAPTER 17

# THE BLACK SEA: DESCENT INTO BUNGLING INCOMPETENCE

The Black Sea Fleet under the command of Ushakov had become a shining example of efficiency, especially when compared with the Baltic Fleet. Under him a continuous regime of training had been introduced, ensuring that ship commanders, or at least those with sufficient aptitude, had a perfect knowledge of the vessels they commanded and how these vessels would perform in any given situation. Equally important was that by being frequently at sea, crews learnt and then retained what they had learnt, both in manning the rigging and in their accuracy and speed in the firing of guns. However, all this changed within a few years of Alexander's accession with the Black Sea Fleet entering a lengthy period of decline leading to displays of incompetence that came to rival the fleet in the Baltic.

An important factor in this decline was a leadership failure. Ushakov, despite all that he achieved, was overlooked by Alexander, the new emperor determined to replace those who had been favoured by Paul, appointing the Marquis de Traversay as commander-in-chief in the Black Sea Fleet. This was a catastrophic error for if Ushakov had been retained, given that he now had an even greater depth of experience, he could have usefully prepared a new wave of seamen for future combat duty. The failure to appoint Ushakov as commander-in-chief, a position to which he was entitled by virtue of him being the highest ranking officer in the Black Sea, while misguided did not have an immediate impact. Senyavin, who had learnt much from Ushakov, was given the post of fleet commander, ensuring that he could continue those regular and frequent training exercises. Only upon his transfer to Riga following his promotion to the rank of rear admiral did the real damage set in. No successor emerged with the calibre of Ushakov or Senyavin, and Traversay seemed quite happy to allow the fleet to spiral in a downward direction. At the same time, Alexander's disinterest in naval affairs and forced economies was also taking effect, leading to a slowing down in the pace of ship construction alongside a growing backlog of ship repair work.

This overall decline in the fighting efficiency of the Black Sea Fleet might well have gone unnoticed if it had not been for the outbreak of hostilities with the Porte that came about in 1806. As well as revealing the otherwise hidden levels of incompetence with the administrators and commanders of the fleet, it also drew attention to a severe shortage of combat-ready ships, with numbers available far short of the twenty or so fighting ships that Chichagov had estimated as necessary to defend Russia's position in the Black Sea. To achieve this a significant expansion in the Black Sea shipbuilding programme would have been required. At the heart of the problem was that of ships built for the Black Sea Fleet having a higher attrition rate than those built for the Baltic, a result of so much unseasoned timber having been used in that initial urgent construction programme. On average, of ships built during the 1780s and 1790s, they ceased to be of any further value after twelve years. Further eating into the number of ships available in the Black Sea was that several ships sent into the Mediterranean to support Senyavin were, following the Porte refusing to allow continued passage through the Bosporus, effectively lost. While ships taken by Senyavin into Lisbon were only ones drawn from the Baltic, most of those he had considered unfit to sail on that projected passage to the Baltic were mostly from the Black Sea. Among them were two seventy-four-gun third rates, two fifty-gun fourth rates, and a frigate. If the Bosporus had remained open, these could have safely returned to Sevastopol and at the very least been available for conversion into troop transporters. A further loss to the Black Sea Fleet was the seamen manning those ships, many not to return for a considerable period and who must be counted as among the best trained of Russian seamen.

A task immediately presented to Traversay on the outbreak of the war in 1806 with the Ottomans was a plan emanating from the Admiralty Collegiate in St Petersburg to reinforce Senyavin by driving a passage through the Bosporus from the Black Sea. To do this it was required that every warship available was to sail out of Sevastopol and whenever an Ottoman ship was encountered it was to be captured. Upon reaching the mouth of the Bosphorus, entry was to be made either under cover of darkness or in fog, with all shore batteries neutralised by overwhelming them with the firepower of the fleet. Once achieved, the fleet would continue passage through the Bosporus until reaching Büyükdere. Here, the Ottoman Fleet, it was assumed, would be found at its moorings, allowing it to be bombarded and destroyed by fireships. In support of this operation, transports carrying 17,000 troops and considerable artillery would accompany the fleet.

It was a bold plan, and one with which Traversay was at first in full agreement. How he came to believe that such an expedition was possible is difficult to fathom. Clearly, he failed to carry out any assessment of available resources, or even the ability of his officers to conduct such an operation. At the very least he should have obtained some basic intelligence regarding the strength and layout of the coastal batteries lining the Bosphorus and the number of ships the Porte had in readiness to put to sea and likely to be encountered, either at sea or during the bombardment of Büyükdere. All such essential detail was unknown and only to be acquired once the fleet was at sea and obtained from any captured Ottoman ships. Here there existed on the part of Traversay and his officer team a naïve assumption that enemy ships would be easily captured, and that those on board any captured ship would not only possess the information required but any information given would be accurate.

Finally, but not until April when the fleet was due to sail, Traversay realised that in agreeing to the plan he had made a gigantic error. It was then and only then that he discovered the number of ships available to him was a long way short of even the minimum number required for the success of the operation. In total, the Black Sea Fleet possessed no more than six ships of the line in a seaworthy state and ready to sail and far too few serviceable transports. Of battleships, at least twenty would have been necessary, and for the 17,000 troops who were to accompany the expedition, at least forty transports or naval warships ships sailing *en flute.* As for the government storehouses in Sevastapol, Traversay was only now becoming aware that these contained nothing like the provisions required to maintain at sea, possibly for several months, thousands of seamen together with the 17,000 troops.

In the tried and trusted manner of those who usually served in the Baltic rather than the Black Sea, Traversay blamed everyone else but himself. To the emperor he wrote that the regiments assigned to the landing were not fully staffed, a good half of the available soldiers were untrained recruits, and there were practically no experienced senior officers. Consequently, the Bosphorus operation was cancelled at this somewhat late stage. Yet Traversay as commander of the Black Sea naval forces should have been aware of what ships and material resources were available to the navy. A simple inspection of Sevastapol would have revealed not just the overall poor state of the fleet but also the number of ships that might eventually sail. Until that letter was sent to Alexander, at no point did Traversay indicate, or that he had possibly even become aware, that all was not right at Sevastapol. To Chichagov he should have been regularly writing of the need for more money, more shipwrights, more resources, and more talented officers. He was lax in this and would be similarly lax when he succeeded Chichagov as minister of the navy.

All this said, it must be admitted that the Black Sea Fleet, even under Traversay, could support military operations against the Ottomans when called upon, but only those of a much smaller scale. After all, some of the men Traversay had under his command had trained under Ushakov and Senyavin, although the total number of proficient officers was in decline. It was good seagoing leadership that explains why on 3 April 1807, and using the template as successfully applied by Ushakov in his taking of the Ionian Islands, that a naval battalion successfully took Anapa. Now a popular resort on the northern coast of the Black Sea, Anapa had withstood two attempts to bring about its capture during the reign of Catherine, but Anapa was taken after a brief two-hour battle. The Russian force, consisting of four battleships, five frigates, two brigs and five gunboats, opened the attack with a barrage of fire directed at both the town and fortress. One participant in the capture of Anapa, signing himself as 'М. П.' ('M.P.'), described the event two decades later, indicating:

> *The garrison and the inhabitants, frightened by the very action of our artillery, and fearing the fire of the entire squadron, hastened to withdraw from the fortress, into the surrounding mountains.*

With the fortress abandoned, troops who had landed 3km above the fortress hastened to occupy it, followed by further reinforcements.

Attempted landings in 1807 were also made on the southern shore of the Black Sea where every effort was made to garner the support of the Greek population of the area. Targeted for attack were the port cities of Pulathane (Akçaabat) and Trebizond (Trabazon), and which could serve as a forward naval base while also directly threatening Istanbul. In February, ships had set out from Sevastopol, first bombarding Trabazon with cannon fire before shelling Akçaabat, destroying in a period of two hours several merchant ships at anchor. Accurate artillery fire from the shore caused considerable damage to several Russian ships, forcing them to retreat, with a north-east wind overnight pushing them further from the shore.

In mid-June, following the capture and destruction of the fortress at Anapa, this same fleet made a second attempt to land troops at Trabazon. It was a force of three battleships, three frigates and several brigs, fireships, bombs, supply, and ammunition ships. A total of thirty-one vessels. On 19 June, a group of six sloops sailing close to the shore fired on Akçaabat, setting fire to one ship and capturing another. This attack lasted four hours with the Russians coming under heavy fire from the shore batteries and losing two of their sloops. Four days later Trabazon was targeted, the attacking ships anchoring on the eastern side of the city and detaching two ships of the line to come close and bring it under bombardment, firing more than 500 cannon shots. While the intention was to land between 3,000 to 5,000 infantry, the defending gun batteries once again proved too much, with several ships heavily damaged, forcing them back out to sea.

After an armistice was signed in August 1807, a conflict-free period of approximately one and a half years followed, during which both sides strengthened the areas they considered strategically important and the Ottomans were allowed to reoccupy Anapa. For his part, Alexander continued to concentrate on strengthening his land forces to the detriment of the navy. The outcome was that when the war resumed in March 1809, the Black Sea Fleet was in an even poorer state than it had been two or three years earlier. As for the Ottoman Fleet, this had been greatly strengthened by the transfer of ships once needed to defend the Dardanelles against Senyavin. In addition, the Black Sea Fleet had a new commander, Vice Admiral Nikolai Lvovich Yazykov, Traversay having now been recalled to St Petersburg to take his appointment as head of the naval ministry as acting minister upon the departure of Chichagov.

The rebalancing of naval forces in the Black Sea would inevitably hamper the effectiveness of the Russian Fleet, including its ability to carry out its primary role of supporting military operations on land. Nevertheless, in June Anapa was successfully retaken, the fortress surrendering with minimal resistance. Here, with the Ottoman Navy not appearing, 1,200 troops had been landed from three transports supported at sea by one ship of the line, two frigates, and a bomb. A much more ambitious scheme for an assault on Varna failed at every level, the navy seeming quite incapable of mustering ships needed to transport a larger number of troops as well as a larger squadron of warships to provide protection for the landings in an area heavily patrolled by Ottoman warships.

Varna was a strategic target, a city just 300 miles by sea from Istanbul, and if captured would place Russian forces in a position to threaten Istanbul. It would also place Russian warships, assuming enough could be brought together, to block the Ottoman Navy from bringing reinforcements into the Black Sea from Istanbul. In turn, of course, it meant that its defences would be greater, with the constant possibility of the landing being interrupted by the hasty arrival of Ottoman warships already at sea or dispatched from the Bosporus.

In September 1809, following a series of lengthy delays in preparing a contingency of warships to bombard Varna, the commander on land, Prince Pyotr Bagration, expressed to Vice Admiral Yazykov, the new commander of the Black Sea Fleet, his exasperation at the non-arrival of the expected force, 'which was supposed to bring fear' into the enemy 'right up to Constantinople itself'. Instead, Bagration found himself 'using ground troops to protect the Black Sea coast', adding that 'many Turkish ships continue to cruise near the Black Sea coast.'

It was only on 22 September that three frigates and a brig finally put to sea, a force that was totally inadequate for the purpose of securing naval dominance in the area or of providing an effective bombardment of the coast to support military operations on land. Indeed, this small Russian contingent came within a hair's breadth of its own annihilation, as once again assumptions were made based on poor naval intelligence. One such assumption was that no substantial Ottoman force would put to sea, despite the area of intended operation being close to several Ottoman naval bases including Istanbul. On 3 October, while cruising off Cape Kalikra, 60km north-east of Varna, the inevitable happened. The Russians came within sight of a powerful enemy force of nine warships that was very much at sea. Fortunately for the small Russian unit, the enemy was tacking in the opposite direction and, despite one of the three frigates, the forty-four-gun *Nazaret*, constantly lagging, managed to outrun the enemy. Continuing the same tack until mid-morning, they were shocked to discover at a distance of only 2 miles that they were facing a substantially more powerful enemy of two 100-gun and three seventy-four-gun ships of the line in addition to three frigates, a corvette and two small vessels. So heavily outgunned, and through being so close to the shore, defeat, unless they could break through the enemy line, seemed inevitable. However, and somewhat miraculously, they were saved by the greater incompetence of the enemy. For instead of changing direction and forcing the Russian ships into a battle, they continued their own pre-set course before disappearing. Apparently, the red pennants flown on the top mast of the Russian ships had been mistaken for Ottoman colours.

Overnight, the laggard *Nazaret* under the command of Captain Second Rank Pavel Lang, continued to fall behind, and in doing failed to see a flagship signal to turn. Consequently, she lost contact with the other two frigates. Her disappearance went unnoticed by the squadron commander and no attempt was made to find her. On board *Nazaret*, it was later revealed that at the time of losing contact, permission had been given to her two watch officers, Lieutenant P. Nevorovsky and A.I. Kovtunovich, to leave the quarterdeck to take dinner in the wardroom. In other words, *Nazaret* was sailing blind. Matters now went from bad to worse. The Ottoman battle fleet, which had been so narrowly avoided, in realising their mistake were now in pursuit and, as morning dawned on 4 October, found they were within easy range of the wayward *Nazaret*, with two powerful battleships opening fire on her. Fortunately for the Russian frigate, an increase in wind forced the enemy to reef sails, allowing *Nazaret* to break away and eventually she joined up with the other two frigates.

On the return of the squadron to Sevastopol on 9 October, a court-marital was summoned to investigate the entire matter, but especially why *Nazaret* had lost contact with the squadron and had then engaged before successfully fleeing two ships of the line. From this it was revealed that Lang was highly unsuited to his command, having not even an elementary knowledge of the marine signalling system while also exhibiting an inability to ensure those under him properly performed their duties. To conceal his guilt, Lang went so far as to make alterations to the navigator's log and for which he was unable to present any evidence to justify those alterations. Two of his officers, Lieutenant Mikhali and Midshipman Volynsky, accused Lang of stupidity and not treating his officers with respect, further stating that he tried to surrender the frigate when threatened by the Ottoman battleships. As for the latter crime, this went unproven as no order could be found for the raising of an Ottoman flag as a sign of surrender. The outcome was that of Lang being found guilty of placing his frigate at risk. In punishment he was demoted to the rank of seaman. Of the accusations made by Mikali and Volinsky, these were viewed to be of malicious intent and both were sentenced to death.

On two occasions in 1810, the Russian Black Sea Fleet came close to engaging the Ottoman Navy in major sea battles, but on both occasions, and despite sighting and pursuing Ottoman ships matching their own in strength, the latter were able to avoid battle. Ordered to Varna and approach the Strait as close as possible, it was here that the confrontations occurred. The first in June, with the Ottoman Fleet escaping to Sivas was helped by the outbreak of a storm. In October, a Russian unit of eight ships of the line, five frigates, one corvette and three small ships encountered an Ottoman naval unit consisting of eight ships, two frigates and one brig. Once again, the Ottoman ships showed no inclination to fight and, following a lengthy pursuit, escaped with the Russian units returning to Sevastopol. Of course, if the seamen and officers on board those chasing Russian ships had been better trained and more adept, it seems not unlikely that on both this occasion and previously, the escaping Ottoman ships would have been forced into battle rather than outsailing their pursuers.

In one more attempt to establish a base at Trabzon and incite the Greeks against the Ottomans, a Russian Fleet under Admiral Sarychev departed from Sevastopol on 6 October 1810. While two attempts were made to land under the covering fire of ship-board artillery, both ultimately failed, defeated by Ottoman artillery and a determined counter-attack. Seemingly, the Russian landing force suffered heavily, many drowning in their attempts to return to the ships that had brought them while others died from bullets and cannon fire. One report, given by Pierre Dupré, the French consul in Trabzon, tells of 300 Russians taken prisoner and, somewhat more gruesome, a further 122 beheaded. A possible estimate is that the Russians suffered nearly 1,000 casualties.

# CHAPTER 18

# THE BALTIC: SEE THE ENEMY AND RUN

Resulting from Sweden's refusal to break away from her alliance with Great Britain, and Olaf IV regarding Napoleon as the 'beast of the apocalypse', Russia, at the bidding of Napoleon, entered a war against Sweden in February 1808. Three weeks later, Denmark also declared war on Sweden. At this time the Danish government was very much open to French bidding, resentful towards Britain following a second bombardment of Copenhagen in February 1808 and carried out for the purpose of preventing the Danish Fleet falling to the French. While this objective had been achieved, sixteen Danish ships of the line and substantial quantities of naval stores removed to England, it had the not surprising consequence of Denmark wanting to take its revenge. The war declared against Sweden was one outcome of that second bombardment of Copenhagen, but alongside this came a desire to obstruct the passage through the Danish straits of merchant shipping either trading under a British flag or those of any flag carrying cargoes bound for or leaving Britain. For this purpose, and to make up for the loss of those ships taken to England, a rapid and large-scale programme of constructing gunboats was begun, these to become a considerable threat to British merchant shipping passing through the straits.

In Alexander's declaration of war against Sweden, Russia successfully invaded and took full control of Finland, a Swedish possession since the Middle Ages. This not only provided greater security for St Petersburg and the naval base at Kronstadt but presented Russia with Sveaborg, an island fortress and formidable naval base immediately to the south of Helsinki. It was a campaign in which the Baltic Fleet played at best only a minimal role, despite military commander Count Frederick von Buxhöwden making a request in May 1808 for support from the fleet, but with Naval Forces Minister Chichagov persuading the emperor not to mobilise any ships for this purpose. Instead, he argued that as the Russian army had, in capturing Sveaborg, also taken possession of 100 Swedish in-shore craft, these would be adequate for the needs of the army. Hidden behind Chichagov's desire to not involve the fleet was his awareness that the navy in the Baltic was not up to the task, especially as some of the best ships had been sent with Senyavin into the Mediterranean. Apart from anything else, there was a shortage of trained seamen, something that happens if ships rarely put to sea and the men in the barracks are given tasks on land. As for the ships of the fleet, several of the larger units were clearly unfit for sea service, being long overdue for substantial repairs, while masts, spars and other essential items were in short supply. To put it another way, the Baltic Fleet was in chaos and nobody was prepared to admit it.

Forcing the issue, and ensuring that the Baltic Fleet would sail, even if the ships and crews were not ready for such a novel idea, was that of the Swedish Navy preparing to sail. If not countered, its presence would seriously disrupt Russian military plans to transfer troops to the battle front by sea, a task that until then required the assistance of only a small number of frigates. Heightening the situation was Great Britain also entering the war in the Baltic and choosing to provide support for Sweden. Under Vice Admiral James Saumarez, a squadron of eight ships of the line, alongside a flotilla of frigates, brigs and sloops, was sent into the Baltic, arriving in July. Assigned to work in conjunction with the Swedish Fleet against the 'common enemy', Saumarez's instructions also included 'the important service of attempting to destroy the Russian Fleet'. This was why he had within his command those eight ships of the line, while the role of his smaller and more agile vessels was for the protection of merchantmen sailing into the Baltic by enemy privateers and the increasing number of Danish gunboats deployed in the straits.

Upon arriving in the Baltic, Saumarez immediately detached two of his ships of the line, the seventy-four-gun third rates *Centaur* (Captain William Webley-Parry) and *Implacable* (Captain Thomas Byam Martin), to the Gulf of Finland. These were under the command of Rear Admiral Samuel Hood, the same Samuel Hood previously mentioned as serving under Nelson in the Mediterranean with *Centaur* his flagship. The first of Saumarez's ships to unite with the Swedish Fleet, *Centaur* and *Implacable* would be joined later by Saumarez and his remaining ships of the line. It was Saumarez's belief that the Swedes alone, even if assisted by two of his own warships, were incapable of achieving victory, but with the assistance of all his larger units, believed a victorious outcome would be inevitable.

In command of the Russian Baltic Fleet, which was now at sea, was Pyotr Ivanovich Khanykov, a full admiral since May 1799. Seemingly both he and Naval Forces Minister Chichagov were in full agreement with Saumarez. Like him, they believed the Swedish Fleet when acting alone was incapable of victory against their own ships, but if supported by British warships, any battle fought would have for Russia a disastrous outcome. Consequently, on learning of *Centaur* and *Implacable* having entered the eastern Baltic, both were in near panic. As for why they so feared even just those two British ships, it is only necessary to consider what Khanykov and Chichagov had experienced just ten years earlier when Khanykov was the Russian commander and Chichagov a captain of the first rank, alongside Duncan's squadron in the North Sea. Here they had witnessed first-hand the efficiency and discipline of British crews and how on every occasion they had outmatched Russian crews. Khanykov, of course, had reported to Catherine that Russian crews might take ten or twelve minutes to reef or unfurl sails. British crews were doing the same in two minutes. Both were aware that on first arriving in British waters their ships had failed even to maintain station with Duncan's ships when under sail, the British admiral for this reason reduced the sail of his own ships. Improvements in the ability of Russian crews might have seen a closing of the gap between the skills of the seamen of the two nations, but since then the Baltic Fleet had lain dormant with a consequent decline in the fighting ability of Russian ships and crews. For this reason, Khanykov received instructions from St Petersburg that he should attempt to meet with the Swedish Fleet in battle but at all costs avoid contact with any British ships. To this was added a further instruction issued on 27 June. This directed Khanykov to search for the Swedish Fleet, 'attack swiftly' and 'seize or destroy', but also stipulated that he should:

> *Maintain constant vigilance so that the English fleet, by its initial union with the Swedish fleet, does not put us in danger or difficulty with its superiority of forces.*

On 5 August and reaffirmed on 18 August, Khanykov was reminded that his object was 'destruction or seizure of the Swedish fleet', but he must protect 'himself from an attack by the English'. With Khanykov sailing out of Kronstadt on 19 August, he received on the following day a *further attack but do not attack* instruction from Chichagov, in which Khanykov was 'to the utmost extent possible to protect himself from an attack by English naval forces'. To this was added permission, 'depending on circumstances', that he might take refuge in the newly captured Finnish stronghold of Sveaborg. However,

**Russian ships under Admiral Khanykov's command, 1808.**

| | **Guns** |
|---|---|
| *Blagodat* (Grace) | 130 |
| *Gavriil* (Gabriel) | 100 |
| *Syevernaya Zvyezda* (Northern Star) | 74 |
| *Borey* (Boreas) | 74 |
| *Orol* (Eagle) | 74 |
| *Zachatie Sviataia Anna* (The Conception of Saint Anna) | 74 |
| *Vsevolod* (named after Vsevolod I, Grand Prince) | 74 |
| *Archistratig Mikhail* (Archistrategos Mikhail) | 72 |
| *Emgeiten* (Emgeiten) | 66 |
| *Geroi* (Hero) frigate | 48 |
| *Bystriyi* (Fast) frigate | 44 |
| *Argus* (Argus) frigate | 44 |
| *Sviatoi Feodosii Totemskii* (St Feodosiy Totemskiy) frigate | 44 |
| *Stchastlivyi* (Happy) frigate | 44 |
| In addition, six small frigates and other smaller vessels | |

any question of fighting the Swedish Fleet unsupported by any British ships was to prove impossible as, wisely, it had been decided by Rear Admiral Henrik Johan Nauckhoff, who was commanding the Swedish Fleet, that it should only put to sea once it had been joined by *Centaur* and *Implacable*. With this achieved on 20 August, the Swedish Fleet soon after left its anchorage in the Örö roadstead that lay within the Finnish archipelago.

Khanykov, the Russian admiral, commanded nine ships of the line, including the 130-gun *Blagodat* and the 110-gun *Gavriil*, in total carrying 738 guns, together with eleven frigates. Technically his was the stronger force if meeting only Nauckhoff's ships in battle. Nauckhoff did have a greater number of ships of the line, but these lacked the weight and power of some of the Russian ships, carrying in total 654 guns. However, with *Centaur* and *Implacable* having joined Nauckhoff, the tables had been completely turned with these two ships bringing a further 148 guns.

On 25 August, the two fleets came within distant sight of one another, with Khanykov, if not already, becoming aware that he could not fight the Swedes without engaging the two British seventy-fours. Ordering his ships to form a line of battle, Khanykov's limited confidence in the ability of those manning his own ships was immediately demonstrated when Khanykov instructed each ship to join the line 'according to ability'. That is, he did not require each ship to take up their established position in the line through careful manoeuvring, but to take up any position they could without endangering any other ship. This went totally against the established procedure, which for success required a much stricter level of organisation. However, despite this attempt at a show of entering battle, Khanykov also ordered his ships to sail on a south-westerly course that was designed to bring them into Russian waters and the safety of a Russian port. Effectively he was preparing for a battle while hastily retreating, a retreat that would eventually turn into outright flight, with some of his ship commanders exhibiting nothing less than absolute panic.

In the chase that followed, it was the two British ships that, through having been coppered before leaving England, were soon leading all the Swedish ships as they closed in upon Khanykov's ships in retreat. By 4 a.m. the following morning, *Implacable*, the best-performing ship of the entire Anglo-Swedish Fleet, was 2 miles windward of *Centaur*, and only 4 or 5 miles behind the Russians. For their part, the Russians were scattered, and still making every effort to get away with several ships setting their own course and speed to avoid the enemy. Hood gives confirmation of this, remarking in his description of the pursuit that the Russian Fleet was 'in the greatest disorder, apparently to avoid a general battle'. Martin, who was commanding *Implacable*, was clearly proud of what the two British ships were achieving, writing to Henry Martin his uncle:

> *This is the first instance of an action between the English and Russians. It was the finest sight imaginable to see twenty-four sail flying before [our] two British ships, which literally was the case, as the Swedes were so far distant.*

As the distance shortened, *Implacable* opened fire on the slowest of the retreating enemy, the seventy-four-gun *Vsevolod,* with Hood providing this description of what followed:

> *Although the enemy's ship fought with the greatest bravery, she was silenced in about twenty minutes: and only the near approach of the enemy's whole fleet could have prevented her then falling, her colours and pendant being both down; but I [Hood] was obliged to make the signal for the Implacable to close me.*

Khanykov, in ordering several ships, including his own flagship *Blagodat* to give some protection to *Vsevolod,* found himself defied by three ships, their captains openly disobeying the order by failing to turn back. Others, however, did come to the aid of *Vsevolod* and, with the Swedish ships still at some distance, and *Implacable* awaiting *Centaur* to join her, this enabled *Vsevolod* to be taken in tow by the frigate *Pollux*. But this proved only a temporary reprieve. Most of Khanykov's fleet, with just a few exceptions had continued to make full sail, resulting in the towing frigate and *Vsevolod* falling behind and which allowed the two British ships to begin a combined attack. As reported by one Russian historian, *Implacable* fired on *Vsevolod*:

> *On a counter course and in an extremely short time turned back and approached Vsevolod from downwind at pistol shot range turning her into a slow-moving burden for the rapidly retreating main force.*

In this attack, *Vsevolod*'s stays and top sheets were broken, her foretop mast knocked down, and her sails seriously shot through. To avoid a continued encounter with *Centaur* and *Implacable,* Khanykov at 8.45 a.m. raised the signal to his rear ships to add sails and abandon *Vsevolod* to whatever fate awaited her. At the same time *Pollux* also threw off the tow line, and resulting from a favourable wind, all Khanykov's ships, apart from *Vsevolod,* made a safe entry into the port of Paldiski on the south side of the Gulf of Finland and about 50km to the west of Tallinn.

As for *Vsevolod,* lacking steerage and her sails much damaged, it was impossible for her to navigate into the port, anchoring outside where boats were sent later in the afternoon to tow her into Paldiski. This prompted *Centaur* to drive off the boats, running across the bow of *Vsevolod* just as she was reaching the harbour. At 8 p.m., having lashed the bowsprit of the Russian ship to her mizzen rigging, *Centaur* opened fire, but having entered shallow water both she and *Vsevolod* ran aground. Forty minutes later, with *Implacable* having continued to fire into her for ten minutes, *Vsevolod* surrendered. This allowed *Implacable* to haul *Centaur* off, but a similar attempt to get *Vsevolod* into deeper water failed, and at 6 a.m. the following morning the British admiral ordered the burning of *Vsevolod*, and a few hours later she blew up.

No subsequent attempt was made to attack and destroy Khanykov's fleet. Admittedly, thought was given to the possibility, a project that might have succeeded if Saumarez and his additional force of British battleships had been available upon the Russian Fleet first entering the bay. However, supported only by ships of the Swedish Navy, which had already proved inferior to the British warships, a successful attack upon Paldiski was not considered feasible. In his own words, Martin wrote:

> *I have no hesitation in giving a decided opinion that the Russian Fleet in Rogerwick [Paldiski] cannot be attacked with any reasonable hope of success, or without the risk of losing some of his Majesty's ships. It would be a hazardous thing with a powerful squadron of British ships to attack an enemy so strongly situated; but with a force composed principally of Swedish ships, I am confident it would end in disappointment if not in disgrace.*

Furthermore, such an attack would soon become even more difficult as the harbour was rapidly strengthened. Apart from the arrival of 6,000 troops from Tallinn, additional guns were placed in the fort overlooking the bay, gun batteries erected on the Pakri Islands that commanded the bay, and a carefully buoyed chain boom laid across the entrance to the harbour. Arriving towards the end of August, Saumarez at first favoured an attack using the full force of the now much enlarged Anglo-Swedish Fleet. But was persuaded otherwise by Martin who viewed the Russian position as having become impregnable.

In choosing to agree with Martin, it is also likely that Saumarez was acting out of political prudence. An attack on Paldiski and destruction of the Russian Fleet would have inflamed Russian pride against any future alliance with Great Britain, something the British government was keen to avoid. While Saumarez's original instructions did allow for his attempting 'to destroy the Russian Fleet', it is likely that he was also aware that opinion in London on the shrewdness of doing this was much divided. From St Petersburg in September of the previous year had come a report from Lord Hutchinson that went completely against the taking of any form of extreme action against the Russian Fleet as such a move, according to Lord Hutchinson's report, would destroy any possibility of Russia returning to Britain as an ally in the war against Napoleon. Hutchinson had been sent to St Petersburg to discover the full nature of the terms that Alexander had agreed at Tilsit. While he was unsuccessful in getting Russia to share the secret articles contained within the treaty, he did learn that among Russian merchants and others of influence, the alliance with France was deeply unpopular and there was a general desire to continue, at the very least, a trading relationship with Britain. In his report, Hutchinson stated:

> *Thinking people here, and indeed the nation at large, inclined very much to a connection with England, the appearance of our fleet before Kronstadt, any attack upon the capital, would change these good dispositions, irritate the whole empire against us, and induce the government to make efforts against our empire in India.*

Knowing that any such attack on Paldiski and the annihilation of Khanykov's fleet would, with certainty, destroy any possibility of renewing the former alliance with Russia, this could well have influenced Saumarez in his decision not to make such a move. If he wanted further evidence of what might be the result of such an attack, he needed only consider the consequence of the recent bombardment of Copenhagen. From a relatively sympathetic feeling towards Great Britain and her war aims, the bombardment had turned virtually every man, woman and child in Denmark against Britain in favour of France.

In Paldiski, Khanykov's squadron, with their yards and topmasts struck, lay moored in the harbour for almost a month. Their only threat was the thought Saumarez briefly gave to the sending in of fire ships. Out of civility, such an attack would first have been notified to Khanykov. Saumarez had indicated to him the perilous danger such an attack would present to the Russian Fleet, 'and the inevitable destruction that must await the town of Baltic Port [Paldiski].' Having finally dispensed with thoughts of any form of attack on Paldiski, Saumarez settled on the alternative of sending to Khanykov English newspapers, porter, and a quarter hundredweight of coffee.

The Anglo-Swedish blockade of Paldiski proved short-lived, continuing only until the end of September. By that time, with no relief ships sent out from Britain and the Swedish Fleet suffering greatly from scurvy and other sicknesses, Saumarez deemed it necessary to abandon the blockade. The Swedish Fleet, on arriving at Karlskrona, landed 3,000 sick, their suffering eased by medicine and fresh provisions supplied by Saumarez from his own ships and which had also come into Karlskrona before making a return to England. Nauckhoff, aware of the inefficiencies of his own ships, for they had been so clearly outsailed during the chase of the Russian Fleet, requested and was permitted to receive the help of some British officers so that Swedish ships would be in a better state to co-operate with the British during the following year. Khanykov no longer under blockade also sailed, taking his ships to Tallinn.

Alexander, thirsty for success on all fronts, now sought retribution on all who he considered responsible for the Baltic Fleet's poor performance, with Khanykov viewed as the main culprit. Brought before a court-martial, Khanykov was charged and found guilty of:

> *Allowing British ships to join the Swedish squadron, of refusing to engage in battle, of too hasty a withdrawal to a Baltic port and of failing to provide assistance to the ship Vsevolod.*

Upon all these he suffered a reprimand, but on a further charge, that of 'oversight weakness in command, slowness, and indecisiveness', he was sentenced to be demoted to the rank of seaman for one month. This sentence was subsequently cancelled by Alexander 'in respect of his previous service', and instead he was sent into dishonourable retirement. As for the three ship commanders who had failed to obey the signal to go to the aid of *Vsevolod*, they too were brought to trial, one acquitted and the other two sentenced to death.

The ships of the Baltic Fleet that had once been under Khanykov's command remained at Tallinn until the spring of 1809 when, upon the Baltic becoming ice-free, most were transferred to Kronstadt. Here engineers were hastily constructing two dozen batteries, some placed on newly created artificial islands. In addition, and between Kotlin and Cape Lisii Nos, were anchored *Aleksei* (74) and *Mikhail* (66), alongside the former Swedish sixty-four-gun *Prince Karl*, among other battleships, all re-armed as floating batteries. Supposedly, the returned ships of the Baltic Fleet were ready to repel any threatened British attack, but everyone knew, except possibly Alexander, that such was no more than a pipe-dream. Even when British ships landed troops on Gogland Island in the eastern Baltic, about 97 miles (176km) west of Kronstadt, where they burned the lighthouse, the Russian ships in Kronstadt did not move.

Occasionally, a frigate of the Baltic Fleet did set sail, but only to escort supply ships sailing through the Gulf of Bothnia to deliver food for troops fighting in Sweden. On one such operation, the thirty-four-gun frigate *Bogoiavlenie Gospodne*, under the command of Captain Lieutenant Mendel and sailing with two brigs, was forced to retreat when attacked by two forty-eight-gun Swedish frigates. On 11 June 1808, *Opyt*, a fourteen-gun cutter launched at St Petersburg in 1806, while returning from Sveaborg was intercepted by the forty-four-gun British frigate *Salsette*. Following a one-hour fight in which *Salsette* fired two full broadsides into the relatively diminutive brig, *Opyt* was forced to surrender. After the surrender, the British captain returned the Russian commander's sword, landing the survivors near Libau (Liepāja). It will be noted in the account given by Captain Walter Bathurst (see below), that *Opyt*, when the wind died back, used sweeps to help her manoeuvre. Sweeps were long oars used by small Russian warships in the Baltic to assist manoeuvring and were especially useful in the tight, restricted waters of the Baltic.

**Captain Walter Bathurst's letter to the Admiralty in London describing the battle fought between the frigate *Salsette*, which he commanded, and the Russian brig *Opyt*, 24 June 1808.**

*Sir I beg leave to inform you; that having yesterday, in his Majesty's ship Salsette, chased a sloop of war under Russian colours to Reval [Tallinn], where a frigate and a brig were laying, and taken a galliot partly laden with spirits that was at anchor in the Roads, in coming out with the latter saw a cutter off the North End of Norgen Island, coming down with sails up, who soon after hauled her wind for the land; made all sail in chase, and closed with her at half past eight but on opposite tacks, and the wind dying away at the time she crossed us with her sweeps out, and returned our fire, by which, I am sorry I have to say, one, a marine, was killed. The wind continuing very light, and the cutter pulling away with her sweeps, prevented our closing again with her for some time, but a sudden squall of a few minutes brought the ship up with her about ten o'clock. Yet, as they were near the shore, and, it just then setting in dark, they persevered in their endeavours to escape after they were completely under and exposed to the fire of most of our guns; but being hailed to lay in their sweeps, at quarter past ten they did so, as it was then impossible for them to get away. On taking possession, she proved to be his Russian Majesty's cutter Apith [Opyt], commanded by Lieut. G. C. Novelski, of 14 guns, carronades, and manned with 61 men, four of whom were killed, the commander and seven wounded. She left Sveaborg at noon the same day, to join the sloop of war we had chased in the morning, belonging to a squadron of four frigates and eight sloops stationed there. The cutter a very fine vessel, about two years old, exceedingly well fitted, and found in everything. I am, Sir (Signed) W. BATHURST.*

## PART SEVEN

# War with France, 1812-1814

The rift with Napoleon that led to the invasion of Russia in 1812 had been simmering for many months, and while several causes are put forward, none was more important than Russia's failure to adhere to the terms of Napoleon's continental system. While a ban on British ships entering Russian ports had been implemented, little attention was given to neutral flagged ships and the trade they were conducting between Russia and Britain. As often as not, these ships were British-owned and carrying papers forged by the British government declaring them to be neutral with a cargo bound for a port neutral or friendly to France. Everyone knew this was how Britain and Russia continued to trade – a fact well known even in Paris. With Alexander refusing to bring it to an end, Napoleon had little option other than to go to war by invading Russia.

For Russia, the continuation of dealings with Great Britain was essential, securing a highly favourable balance of commerce, paid for in ready cash by British merchants; a business that if lost would result in untold economic damage. To Britain it guaranteed a supply of naval stores in quantities unavailable anywhere else in the world. Should Britain be cut out of this trade, the number of ships she could put to sea would be greatly reduced, threatening in consequence her position as the world's richest trading nation. Seen in this way, Napoleon was operating a two-pronged attack on the British economy, attempting to both deny Britain access to European markets and destroy how Britain operated.

If successful, Napoleon's invasion of Russia would not only prevent Britain obtaining naval stores from Russia, but allow those same stores to be directed entirely to France. Once in the hands of Napoleon, they could be absorbed into his own warship-building programme that was designed to give the French Empire sufficient warships to eventually outnumber and overpower the British Navy. As well as ensuring the materials needed for the ambitious shipbuilding programme already underway, Napoleon saw a further bonus that would emanate from a successful invasion of Russia: the gaining of ready-built ships of Russia's Baltic and Black Sea Fleets, alongside naval dockyards that could be used to build an even greater number of ships.

# CHAPTER 19

# ESCAPE TO ENGLAND

Five months after Napoleon's army had begun its march on Moscow, Russia's Baltic Fleet, or at least a considerable part of it, together with ships based at Arkhangelsk, fled to England. It was an arrangement made with the British government and one that worked much to the advantage of Great Britain, as it gave absolute surety that most Russian warships would not fall into the hands of Napoleon. With that fleet locked into a British harbour, even if the Russian emperor reversed his position and became once again an ally of France, most of his navy would be lost to him. But of much greater importance to Britain, this navy would be lost to Napoleon. How hard Alexander was pressed by the British government to send his fleet to England is unknown, but his agreement does demonstrate the Russian emperor's lack of interest in naval affairs and what could have been achieved by a fully operational Baltic Fleet. It also demonstrated Britain's own attitude towards the Russian Fleet, viewed in London as a liability if it remained under Russian control but a potentially strong fighting unit if it fell into the hands of Napoleon and re-officered by competent French naval personnel.

Since its brief encounter with the Anglo-Swedish Fleet in 1808, the Baltic Fleet had remained in port, determined to avoid a possible future battle with Saumarez. Each year following the encounter with *Centaur* and *Implacable*, Saumarez brought ships into the Baltic to safeguard the passage of merchantmen bound for Britain carrying naval stores and other essential imports. From Sweden, Russia, Finland and Prussia, merchant ships in autumn and before the sea became ice-bound assembled in Hanö Bay, on the south-east coast of Sweden. From there, under the protection of Saumarez's ships, a hundred or more would sail in one massive convoy. In 1811, 129 merchantmen were escorted by five ships of the line and three gunboats while other ships provided further protection by holding station in areas along the sea route that were vulnerable to attack. In addition, Saumarez had to be prepared to take on the Russian Navy should it once again sail into the Baltic. Admittedly, this was always seen as unlikely for, if it did sail, the outcome for Saumarez was certain victory. The state of the Russian Fleet made this inevitable. Apart from those manning the ships being poorly trained through being at sea so infrequently, few ships were combat-ready having undergone insufficient repairs and little maintenance. Despite Paul's attempts to curb corruption, this was still a major problem, ensuring that even when ships were taken into dry dock, timbers and other items needed to undertake repair work were often not available, either paid for and not delivered or stolen after arrival.

Of this, Alexander himself was aware, declaring somewhat dramatically, when referring to the officials of the Kronstadt naval base, that 'they would have stolen my military battleships if they had known where to hide them.'

By late June 1812, when Napoleon was crossing the Neman and beginning his entry into Russia, the Baltic Fleet possessed no more than six seaworthy ships of the line. As for the remaining ships and frigates, these were listed as fireships, floating batteries, transports and blockships. Nevertheless, if taken by the French and brought back into a seaworthy condition by their own skilled shipwrights, those discarded ships could have been employed to advantage. For while Great Britain may have possessed the world's largest and most powerful navy, it was hopelessly over-stretched. Apart from the need to maintain a continuing presence in the Baltic, and one now requiring even more ships, others were deployed on blockading French ports, both those facing on to the Atlantic and Mediterranean and other ports in the North Sea, Atlantic and Adriatic. Elsewhere, British naval ships were supporting Arthur Wellesley on the Iberian Peninsula, while on the far side of the Atlantic a new war had broken out in June 1812 against the USA. This, in turn, would soon require more ships to not only blockade American ports but to combat US-manned privateers on whichever ocean they chose to strike.

Of course, had the Russian Fleet been in a better state of preservation, and with the British government trusting that Alexander would remain bound to Britain, Russian ships could have been usefully deployed in the Baltic. This would have relieved the British Navy of some of the pressures it was under. But that trust in either Alexander or the ability of Russian ships to perform such a task was just not there. At the very least, Russian warships could have secured the safety of passage through the Danish straits. Instead, this was a task still to be undertaken by British warships, with Saumarez once more undertaking the role in 1812. Nor, in that year, was it made any easier when it was realised that two of the most important ports used in the commercial trade, Liepāja and Tallinn, were under threat of landward attack by the French. In these two ports, British ships were collecting naval stores and other cargoes bound for England, and for their protection Saumarez was forced to dispatch two seventy-four-gun third rates, *Aboukir* and *Orion,* into the eastern Baltic.

To digress for one moment. The Baltic, even before the French invasion, and discounting any threat from a suddenly resurgent Russian Navy, was a very dangerous sea for ships carrying cargoes to Britain. When passing anywhere close to its northern shoreline, any stray merchant ship would immediately excite the interest of enemy privateers, especially those occupying the heavily defended port of Danzig (Gdansk). Having withstood this danger, the Danish straits presented even greater peril. These were the narrow stretches of water, namely the Great Belt, the Sound (Øresund), and the Little Belt, through which ships had to pass before entering the North Sea by way of Kattegat and Skagerrak. It was a passage that brought those convoyed ships dangerously close to the coastline of Denmark, a nation in alliance with France. Following the attack on Copenhagen carried out by the British Navy in 1801, and a further bombardment of the city in 1807, combined with the capturing and taking by Britain of the Danish sailing fleet,

Denmark remained true to France. In truth, the Danish government was more fearful of a full-on French invasion than a seaborne attack from Britain. To compensate for the loss of her fleet, Denmark had created a substantial force of gunboats that were used against merchant convoys under British escort operating out of numerous bases on the coasts of Skagerrak, Kattegat, Sound, Great Belt, and some of the Baltic islands. From these bases, any merchant ship straying out of sight of an escorting warship would become an immediate target. This was why the presence of a British fleet in the Baltic had become and continued to be of such importance. Yet it was a role to which the Russian Fleet could have easily adapted. Instead, and when finally ready to sail for England towards the end of the year, the Russian Fleet itself had to be escorted through the Danish straits by Saumarez's already overworked warships.

Following negotiations with Lord Cathcart, the British Ambassador Extraordinary to the Court of Russia, it was agreed that Russia's entire Baltic Fleet, or as many as were in condition to sail, would proceed to England. Serving as nothing more than a face-saver, it was also agreed that those ships might work alongside the British Navy 'as should be deemed by the Government of Great Britain to be most advantageous to the general interest'. To attract less attention while sailing, the ships of the Russian Fleet sailed in three separate units. The first, commanded by Rear Admiral George Tate, consisted of ten battleships sailing out of Kronstadt at the end of October. Two weeks later a second unit of eight ships left Kronstadt under Rear Admiral Maxim Petrovich Korobka. Among his ships was the seventy-four-gun third rate *Iupiter*, a ship launched at St Petersburg only five weeks earlier with the need to await that ship determining the date on which the second unit sailed out of Kronstadt. *Iupiter*, upon arrival in England, would be completed and fitted out, this work performed at Chatham naval yard early the following year.

The third unit comprised ships from Arkhangelsk sailing under the command of Vice Admiral Roman Vasilievich Crown. Before sailing to England, it was required of Crown that he should sail into the Baltic and, through a relay of his ships, convey 25-30,000 soldiers of the Finland Corps from Sveaborg to Riga, the latter under threat from Napoleon's invading army. What should have been a relatively easy assignment became an unmitigated disaster. Off the Shetland Islands, following Crown's departure from Arkhangelsk, a violent four-day storm was encountered, a storm for which the shallow-draughted Arkhangelsk-built ships were never supposed to encounter. Many suffered considerable damage made worse by several having their outer planking so poorly caulked that large amounts of water were constantly leaking into these ships through the seams. For many on board who had never previously experienced the open seas, it must have been truly terrifying. But for those with more experience, it would still have been greatly alarming. Unable to continue, Crown was forced to take his squadron into Gothenburg, with one ship so badly damaged she had to be taken into the nearest of the Norwegian ports. This was *Vsevolod*, a seventy-four-gun third rate launched in May 1809 to replace the *Vsevolod* lost at sea following her encounter with *Centaur* and *Implacable*. Of her crew, *Vsevolod* suffered the loss of ninety-seven, but while some were fatalities that might have been related to the storm, the majority were taken by avoidable diseases.

Scurvy and pneumonia were especially rife, while rancid food brought on board before leaving Arkhangelsk may also have added to the death toll. In addition, 225 of *Vsevolod*'s crew of around 600 reported sick.

With Crown's unit of ships forced to remain in Gothenburg until October, this left the Finland Corps languishing in Sveaborg unable to reach Riga. Eventually, a much smaller number, around 5,000, were to be transported to Riga, not by the ships of the Baltic Fleet but by Russia's entirely separate rowing fleet. Crown was now ordered to rendezvous with Rear Admiral Korobka's squadron and with him sail directly for England. Even that did not go according to plan, for upon leaving Gothenburg prior to meeting with Korobka, a second ship, *Saratov,* was lost on 28 October, striking an underwater rock off Harmano in Skagerrak. Fortunately, her entire crew was rescued but *Saratov* sank two days later.

The two units from Kronstadt under Korobka and Tate were more fortunate, but this might well have been through assistance provided by Saumarez, with the British admiral instructing his captains on 24 October that the safety of the Russian ships were to be their 'chief and primary object of attention'. Apart from ensuring that no Danish gunboat came within sight of any Russian ship, much more important was the supplying of navigational assistance, including the sending to each Russian ship a British pilot. Hidden rocks and areas of shallow water had since Nelson's attack on Copenhagen in 1801 been carefully mapped by British naval hydrographers and navigators, with accurate charts made available to those commanding Saumarez's ships. The Russian Navy had nothing like this. While Paul had recognised the importance of mapping areas of ocean, assembling a collection of nautical charts and foreign atlases with a view to carrying out more detailed surveys, this had been abandoned by Alexander. It was the British charts used by the on-board pilots that ensured safe guidance of the Russian Fleet through the Danish straits, and it was the Russian failure to have surveyed for themselves those same and adjacent waters that had resulted in the loss of *Saratov.*

The naval base at Chatham, because of its geographical location, possessing the nearest major dockyard to the North Sea, was to receive the bulk of the Russian warships, an order sent to the commissioner of the yard that the officers and ships' companies of the Russian Fleet were to be allowed free entrance into the dockyard, in like manner to ships of the British Navy. On arrival off Sheerness at the mouth of the River Medway, pilots were again assigned to each ship, taking responsibility for navigating them through the various twists and turns of the river before claiming their assigned moorings in Kethole Reach. As might be expected, the arrival of these Russian ships was widely reported in both regional and London newspapers, with an account given by an officer serving on *Podargus*, a brig-sloop that had accompanied the second division, appearing in the *Kentish Gazette*:

> *This ship [Podargus] arrived here yesterday from the Baltic, with six sail of the Russian line of battle ships in company. We left Gothenburg on 3d Dec. in company with 26 sail of men of war, English and Russians. The*

> *squadron brought by us is commanded Vice Admiral Crown, who has brought his lady and family with him; the remaining part of the fleet we left off Orfordness. Admiral Hope landed here last night, and immediately set off express to London, with the intelligence of our arrival. The Podargus is the first vessel arrived belonging to this large fleet.*

The fact of the fleet being commanded by two officers, Tate and Crown, both of whom were British by birth, also gained newspaper attention:

> *The liberal reliance of the Russians on British good faith, is as honourable to that nation as complimentary to this. What a racket about romantic confidence would a certain part of John Bull's body politic make, if we were to send a fleet British men war to winter in a Russian port, under the command of native Russian officers!*

Rear Admiral Tate was English by birth, born on 14 June 1746 near London. His father had also served in the Russian Fleet and later acted as an agent for securing mast timbers from Russia. Active in several naval campaigns, Tate had been present at Çeşme and the Baltic campaigns against Sweden. Following the Treaty of Tilsit and the declaration of war against Great Britain, he had been placed on shore duties but brought back into the seagoing navy following Napoleon's invasion of Russia. Vice Admiral Crown was born on 21 December 1753 near Perth, Scotland, and had served in the British Navy. Placed on half pay following the American Revolutionary War, and with little prospect of promotion, he transferred to the Russian Navy in 1788. Initially given the rank of captain lieutenant, his promotion to vice admiral came in February 1804. Like Tate, upon declaration of war against Great Britain, he had also been placed on shore duties, returning to sea service on the outbreak of war with France.

The arrival of the Russian Fleet in the Medway was to put considerable strain on the already overburdened dockyards and naval facilities at both Chatham and Sheerness, but no more so than on the medical services. Even upon their first arrival in the Medway, the Russian ships, including of course *Vsevolod*, were experiencing high rates of mortality, a fact reported by several newspapers, including the *Kentish Weekly Post*:

> *Since the arrival of the Russian Fleet at Chatham, the crews of several of the ships have been affected with contagions distemper, of which some have died. Change of diet, and want of cleanliness, have been assigned the causes of this disorder the violence of which, however, is now subsided, through the mode prescribed by the medical practitioners who were sent from town.*

As a matter of urgency orders were given by the Admiralty in London for the hospital ships *Argonaut* and *Trusty* to be cleared of the sick they had on board to make room

**Russian ships arriving at Sheerness, 11-12 December 1812.**

| Name | Guns | Ship commanders and notes |
|---|---|---|
| *Khrabryi* (Brave) | 120 | Commodore Butchensky. *Khrabryi* closely based on the design of the British *Caledonia.* |
| *Smelyi* (Fearless) | 88 | Captain First Rank Ogilby. *Smelyi* designed by the French Constructor Le Brune. |
| *Iupiter* (Jupiter) | 80 | Commodore Boyle. *Iupiter* launched at St Petersburg in September 1812, completed and fitted out at Chatham. |
| *Trekh Sviatitelei* (Three Saints) | 74 | Captain First Rank Rose. |
| *Severnaya Zvezda* (Northern Star) | 74 | Captain First Rank Povahehen. |
| *Ne Tron'Menia* (Don't Touch Me) | 74 | Captain First Rank Mitkov. |
| *Borey* (Boreas) | 74 | Captain First Rank Ratmanov. |
| *Sviatyk zhen mirono sits* (The saint of the myrrh-bearing women) | 74 | Captain First Rank Moore. |
| *Nord-Adler* (North Eagle) | 74 | Captain First Rank Hamilton. Flagship of Vice Admiral Crown. *Nord-Adler* lost topmasts in storm off Shetlands (September 1812). |
| *Sviato Slav* (Holy Glory) | 74 | Captain First Rank Stepanov. |
| *Trekh Ierarkhov* (Three Hierarchs) | 74 | Captain First Rank Ternossky. |
| *Ches'ma* (Çeşme) | 74 | Captain First Rank Shishmanov. *Ches'ma* named after the battle fought in 1770. Her design copied from the British first rate *Victory.* |
| *Orol* (Eagle) | 74 | Captain First Rank Dernov. *Oryol* named after the city on the Oka river. |
| *Pamiat' Evstafii* (Memory of Evstafii) | 74 | Captain First Rank Butchensky. Flagship of Rear Admiral Korobka. Had been serving as a floating battery in Tallinn. |
| *Pobedo nosets* (Victory bearers) | 66 | Captain First Rank Disvowith. |

| Name | Guns | Ship commanders and notes |
|---|---|---|
| **Frigates** | | |
| *Venera* (Venus) | 56 | Captain First Rank Hildebrand. |
| *Sveaborg* (Sveaborg) | 46 | Captain First Rank Butchensky. Admiral Tate's flagship. |
| *Bystryi* (Fast) | 44 | Captain Second Rank Nivetsky. |
| *Arkhipelag* (Archipelago) | 44 | Captain Second Rank Polozov. |
| **Corvettes** | | |
| *Mel'pomena* (Melpomene) | 22 | Captain Lieutenant Waselessky. *Mel'pomena* named after the Greek muse of tragedy. |
| *Germion* (Hermione) | 22 | Captain Lieutenant Bojodanov. |
| **Brig** | | |
| *Gonets* (Success) | 22 | Captain Lieutenantt Gesimges. |
| **Transport** | | |
| *Sharlota* (Charlotte) | | Formerly a corvette purchased in France. |

for the Russians. Later, during early winter 1814, typhoid also struck, claiming several hundred Russian lives.

The treaty of alliance between Great Britain and Russia automatically required attention to be given to the seven ships of the line and the frigate that had to be returned to Russia in accordance with the articles of the Cintra Convention (see Chapter 16). Initially, it was intended that following essential repair work they should be sailed to Russia to join the rest of the fleet, with Lord Cathcart's primary instruction on being appointed ambassador to the imperial Court that of arranging for the return of those ships. Complicating the entire matter was the poor condition of these vessels, all much in need of repair. A survey carried out in October 1812 considered the expense of repairing and equipping the ships for a return voyage to Russia compared to their value if sold in this country. The expectation was that the Russian government would either pay for the repairs or agree to the sale of the least seaworthy with the money paid over to Russia. In February 1813, a more detailed survey was conducted in which Tate and Crown were present and the conclusion reached that five of the ships of the line should be sold together with a frigate, with only *Sil'nyi* and *Moshchnyi* to be retained.

# CHAPTER 20

# WAR AND PEACE

In gaining Alexander's agreement that the most powerful ships of his fleet should be removed to England, the British government agreed to pay £500,000 annually to Russia for their upkeep while they remained in British waters. In defending this large payment, Lord Robert Castlereagh, Britain's foreign secretary, in a statement made to Parliament in November 1813, reminded the House of the difficulties that were then facing the British Navy and of it not being 'effectual for all purposes' for which it was then required. In his words, as reported by Hansard:

> *The House and the country ought to know, that, notwithstanding the immense pressure which had been made on the enemy's naval resources for many preceding years yet he [Napoleon] had not relaxed his maritime efforts; and that he had still fleets in most of his leading arsenals, ready for sea...accumulating his marine forces by rapid strides.*

Going on to refer to the presence of Russian warships as 'eminently useful', he no doubt had in mind ongoing activities off the mouth of the Scheldt. Here, Russian ships under the charge of Korobka were blockading the movement of all French shipping. This had been first reported to the British public in May when news had been given of five Russian sail of the line and a frigate bound for the Scheldt to relieve 'the same number of British men of war'. In consequence, it was further reported, the same number of British ships could now be sent 'to the American station'.

The sending of Russian warships to the mouth of the Scheldt certainly had value. If nothing else it took some of the pressure off the British Navy, for the Scheldt in French hands was a very real danger to Britain and one that required a blockading force of considerable strength. At the mouth of the Scheldt lay Vlissingen, a vast natural harbour that was giving protection to a small fleet of naval ships or those carrying letters of marque. Should any sail, and given that the mouth of the Scheldt was in close geographic proximity to the Thames Estuary, they became an immediate threat to merchant shipping entering and leaving the port of London. Especially vulnerable were those carrying naval stores from the Baltic as they had to pass close to the mouth of the Scheldt. Also, not far distant lay the vast anchorage of the Downs where hundreds of merchantmen awaited a suitable wind before continuing their passage. Lying further upriver from Vlissingen was

Antwerp, which offered a threat as great or even greater than that of Vlissingen. Here, a huge warship-building programme was underway with no less than fifteen line of battle ships launched between 1807 and 1811. It was a rate of new launchings that exceeded the entire output of all six of Britain's naval dockyards. While not ready to sail, the materials needed for the continued construction of this fleet could most easily be brought to Antwerp by way of Vlissingen, a further reason for blockading the Scheldt. Thus the reason many naval ships were required to patrol the North Sea and be constantly within sight of the Scheldt

During the summer of 1809, an attempt was made to destroy the port at Vlissingen and the shipbuilding and repair facilities at Antwerp, but this had failed. While Walcheren Island at the mouth of the Scheldt had been successfully secured and the dockyard at Vlissingen destroyed, nothing else was achieved. A fleet of ten or so warships in moorings escaped capture, successfully removed towards Antwerp, while a planned sailing of a fleet of warships along the Scheldt towards Antwerp, where the city and naval complex were to be bombarded by mortar and cannon fire, never materialised. Now, through the availability of the Russian ships, and despite the British Navy's shortage of ships, a second attempt to capture and destroy the Scheldt naval facilities was put into action. An operation that began in January 1814, Russian ships were used to bombard the defences of the Scheldt with 4,000 Russian seamen drawn from ships moored in the Medway drafted into the Russian Army to support the siege. It was to meet with no more success than the assault of five years earlier. A strong defence of the heavy fortifications around the Scheldt, but especially the two substantial forts at the mouths of the Scheldt, Lillo and Liefkenshoek, aided by a French naval flotilla, were key to a successful resistance, with surrender only coming after Louis XVIII of France signed an armistice upon Napoleon's abdication.

While the major fighting ships of the Russian Fleet had been taken to England, several smaller ships remained to oppose Napoleon's invasion. Particularly active was the forty-four-gun frigate *Amphitrite*, commanded by Captain First Rank Toubolov, his orders during the summer of 1812 'to capture all French vessels and to protect all vessels under British colours'. Initially he sailed to Liepāja, where twenty merchant ships were rapidly loading corn belonging to the Russian government, with fourteen more preparing to sail for England and six to Sweden. They were vulnerable not just to the arrival of the French by land, but to enemy privateers. Only 152 miles to the west lay Gdansk, a principal base for Danish and French ships carrying letters of marque and now ready to be unleashed on any ship leaving a Russian port.

Soon after, in early July, Toubolov was joined by the British admiral Byam Martin and the two seventy-fours, *Aboukir* and *Orion*, he commanded. Initially, Martin was tentative in his approach, for while Russia was now at war with France, the future intentions of Alexander and his relationship with Britain were still undefined. While Napoleon might have invaded, it was always possible that Russia would again strike a peace deal and turn against England. To Saumarez he requested 'another line-of-battle ship' to make him safe 'against any hostile efforts' by the Russian Fleet 'coming out of Kronstadt'. Chichagov, now holding the post of commander-in-chief of the Army of Danube, was in Riga and equally perplexed as to how matters with Great Britain would untangle, allowing Martin to take on any refreshments he might require but on condition that any boat sent into the port, 'would be expected to bear a flag of truce'. Only upon receiving word from Toubolov that Russia was at peace with Britain and that British merchant ships would receive protection, did Chichagov relax his position to become more accepting of the British presence in Riga.

While Liepāja was under a more immediate threat of occupation by the enemy, Riga was also vulnerable. Here were many warehouses containing wheat and naval stores (hemp, flax, masts and iron) with several hundred merchantmen in the Daugava, the river running along the east side of the town, waiting to take on those stores. In mid-July, Martin reported to Saumarez that about seventy ships, mostly laden with corn, would be ready to sail for Hano within a few days, while a similar number had already sailed. Nevertheless, he warned Saumarez that 'vast quantities of grain' and other stores 'will still remain after all the ships are gone'. For this reason, the government in London was arranging for the arrival of further merchant ships, with Saumarez advising that they should sail empty and not bring any cargo with them. This large amount of grain and hemp now being shipped to England led Marttin in writing to his father to quip that in England, 'If hungry you will have plenty of bread; if miserable, plenty of rope to hang yourselves.'

To strengthen Riga's defences against the imminent arrival of the French, Martin instructed the building of ten gunboats to be used to disrupt enemy movements along the coast or where they were vulnerable on the Daugava. For this he issued instructions that 'from the *Orion* as many carpenters as she [could] with propriety spare' should help in their construction while equipping them with ordnance offloaded from *Aboukir* and *Orion*. When completed in late-July, these gunboats were to be manned by a mix of British and Russian crews, with Captain Stewart of the British Navy, as the Russians were unable to find a suitable officer, appointed as commander of the gunboats. Long promised but still languishing in Sveaborg and awaiting the arrival of Crown's much delayed detachment of ships from Arkhangelsk, was the 30,000-strong Finland Corps. Only on the last day of August would they finally appear, or at least a somewhat smaller detachment of 5,000, conveyed to Riga by gunboats of the rowing flotilla.

Prior to the arrival of the reinforcements from Sveaborg, events in Riga had begun to move fast. Of the ships loading for England, these had sailed to the convoy assembly point in the Bay of Hano, the total number that year eventually rising to 224, of which 124 had sailed from Riga. The gunboats commanded by Captain Stewart were also active, stemming an enemy incursion by preventing an advanced division crossing the river at a narrow point 8 miles above the city. Commanding the newly arrived gunboats of the rowing flotilla was Rear Admiral A.V. Muller, who now took responsibility for the protection of Riga and patrolling the Gulf, and in so doing captured several enemy batteries on the outskirts of the city. Later, in October 1812, gunboat activities were extended to the Courland coast, shooting down coastal batteries and landing a force sufficient to take back from the French the ports of Mitau (Jelgava), Liepāja and Vindava (Ventspils), all of which had been captured during the summer.

The arrival of Muller allowed Martin to consider himself at 'liberty to go to such other parts' as might appear 'most desirable for the common interest'. The return of *Amphitrite* to Riga in mid-August, along with a corvette, *Sharlottta* (Captain Stanitsky), and a brig *Feniks* (Lieutenant Doctorov), provided him with a strengthened force, as St Petersburg had agreed that they should act under his authority. Initially, Martin gave thought to harassing the enemy occupying Liepāja and nearby Memel by making a close run along the Courland shoreline. In discarding this idea, he determined instead upon using *Amphitrite, Sharlottta* and *Feniks* to support a landing of the Finland Corps at Gdansk. The purpose was to disrupt the French supply chain, for Gdansk was the central point of supply for Napoleon's forces occupying the Courland coastline and threatening Riga, its storehouses crammed with food, munitions, forage, weapons and clothing. Heavily defended, Martin soon realised that any direct assault on the city would bring little reward, choosing instead to use his combined Anglo-Russian force to bombard the city from the sea.

The bombardment of Gdansk conducted by Martin in October was a comparatively minor operation with what was to come. Nevertheless, it does represent the precursor of a considerably more intensive siege of the city, which was to begin with the landing of 7,000 Russian Cossacks in January 1814. Eventually, Gdansk would be surrounded on its landward side by a military force of around 80,000 and blockaded at sea by as many as fifty ships. Inside the besieged area, the forces loyal to Napoleon had a nominal strength of 35,000, but with only 10,000 fit for action. Having once been a supply centre for the French advance into Russia, it was now a place of refuge for thousands of cold, starving, dispirited troops retreating from Moscow. This explains why so many of those defending Gdansk were unfit for the task. Outlying areas of the city, and still held by the French, provided a limited source of food, but quite naturally came under heavy attack from the besieging army. At sea, blockading warships, both British and Russian, unleashed frequent and concentrated bombardments on the city and its fortifications, with one period of bombardment in August lasting fifteen days. According to an eye-witness, 'the Anglo Russian fleet...fired five hundred thousand shot of every calibre' into the city during three of those fifteen days.

By March, conditions were so bad within the confines of Gdansk that on average around 150 were dying each day from starvation, typhus or typhoid, but also injuries resulting from the constant artillery pounding. As for the besieging troops, they were receiving plentiful supplies of all they required from Russian ships and an English transport fleet bringing artillery, mortars. gunpowder, ammunition, and provisions. Also in January, Rear Admiral Tate arrived in the Baltic with five ships of the line and a frigate drawn from the Russian Fleet in the Medway. However, Tate's assignment was unconnected with the siege. Instead he had been tasked with collecting from Kronstadt 15,000 poods (240 tonnes) of hemp. This was to be taken to England in exchange for finished rigging. In May, Rear Admiral Greig brought into the Baltic another squadron from England, this time joining the sea component off Gdansk but through the ships of Greig's squadron having deep draughts, for they were St Petersburg- and Kronstadt-built ships rather than the shallower draughted ships built in Arkhangelsk, they were unable to close in on the city and, therefore, could not contribute to the shelling of the fortifications. Instead, but not until July, they were replaced by a contingent of mortar-armed inshore craft of the rowing flotilla. In October, the blockading fleet was significantly strengthened by four newly completed Russian seventy-four-gun third rates from Arkhangelsk, *Berlin*, *Hamburg*, *Dresden* and *Lübeck*. Constructed with the shallower draught of ships built specifically for operations in the White Sea, they were better suited to the inland waters of the Baltic and successfully worked alongside the rowing flotilla. Eventually, on 2 January 1814, the French and their remaining allies left the city with colours flying while at the same time, from the opposite side of the city, the victorious Russians and Prussians under Duke Alexander entered Gdansk.

# EPILOGUE

# THOUGHTS OF A FUTURE WAR

The exploits of the Russian battle fleet in the North Sea and other ships of the fleet in the Baltic represented the final actions of the Russian Navy during the French wars that stretched from 1793 to 1814. In connection with Napoleon's 100 days following his breakout from Elba, there was no connected Russian naval activities. On board the various Russian battleships that had been based on the Medway, Napoleon's surrender and abdication in April 1814 was met with great joy. Now these ships could sail back to Russia, but first one other mission had to be completed: the transporting to Kronstadt of Russian troops now in France. These were soldiers of the Imperial Guard, men who had fought their way across Europe in the wake of the French retreat, reaching on the day of surrender the very suburbs of Paris. Leaving England in mid-June, Rear Admiral Tate sailed with twelve battleships and six frigates accompanied by supply ships and transports to convey a division of the Imperial Guard from Cherbourg. Due to insufficient available shipping, it was not possible to transport the entire body as a single unit leading to a second and separate division of warships under Vice Admiral Crown embarking troops at Portsmouth, the transports accompanying his ships being primarily British warships sailing *en flute*. To each ship a British naval surgeon had been assigned.

One of those British naval surgeons, James Prior attached to *Smelyi*, was soon to realise that not all was well on those returning ships. In a record he kept of the voyage, he writes of the Russian seamen suffering high levels of morbidity and mortality, which he viewed as resulting from the unhygienic conditions under which those of the lower deck served. As a surgeon this naturally worried him, attempting to persuade disinterested officers that they needed to give greater attention to ensuring that the men regularly washed and changed their clothing. In this he failed, it not regarded as something to which a Russian naval officer should give attention. While troubling him as a surgeon but recognising that his recommendations were being completely ignored, he turned to another matter bubbling under the surface. Many of the officers on board were talking of war, not the war that had just been fought, but a future war – a war not against France but a war against Britain.

Despite Russia and Great Britain having successfully allied themselves in bringing Napoleon's empire to its knees, on *Smelyi*, and doubtless other ships of the returning Russian Fleet, there was deep resentment among the officers to whom he spoke. One holding such views was the ship's captain, named only by Prior as 'Captain R'. He was irritated by the way Britain had conducted herself during the wars recently fought, believing that Britain had fought against Napoleon with only one object in mind: that of grabbing every available commercial opportunity while denying the same to friend and foe alike:

> *The selfishness of England was disgusting; – it was more – it was both galling and insulting. Money seemed to be the god of the country...For Russia she had done nothing.*

During the recent French wars, the British government had worked long and hard at financing a war that had brought massive monetary gain to Great Britain. Throughout the world Britain had gained a considerable number of colonies taken from the French, Danes and Dutch, and which, during that wartime period, reaped huge financial profits. Of pertinence to those on *Smelyi* would have been their own personal experiences and the experience of those they knew and trusted. On those returning ships were some of the 3,000 men who had served between 1805 and 1808 under Senyavin in the Mediterranean. They had witnessed a senior British naval commander, Vice Admiral Duckworth, despite supposed orders to the contrary, deliberately choosing not to co-operate with Senyavin in what for Russia was a vital operation designed to prevent an Ottoman alliance with the French. Others on those ships returning to Kronstadt were familiar with difficulties that had been placed in the way of Vice Admiral Ushakov by the much-revered Nelson. In the eyes of 'Captain R' and others, Britain appeared to view 'foreign enterprise as a crime' and 'foreign colonies, as standing eye-sores'. Providing further detail, Prior added:

> *Sooner than see a foot of ground subject to another flag, she [Britain] would gladly garrison, at an enormous expense, and with no possible profit, all the barren rocks of Europe, and of both Indies. Even her assistance was not disinterested. Her money had been scattered throughout Europe, solely to annoy France; and in fighting the battles of Spain and Portugal, she merely defended herself. For Russia she had done nothing.*

Admittedly that future war, as predicted, did not come until 1855, but the genesis, the cause of that war, lies embedded in the beliefs held by those naval officers and others of high rank following experiences gained during the French war period. Russia was a country striving to gain commercial leverage in the world but finding itself blocked by Britain at every turn. The two nations, of course, were playing geo-politics at the highest level, both attempting to take from the world what they could. In doing so, neither came to trust the other. That those Russian officers felt so slighted was not just because Russia was losing the geo-political global economic war but because they felt Britain had used Russia to achieve the profitable outcome she achieved in fighting the war against Napoleon. Malta and Corfu, valuable bases that could serve Russia's naval and trade aspirations, had either fallen or were about to fall entirely within the British sphere of influence. In other areas of Russian interest, including the Black Sea, Caspian and Pacific, Britain was now a direct competitor.

Adding to the likelihood of a future war between Britain and Russia was that in Britain there was beginning to emerge a reciprocal fear of Russia and a concern that Russia might come to interfere in Britain's newly acquired global reach as a product of the war fought against Napolean. *Bell's Weekly Messenger* in May 1814 spoke of the importance of Malta being retained by Britain for no other reason than of it being a base from which the British Navy could 'prevent the Russian Fleet from passing into the Dardanelles, and check the declaration of the Greek States in their favour'.

A few days later an editorial opinion published in the *Morning Post* expressed the need to 'curb' Russia's 'ambitious movements' for the purpose of preventing 'the recurrence of projects, hostile to the tranquillity and interests of the world'. Although adding only when 'the disposition' of Russia is fully manifested, concluding that otherwise:

> *It would indeed be a dangerous refinement in diplomacy to torture speculative aggression and possible encroachment into a cause for insult and oppression. The jealousy of Russia is the jealousy of a weak mind. It is absurd in principle, and would be dangerous in practice.*

*The Morning Chronicle* also spoke of a future war with Russia, but only if Russia continued to expand at the expense of Europe or Britain's trading empire:

> *What then, it is asked by those who wish to perplex the question, would you go to war with Russia because she is too powerful? Certainly not. However unjustly Russia may have acquired some of her possessions, as it is impossible to take them from her, and she must be allowed to retain them. But Europe ought no longer to be deprived of the means by which, should further aggressions be attempted, they may be resisted with some prospect of success.*

The *Courier* saw action against Russia, if required, to be in the long distant future:

> *Russia will find enough to do for many years to come, in civilizing her population, and promoting her internal prosperity.*

In the meantime, and among the general population of the country, there was nothing but adulation for Russia and Alexander I, and the important role of the Russian Army, in defeating Napoleon. Travelling to England in July 1814, Alexander was treated with great reverence – dubbed by one London newspaper 'Alexander the Liberator'. Remaining in the country for just over three weeks, his itinerary included the Royal Pavilion at Brighton, Petworth House in Sussex and the naval town and dockyard of Portsmouth. In travelling along the Portsmouth Road, the *Evening Mail* reported a vast and enthusiastic crowd lining much of his route:

> *All flocking to behold what they could not expect the opportunity of seeing again – all crying out for Alexander...*

# NOTES AND REFERENCES

**Prologue:** In general, there are few books written in English covering the Russian Navy of the eighteenth century other than Woodward (1965), Jane (1899 reprinted 1983), and Sozaev and Tredrea (2010). In providing an assessment of the size of Russia's Navy in 1790 and that of other world navies, Fulton's estimates are useful but not definitive. The two quotes ascribed to Empress Catherine are drawn from Troyatt (1979, pp.137-8) and the *Collection of the Russian Imperial Historical Society* Vol. X (1876 p.28). Especially useful in assessing Catherine's attitude towards her navy are Herlihy (1986) and Kaplan (1995).

**Chapter 1:** In referring to both Greig and Knowles in Russia I drew upon Cross (1974 and 1997), but specifically for Knowles, Abksandrenko (1884) and Clendenning (1975) were invaluable. In addition, the National Archives (Kew) holds original correspondence between Catherine and Knowles. I also made use of published correspondence, in French and Russian, between Greig and Semyon Vorontsov, the Russan ambassador in London, as published in Moscow and available in the National Library of Belarus. Sands (1830, p.462) for the quote ascribed to John Paul Jones. The following description of the use of camels for lifting ships over shoals and sandbanks is given by Faulkner (1815 p.66):

> *A camel is composed of two separate parts whose outside are perpendicular and whose insides are concave, shaped so as to embrace the hull of a ship on both sides. Each part has a small cabin with 16 pumps and 10 plugs and contain 20 men. They are braced to a ship underneath by means of cables and entirely enclose its sides and bottom. Being then towed to the bar, the plugs are opened and the water admitted until the camel sinks with the ship and runs aground. Then the water being pumped out, the camel rises, lifts up the vessel and the hull is towed over the bar.*

**Chapter 2:** In addition to the major shipbuilding yards to the north, Russia also possessed a number of smaller state-owned yards for the construction of small ships, galleys and other oared craft, the Olonetskaya shipyard north-east of St Petersburg, the St Petersburg Galley yard downriver from the Admiralty, Galernaya Dockyard at the mouth of the Fontanka River just south-east of St Petersburg, and the Okhta yard on the Okhta river close to St Petersburg. Potemkin's remarks on Gannibal made in May 1783 were requoted from Eliseeva (2005, p.292); Katasanov's description of Kherson from the Archive of the Counts Mordvinov. Vol. 2; the state of the Russian Fleet in 1824 from the papers of Vice Admiral V.M. Golovin (1861, pp.36-38); the account of the visit to Sevastopol made in 1787 from Montefiore (2010, pp.433-5); the description of the state of ships from letters to and from Ushakov and Mordvinov (Volume 2, pp.165, 394-395). Of the three ships of 110 guns constructed by M.K. Surovtsov and launched at Kherson between 1800 and 1814, all survived into the 1830s while of thirteen seventy-four-gun 'Anapa' class third rates built at Kherson between 1807 and 1825, one was to see a service life of thirty years. Otherwise, the average of all these ships was slightly over seventeen years.

**Chapter 3:** That Pitt was prepared to allow Gascoigne to transfer men and materials to Russia was, as stated, his desire to strengthen the existing bond between Great Britain and Russia, for Russia supplied huge quantities to Britain of what were termed naval stores, primarily fir, flax, tar, hemp and bar iron, the essential commodities for the upkeep of Britain's naval and mercantile fleets. Following the American Revolutionary War, dependence on Russia for the supply of these materials had greatly increased, with Russia having a near-monopoly on the supply of some of these stores. It is a subject I deal with in detail in MacDougall (2022). For that book I relied heavily upon ledgers of imports and other customs and excise papers held at the National Archives (Kew) and which equally support statements made in this book regarding the flow of naval stores into Britain from both Russia and other countries. Tucker (1981) provides an excellent background account on naval ordnance for the period of the French wars, but more specifically on matters relating to Russian ordnance see Morin (2011), Grebenshchikova (2007) and in Russian Veselago (1872). Supporting my account of Gascoigne establishing an ordnance manufactory in Russia, alongside bringing to Russia the carronade, I relied heavily on the Vorontsov papers, and letters between Gascoigne and Pitt, while Norris (1958 pp.136-145) and Cross (1974, p.257) also proved useful. For a short biography of Gascoigne, see his entry in the *Dictionary of National Biography* (Robinson, 2004). Catherine's remarks on the limited skills of the fleet were taken from a letter to Panin, reproduced in the Papers of Empress Catherine published in *Collection of the Imperial Russian Historical Society* Vol. X (vol 10, pp.23-5). The quotes from Elphinston illustrating the nature of Russian gunnery skills were taken from his own hand-written journal held by Princeton University (New Jersey), available online.

**Chapter 4:** For the insight into Catherine's scrutiny of naval affairs, this is once again taken from Elphinston's journal. In considering the officer corps of the Russian Navy, the work of Cross (1974 and 1997) again proved invaluable. Of Dugdale, little is generally known other than he was appointed to the rank of captain following the Battle of Çeşme. MacKenzie, also appointed to captaincy rank following the battle, had been court-martialled and cashiered out of the Royal Navy in 1761 (TNA ADM1/5300). Cross (1974, p.252) names William Roxburgh, Douglas Cleland and William Gordon as being kinsmen of Greig who, in common with Greig, entered the Russian Navy in 1764. Although much more will be said about Chichagov, here his reference to the effect of Russia possessing too many foreign recruited naval officers is taken from Yulin (2018, p.323).

**Chapter 5:** In assessing the reasons behind the differing operational abilities of the Baltic Fleet compared with the Black Sea Fleet, several sources mentioned in the bibliography proved of value, but especially the letters of Ushakov (Mordvinov, vols. 2 and 3, 1952) and Stanislavskaya (1962, pp.10-56). Aleksandr Radischev was writing during the early nineteenth century and while I used an earlier Russian language publication (Radischev 1920, 49), his work is available in English, Radischev (2020). Howard's nineteenth-century biographer is James Baldwin Brown (the Elder), see Brown (1823, pp.625-8). Mikhailov (1957, p.45) in a detailed study of the medical service of the Baltic Fleet in the eighteenth century, confirms that lower deck sanitary conditions were extremely poor. Insight into the lack of care provided by those of the lower deck serving in the Baltic Fleet is given by James Prior (Anon, 1822, pp.20-21), a British naval surgeon attached to the Russian warship *Smelyi* during the summer of 1814. Seemingly, the lower decks of these Baltic Fleet ships were rarely scrubbed or kept ventilated. According to Prior, the men of *Smelyi's* lower deck were rarely provided with an adequate supply of alternative clothes while for the washing of clothes 'not [one day] was appropriated to this purpose during my stay on board', a period of six weeks. Russian squadrons entering British coastal waters in both 1795 and 1798 suffered extensive outbreaks of typhus, with the hospital ship *Union,* moored off Sheerness, between 3 September 1795 and 28 January 1796 taking 479 typhus sufferers from Russian warships. Scurvy was also a greater problem on Russian warships compared with those of other nations. A useful tally of the range of medical conditions suffered onboard Russian ships can be gauged from the records of the naval hospital at Deal (TNA ADM102/191) during 1813 when Russian ships were in the Downs, with Russian seaman first received on 22 May when three crew members of *Smelyi* were admitted, one suffering from scurvy and two from pulmonary conditions. During the last few days of May, fourteen admissions of Russian seamen were received, with the number during the whole of June falling to three with no further admissions in July and August. From then, the number of admissions began to escalate, with forty-two received in November, including more from scurvy and some with fever and scurvy. Seemingly the unhealthiest ship was *Sviato Slav*, the hospital at Deal receiving seventeen from her in November, while a few earlier admissions from *Sviato Slav* were suffering from 'fever', the vast majority in November had their illness described as 'pulmonic'. Vladimir Bogdanovich Bronevskiy (Bronevskiy 2019, 72-30), a midshipman in a Russian squadron detached from Kronstadt to the Adriatic and Aegean in 1805, provides a very different account of how officers treated those who served under them, Senyavin, the officer commanding the squadron, adhering strictly to the rules laid down by the Admiralty, with the officers on each of the ships of the squadron 'acting in accordance with instructions given to us for the preservation of the men's health'.

**Chapter 6:** Virtually every book written on eighteenth-century naval battle tactics in English concentrate exclusively on the British Navy. Tactics developed by the Russian Navy are ignored. Valuable on the subject, however, are biographies of Howe (Syrett, 2006), Rodney (Hannay, 2018), St Vincent (Davidson, 2020), and Nelson (Tracy, 2002). Specifically looking at naval tactics is Willis (2008). Useful works in Russian discussing Russian naval tactics are Taras (2007), Kurordov (1999) and Lebedev (2020). On supporting landings against an enemy-defended shoreline, Hore (2001) is recommended for how the British Navy undertook such operations, but for the Russian Navy it is necessary to resort to the Russian language books cited.

**Chapter 7:** Among the captains under Khanykov's command, several were foreign, including Captain Second Class Brown, who commanded the forty-four-gun frigate *Michael* and who was Scottish by birth. That the arrival of the Russian Fleet was closely scrutinised from the Deal shoreline is recorded by Chichagov in his journal (Chichagov, 1862) while a local newspaper correspondent submitted several accounts to the *Kentish Weekly Post or Canterbury Journal* (October 1795). The Dutch officer whose letter is quoted was an officer on board one of the ships of the Dutch squadron and his letter was first published in a Dutch newspaper before being reprinted in translation in several British newspapers including the *Cumberland Pacquet and Ware's Whitehaven Advertiser* (15 September 1795). Also referred to are Camperdown (1898) and Brenton (1823, vol. II, p.98). *Dispatch* was an eighteen-gun Albatross-class brig-sloop, built on the Medway that entered the Russian Navy in February 1796.

**Chapter 8:** The mutineers at the Nore failed to achieve their aims, with many of their leaders executed. Among Russian seamen a level of incredulity existed towards the mutiny, for they were used to only total subservience to their officers; this a product of their feudalistic servile status on land and the hold placed over them by the Russian Orthodox church. Vorontsov's punishment is recorded in Labanov-Rostovsky (1968 p.16). In outlining the preparations for the Anglo-Russian invasion of the Texel, the following proved of value: Popham to First Lord of the Admiralty, Earl Spencer quote from Corbett (1913 Vol I, p.38); TNA WOI/411 (ff. 33I-8). Popham produced a set of regulations for the sailing of the troop transports and these are reproduced in full in Mackesy (1970 pp.229-23). The first of the transports arrived at the Downs on 16 September. More generally on the expedition itself and the outcome see van Uythoven (2018) and Piechowiak (1962).

**Chapter 9:** While British naval historians have written extensively on the life and command experiences of Nelson, they generally brush over his negative attitude towards Ushakov together with his inability to effectively work alongside navies of partner countries, such as, in this case, that of Russia during this time of joint assignment. Of the many biographers of Nelson, only a few refer to the negative attitude he displayed towards Ushakov, but in doing so they make little attempt to explain its cause or the overall impact it had upon the war being fought. Lambert (2005, p.237) refers to Nelson being 'unusual in the vehemence of his warnings that the Russians [Ushakov and his squadron] were not to be trusted,' to which Knight (2006, pp.333 and 675) adds that 'Nelson disliked him' and 'thought little' of Ushakov with Sugden (2014, p.213) suggesting that it resulted from the 'lack of a coordinated plan'. Pocock (1988, p.287) makes the statement that the 'two men did not take to each other' before attempting to provide Nelson with an excuse, noting that Nelson was called upon to work alongside Ushakov during a period of 'emotional turmoil', for at that time he was in a formative period of his attachment to Emma Hamilton, the wife of William Hamilton, the British Envoy Extraordinary to the kingdom of Naples. For Ushakov's correspondence see Mordvinov (vols. 2 and 3, 1952) and for Nelson see Nicolas (1845, vol 3). Several Russian and English language secondary sources were also used in the writing of this chapter. In Russian: Ovchinnikov (2015), Tarle (1966), Firsov (1992). In English: Constantine (2001), North (2018), Frumin et al (2013), Stanislavskaya (1962, pp.115-79), Sugden (2014). The fictionalised meeting between Ushakov and Nelson appears in a Russian novel, Leonty (2020, 316).

**Chapter 10:** The Greek Orthodox population of the Ionian Islands, while favourable to being freed from French rule by the Russians under Ushakov, were unhappy at the presence of the Ottomans, and at Zante it became necessary for Ottoman warships to fly the Russian ensign. The increasing friction between Ushakov and his Ottoman counterpart came much to the fore during the escape of *Genereux*. While Ushakov claimed it resulted from the indifference of the Ottoman commanders patrolling the entrance to the channel from which *Genereux* escaped, Abdülkadir, in a letter to the Porte, blamed the Russians, who had failed to prevent *Genereux* leaving the channel and then, in attempting a pursuit chose to anchor at the exit of the channel rather than continuing the pursuit. Under the title of the Septinsular Republic, the Ionian Islands would briefly gain the right to self-governance under Ottoman suzerainty but with Russia the guarantor of the rights and territorial integrity of the newly founded republic. Primarily this chapter was informed by Ushakov's letters (Mordvinov 1952, vols. 2 and 3) and Nelson letters (Nicolas, 1845, vols. 3 and 4), together with Sakul (2009).

**Chapter 11:** On the assassination plot and possible British involvement, Lord Whitworth's correspondence held at the National Archives (Kew) was consulted: (ADM 2/141, 17 April 1801), FO65/34-47, FO65/75 (Whitworth to Canning, November 15) and FO/323/4. Particularly compelling in its support of Whitworth's use of English money in supporting the assassins, if not with the intention of his murder, is Kenney (1977). Also referred to, Pronkin (1907), Sablukov (1907) and Rey (2012). Paul's instruction to Ushakov to return his squadron to the Black Sea was quoted from Mordvinov (vol. 3, Letter 170, 3 February 1800). In Sutherland (1885, pp.34-6), Captain Pulteney Malcolm, in a letter to Lord Elgin (23 March 1801), considers the possibility of an invasion of India by the Russians. Fleurieu's speculations on the benefits of the trade agreement with France was given to the National Assembly on 29 November 1801 (*Weekly Dispatch,*

6 December 1801). Further information regarding the growing closeness of Paul with France is given in Labanov-Rostovsky (1968, pp.63-4) while Waliszewski (1913) and Mourousy (1997) both provide detail on the reign of Paul. According to Aleksandr Sablukov, vice president of the College of Manufacturers during the reign of Paul in notes later published (Sablukov 1907, 72), Paul was planning on a naval war against Britain, while instructions sent to Makarov are electronically available (www.drevlit.ru/docs/russia). Accounts of Nelson approaching Tallinn and his likely attack on this Russian naval base is provided by Chichagov (Tchitchagof, 1909, p.49) and Waliszewski (1913, p.379). Chichagov's assessment of the events he witnessed during the first four months of 1801 as 'glorious for the British Navy' and 'shameful for the Russian Navy' is given in Vorontsov (1-26, Letter 23, 5-17 August 1801, p.15). The arrival of Nelson off Tallinn was a further example of the British admiral's disdain for Russia, demanding to enter the harbour under the pretext of purchasing provisions. That entry and the poor defences of the harbour are described in Tchitchagof (1909, p.6), Pope (1972, p.502) and Arens (1899, p.6). That Nelson, in leading his ships away from Tallinn and ultimately out of sight of the Russian shoreline, conducted this in anger is a point made by Knight (2006, p.394) who suggests Nelson was in a fit of pique while the Admiralty in London saw this action as disrespectful to the new emperor (Nicolas, 1845, IV, p.412). Some amends were made by Chichagov who, after Nelson's departure, had with Nelson at sea a six-hour meeting (Voelker, 2009, p.21).

**Chapter 12:** Evidence of the Imperial Russian Navy continuing to fly the flag of the Order of St John comes from Testa (1997, p.614), Bergen (1879), and reports in various newspapers including the *Hampshire Chronicle* (2 June 1800). Several newspapers, including the *Hull Advertiser* (28 February 1801), reproduce the referred-to discussion paper written by a St Petersburg merchant. Catherine at the time of the American Revolutionary War had sought, through negotiation, to also acquire from Britain possession of Menorca. For the new direction on foreign policy Stanislavskaya (1962 pp.196-204) proved useful. For matters relating to the committee to examine ways to 'bring the fleet into better condition' and the views held by Alexander Vorontsov and Chichagov, see Bartenev (1880, Letter 25, p.285), Dotsenko (1992, vol. 2 p.52), and Tchitchagof (1909).

**Chapter 13:** The quote regarding Chernyshev was taken from Waliszewski (1913, p.133) alongside other material relating to senior naval officials of this time. Also referred to was Woods (2000, pp.87-8). The letter in which Chichagov admits to Semyon Vorontsov of his involvement in the assassination of Paul is reprinted in Bartenev (1880, Letter 25, 3 December 1802, p.55). In the Admiralty yard, Le Brun was responsible for constructing *Chrabryi*, a first rate of 120-guns, the design based on *Caledonia*, a British design, of which her draught drawings had been acquired by another of the Russian shipwrights sent to England to experience British shipbuilding methods. For details of reforms introduced by Paul I and Kushelev, the following were of particular value: Barykina (2001, pp. 259, 268), Waliszewski (1913, pp.208, 259, 268), Woods (2000, p.68), and the website *About Grigory Grigorievich* (О Григории Григорьевиче Кушелеве) available at Kushelevhttps://www.geni.com/people/Grigory-Grigorievich-Kushelev/6000000011799275720; the Gatchina Palace website https://spb-pearl.ru/Gatchina/Ansambl-Gatchinskogo-Dvorca/Dvorcovyi-Park/Admiralteistvo/. The title of the signalling arrangements authored by Kushelev is *Discourse on Naval Signals Serving at the Disposal of Naval Fleets* (1st part – 1797, 2nd part – 1799). A discussion on naval administration, especially as that adopted in Britain, can be found in one of my earlier books, *London and the Georgian Navy* (2023), with a more detailed account in my unpublished doctoral thesis, *Somerset Place to Whitehall* (1994). For Chichagov's claim that boys trained for the navy failed to enter the navy due to 'lack of opportunity', see Bartenev (vol. 19, 1881, p.290). Rumyantsev's claim that 'the navy has a special leader' was made by Armand de Caulaincourt to Napoleon on 10 March 1808 and reproduced from Mikhaïlovich (1905, vol. 1, p.219). For Chichagov's threats to resign and Alexander I's responses see Woods (2001, p.150). For improvements to harbour defences, see Bartenev (1881, Letters 178 and 289), Chichagov (1862, p.289), and Chatelet (1996). Traversay remained in office until March 1828. The navy during that post-war period was forced to suffer severe economies following the war. Consequently, fleet manoeuvres in the Baltic and Black Sea became something of a rarity, with the Baltic Fleet constrained to Neva Bay, the easternmost part of the Gulf of Finland, with this area of water becoming known facetiously as 'The Marquis' Puddle'.

**Chapter 14:** The importance to Russia of Corfu is informed by Bronevskiy (2019, p.93), Semyon Vorontsov (Arkhiv Vorontsov, vol. 19, pp.121, 440) and Stanislavskaya (1962, pp.423-4) for plans regarding the creation of several independent Slavic and Greek states. For Collingwood's view that Russia was using Corfu as a springboard for expansion of the Russian Empire, this was in a letter to Hugh Elliott (Collingwood, vol. 1 1828, 23 February 1806). Tarle (1966, p.385) and Bronevskiy (pp.48, 58, 209, 361-2) proved invaluable informants for both this and the following chapter, Bronevskiy being a junior officer on the expedition and writing a very detailed description of the voyage that was first published in four parts between 1818 and 1819 in St Petersburg with an English translation published in 2019 from which I have quoted. *Iaroslav* was a seventy-four-gun ship of the line, while *Ekspeditsion*, *Letun* and *Azard* carried sixteen, twelve and fourteen guns respectively. Quotes from the correspondence of Admiral Collingwood are taken from my own copy of Collingwood (1828, pp.254-5). While the squadron led into the Mediterranean by Senyavin was drawn from the Baltic, Senyavin had gained most of his experience with the Black Sea Fleet, having served under Ushakov but, in 1804, had been promoted to rear admiral and entrusted with the administration of the Tallinn naval base. For Duckworth's entry into the Bosporus and the resulting outcome, reliance, apart from Bronevskiy (2019), was placed on letters of Collingwood to Duckworth, (*The Naval Chronicle*, xix, p.273) and the correspondence of Charles Arbuthnot (FO78/55, 8, 15 February, 12 June 1807) and Anderson (1952, p.438-444). In addition, Firsov (1992, p.354), Tarle (1966, p.380), Driault (1900, p.54), Skritsky (2013 p.187), and Harrison (1996, p.25). Finally, Alexander's remarks to his foreign minister, von Budberg, are recorded in the Moscow Archive of Foreign Policy, F. Chancellery of the ministry of foreign affairs 1806 I 7891, A212 as re-quoted from Tarle (1966, p.382). In the event, the British landings in Egypt, designed to secure the land passage to India, to which any threat from France had long receded, achieved nothing. Apart from successfully occupying Alexandria, attempts by British forces to gain further territory proved impossible with a withdrawal to Sicily undertaken just six months later.

**Chapter 15:** The major sources for this chapter were Anderson (1952, pp.453-4), Bronevskiy (2019, pp.388-93), Lebedev (2020, pp.314-5), Lebedev (2013, pp.28-35), Panafidin (1806-9, letters 25-43), and Tredrea and Sozaev (2010, pp.98-102). Ottoman ships present at the Battle of Athos according to Bronevskiy (2019, pp.415-6) were *Mesudiye* (120), *Sadd al-bahr* (84), *Anka-yi Bahri* (84), *Taus i Bahri* (84), *Tevfik-Numa* (84), *Besharet* (84), *Sayyad-i Bahri* (74), *Mal-beik Nusrat* (74), *Jebel-Andaz* (74), *Kilik-I Bahri* (74), *Meskeni-Ghazi* (50), *Bedr-i Zafar* (50), *Nessim* (50), *Iskenderiya* (44), *Metelin* (32), *Rahbar-i Alam* (28), *Denyuvet* (32), *Alamat i Nusrat* (18), and *Melankai* (18). Although it is generally stated that the Ottomans lost two battleships and two frigates, Anderson (1952, p. 453) without indicating a source suggests that the Ottomans destroyed another battleship and a frigate off Thasos while two more frigates or a frigate and a sloop sank near Samothrace while attempting a return to the Dardanelles.

**Chapter 16:** *Kentish Gazette* (24 November 1807) and *Caledonian Mercury* (26 November 1807) both provide an explanation as to why the British government was pledging the safety of Russian warships during this time of potential hostility. Quoted letters from Collingwood (Collingwood, 1824, pp.313 and 315), were to Ball dated 22 September 1807 and to Lord Mulgrave dated 16 October 1807. The Russian Fleet taking shelter in the Tagus under the orders of Admiral Senyavin were *Tvyordyi*, *Rafail*, *Sv Elena*, *Retvizan*, *Arkhangel Selafail*, *Sil'nyi*, *Skorii*, *Iaroslav*, *Moshchnyi* and *Kildyuin*. This last was a thirty-two-gun frigate. The journal of Rear Admiral Charles Tyler (TNA ADM 50/50, 11 Sept -11 Oct 1808) provides details of the voyage of Senyavin's ships to Portsmouth under escort. British newspapers providing detail for this chapter were *Morning Chronicle* (18 January 1808) for the arrival of the Russian squadron in Lisbon; *The Scots Magazine* (1 March 1808) regarding members of the British community in Lisbon sheltering on board Russian ships; *Kentish Gazette* (5 April 1808) on food shortages in Lisbon; and *The Examiner* (9 October 1808) describing the arrival of Senyavin's squadron in Portsmouth.

**Chapter 17:** Of value for this chapter were Arens (1899), Dotsenko (1992), Yilmaz (2019, pp.461-90); and Lebedev (2020, pp.310-18). Regarding the overlooking of

Ushakov as commander of the Black Sea Fleet and the reasons behind Alexander's decision, see Fydor (2002, pp.75-77), who discusses this in greater detail.

**Chapter 18:** In writing this chapter the *Caledonian Mercury* (4 February 1808) and *Hull Packet* (20 September 1808) were of value. The letter of T.B. Martin to Sir Henry Martin (27 August 1808) was reproduced from Hamilton (1898, pp.47-8) and Captain Bathurst's letter to the Admiralty from ADM 1/1542. Also referred to were the secret instructions given to Saumarez prior to his first departure into the Baltic (TNA ADM2/1365 and Ross, 1838, pp.100-101), letters from Saumarez to the Admiralty, especially one dated 30 August 1808 (TNA ADM1/7), and the logbooks of *Centaur*, *Implacable* and *Salsette*, all held at the National Archives (ADM51). Voelcker (2008) was of considerable value. Russian sources used for this chapter included Arens (1899), Dotsenko (1992), and Lebedev (2020, pp.310-18). It was during the first half of July that the Russian squadron under Khanykov first put to sea, meeting with one success, the capture of the Swedish brig *Falk.* On 25 July, the squadron reached Gangut, ensuring the passage of rowing vessels to the Åland Islands. On 10 August, the squadron moved to the Jungfersund Strait, where the Allied ships were moored. The quote from Lord Howard's report following his mission to Russia was taken from Voelcker (2008, p.57) with the full report held by the West Yorkshire Archives Service (WYL250/8/44).

**Chapter 19**: My earlier book, *The Great Anglo-Russian Naval Alliance of the Eighteenth Century and Beyond* published in 2019 (see bibliography) assesses in detail the growth and importance of the Russian naval stores trade to Great Britain and why Napoleon needed to invade Russia to bring this trade to an end. For the assistance given to the Russian ships by the British Navy in sailing to England I referred to Ryan (1968, especially pp.255-7 and 263). Observations made in England on the first appearance of the Russian Fleet were taken from the following British newspapers: *Kentish Gazette* (15 December 1812), *Stamford Mercury* (25 December 1812), and *Kentish Weekly Post or Canterbury Journal* (12 January 1813). For a fuller discussion on hydrography and the maps and charts in possession of the British Admiralty, Barritt (2024) must be recommended. For detail on the outcome of the survey conducted on the Russian ships held at Portsmouth I referred to the original survey notes held at the National Maritime Museum (ADM 359/32C/89, 30 October 1812).

**Chapter 20:** Details of the 'Convention between his Britannic Majesty, and his Majesty the Emperor of all the Russias' is to be found in State Papers (1813, London: Printed by R.G. Clarke); the debate in the House was informed by *Hansard* (Committee of Supply, 10 November 1813, vol. 27, col.72) and the reference to Russian sail of the line and a frigate bound for the Scheldt from the *Leicester Chronicle* (22 May 1813). Quoted correspondence of Sir T.B. Martin was taken from Hamilton (1898, pp.192-240). Marchangy (1813) provided the eye-witness account of the Danzig siege. For detail on

Napoleon's ship construction programme at Antwerp, see my own paper entitled 'A Birthday Present for the Emperor Napoleon I – Naval Complex on the Scheldt' available on the academia website.

**Epilogue:** Prior's account was published anonymously (anon (1822). The author, James Prior (c.1790-1869), was a surgeon and already the author of accounts of earlier voyages with the British Navy, when he was assigned to the Russian squadron under Tate, returning to Kronstadt from Sheerness in June 1814. Prior rose to be deputy inspector of hospitals and was knighted in 1858. He was the author of biographies of Burke and Goldsmith, and other works. British newspapers referred to in respect of a possible future war with Russia were *Bell's Weekly Messenger* (22 May 1814), *Morning Post* (18 September 1817), *Morning Chronicle* (22 September 1817), *Courier* (October 1818), and *Evening Mail* (24 June 1814).

# BIBLIOGRAPHY


## Primary sources: Unpublished

### The National Archives (TNA), Kew

| | |
|---|---|
| ADM1/7 | Letters from commander-in-chief, Baltic: 1808 |
| ADM1/1542 | Letters from Captains, Surnames B: 1808 |
| ADM2/141 | Admiralty Out-Letters: Orders and Instructions |
| ADM2/1365 | Secret Letters |
| ADM50/50 | Journal of Rear Admiral Charles Tyler, 11 September – 11 October 1808 |
| ADM51/1975 | Captain's log: *Implacable* |
| ADM51/2247 | Captain's log: *Centaur* |
| ADM51/4044 | Captain's log: *Salsette* |
| ADM98/224 | Office of the Commissioners of Sick and Wounded Seamen: Chatham Agent |
| ADM102/17 | Naval Hospitals' and Hospital Ships' Musters: Deal, 1789-96 |
| ADM102/191 | Hospital Muster Book, Deal (Russians) |
| CUST4/3-40 | Ledgers of Imports Under Countries, 1806-1845 |
| CUST10/1-46 | Ledgers of Exports of Foreign and Colonial Merchandise Under Countries, 1809-1855 |
| CUST17/1-30 | States of Navigation, Commerce and Revenue, 1772-1808 |
| FO65/34-47 | Correspondence of Lord Whitworth while ambassador in Russia, 1796-1800. |
| FO78/55 | Correspondence of Charles Arbuthnot, ambassador to the Porte, Jan-July 1807 |
| FO/323/4 | Correspondence of Lord Whitworth while ambassador in France, 1802-3 |
| LBK/80 | Correspondence between Empress Catherine II of Russia and Admiral Sir Charles Knowles |
| WO/4I I | Captain Home Popham's mission to enlist Russian aid for the Helder expedition |

**National Maritime Museum (NMM)**

ADM359/32C/89 30 October 1812. An account showing the expense of equipping the Russian ships for a voyage to Russia, what their value would be if sold in this country. and what expense each of them will require for their thorough repair.

**Princeton University (New Jersey)**

John Elphinston papers relating to the Russo-Turkish War, 1769–71, available at https://findingaids.princeton.edu/catalog/C0951_c013

## Primary Sources (Published)

### English Language

Bronevskiy, Vladimir Bogdanovich, 2019, *Northern Tars in Southern Waters: The Russian Fleet in the Mediterranean, 1806-1810* (Warwick)

Collingwood, G.L. Newnham, 1828, *A selection from the public and private correspondence of Vice Admiral Lord Collingwood; interspersed with memoirs of his life* (London)

Faulkner, 1815, *A New Universal Dictionary of the Marine* (London)

Hamilton, Sir Richard Vesey (ed), 1898, *Letters and Papers of Admiral of The Fleet Sír Thomas Byam Martin* (Navy Records Society), Vol. II

Marchangy, Louis Antoine François de, 1815, *The Siege of Dantzic, in 1813* (Dublin) Available at https://archive.org

Nicolas, Nicholas Harris (ed), 1845, *The Dispatches and Letters of Vice Admiral Lord Viscount Nelson, with Notes* Vols. III and IV (London)

Ross, Sir John, 1838, *Memoirs and Correspondence of Admiral Lord Saumarez*, 2 volumes (London). Available at https://archive.org

Ryan, N., *The Saumarez Papers: The Baltic 1808-1812: Selections from the Baltic Correspondence of Vice Admiral Sir James Saumarez, 1802-12* (London, 1968)

Schembri, Guzeppi, 1990, *The Malta and Russia Connection: A History of Diplomatic Relations between Malta and Russia (XVII - XIX cc.) based on Original Russian Documents* (Valletta)

### French Language

Chichagov, Pavel Vasil'evich, 1862, *Mémoires de l'amiral Tchitchagoff* (Leipzig)

Mikhaĭlovich, Nikolai, Grand Duke of Russia, 1905, *Les relations diplomatiques de la Russie et de la France d'après les rapports des ambassadeurs d'Alexandre et de Napoléon, 1808-1812* vol. 1 219 (St. Pétersbourg)

Available at https://archive.org/details/lesrelationsdip00napogoog

### Russian Language

Golovin Papers

Imperial Russian Historical Society, 1876, *Collection of the Imperial Russian Historical Society* (St Petersburg: Imperial Russian Historical Society) Vol. X

[Императорское Русское Историческое Общество, 1876, *Собрание Императорского Русского Исторического Общества* (Санкт-Петербург: Императорское Русское Историческое Общество) Том. X]

Available in Russian at https://ru.wikisource.org/wiki/%D0%9E_%D1%81%D0%BE%D1%81%D1%82%D0%BE%D1%8F%D0%BD%D0%B8%D0%B8_%D0%A0%D0%BE%D1%81%D1%81%D0%B8%D0%B9%D1%81%D0%BA%D0%BE%D0%B3%D0%BE_%D1%84%D0%BB%D0%BE%D1%82%D0%B0_(%D0%93%D0%BE%D0%BB%D0%BE%D0%B2%D0%BD%D0%B8%D0%BD)

Abksandrenko, V.N., *Russian diplomatic agents in London " XVIII Peke*, Vol. II (Warsaw, 1897)

[Abksandrenko, V.N., *Ruukie diplomaticheskie agenty 11 Londone " XVIII Peke*, Том 2]

Available at https://play.google.com/books/reader?id=W20rAAAAYAAJ&pg=GBS.PA184&hl=en_US

Bartenev, P.I. (ed), 1881, *Alexander and Seman Romanovich Vorontsovs Correspondence with P.V. Chichagov and Greig* (Moscow: University Printing House)

[Бартенев П.И. (редактор), 1881, Александр и Семан Романовичи Воронцовы Переписка с.В. Чичаговым и Грейгом]

Barykina I.V., 2001, *Statesmen of Russia as Seen by Contemporaries: Paul I* (St Petersburg)

[Барыкина И.В., 2001, Государственные деятели России глазами современников: Павел I]

Grebenshchikova, G.A., 2007, *The Baltic Fleet during the reign of Catherine II* (St Petersburg: Nauka)

[Гребенщикова, Г.А., 2007, Балтийский флот в периоа правления Екатерины II (Санкт-Петербург: Наука)]

Mordvinov, R.N., 1952, *Admiral Ushakov*, vol. 2 and 3, (Moscow)

[Мордвинов Р.Н., 1952, Адмирал Ушаков, Том 2]

Available in Russian at https://www.prlib.ru/item/397141

Panafidin, P.I., *Letters of a Naval Officer* (1806-9)

[ПАНАФИДИН П. И. ПИСЬМА МОРСКОГО ОФИЦЕРА]

Available at https://drevlit.ru/docs/turky/XIX/1800-1820/Panafidin_P_I/text1.php

Sablukov, N.A., 1907, *Notes of N.A. Sablukov in Regicide 11 March 1801: Notes of Participants and Contemporaries* (St Petersburg)

[царЕубийство 11 марта 1801 года: Записи участников и современников]

Vorontsov, Alexander, Vorontsov, Semyon, Bartenyev, P.I., 1881, *Papers of Counts Alexander and Semyon Romanovich Vorontsov. Correspondence with P.V. Chichagov and the Greigs*, Book 19
[Архив князя Воронцова. Книга 19. Бумаги графов Александра и Семена Романовичей Воронцовых. Переписка с П.В.Чичаговым и Грейгами. 1881]

## Secondary

### English Language

Anderson, R.C., 1952, *Naval wars in the Levant, 1559-1853* (Princeton: Princeton University Press)
Anon., *A voyage to St. Petersburg in 1814, with remarks on the imperial Russian Navy* (London, 1822)
Barritt, Michael, 2024, *Nelson's Pathfinders: A Forgotten Story in the Triumph of British Sea Power* (New Haven: Yale University Press)
Bergen, von, E., 1879, *The Maltese Order and its Relations with Russia* (Riga)
Brenton, Edward, 1823, *The naval history of Great Britain from the year MDCCLXXXIII to MDCCCXXII* (London)
Brown (the Elder), James Baldwin, 1823, *Memoirs of the Public and Private Life of John Howard, the Philanthropist; compiled from his own diary* (London)
Camperdown, Robert Adam Philips Haldane Duncan, Earl of, 1898, *Admiral Duncan* (London)
Chatelet, du, Madeleine, 1996, *Traversay: A Frenchman, Minister of the Navy of the Tsar* (FeniXX digital reissue)
Clendenning, Philip H., 'Admiral Sir Charles Knowles and Russia, 1771–1774', *The Mariner's Mirror*, 61:1 (January 1975), pp.42-3
Constantine, David, 2001, *Fields of Fire: A Life of Sir William Hamilton* (London)
Corbett, J.S., 1913, *Private Papers of George, 2nd Earl Spencer, 1794-1801* vol. 1 (Navy Records Society)
Cross, A.G., 'Samuel Greig, Catherine the Great's Scottish Admiral' in *The Mariner's Mirror*, (1974) 60:3, pp.251-265
Cross, A.G., 1997, *By the Banks of the Neva* (Cambridge)
Davidson, D.G., 2020, *Admiral Lord St. Vincent: Saint or Tyrant? The Life of Sir John Jervis*, Nelson's Patron (Stroud)
Desmond, Gregory, 2010, *The Ungovernable Rock: A History of the Anglo-Corsican Kingdom and its Role in Britain's Mediterranean Strategy During the Revolutionary War, 1793-9* (Madison, NJ)
Emerson, Barbara, 2024, *The First Cold War: Anglo-Russian Relations in the 19th Century* (London)
Frumin, Mitia and Şakul, Kahraman, 2013, *Reading Between the Lines: Admiral Ushakov's Relations with Kapudane Abdülkadir Beg According to Russian and*

*Ottoman Sources* in International Symposium on Piri Reis and Turkish Maritime History 26-29 September 2013

Proceedings, vol. 4, pp.71-96

Gribble, Francis, 1912, *The Comedy of Catherine the Great* (London)

Hannay, David, 2015, *Rodney: The Admiral Who Broke the Line* (London)

Harrison, Robert T., 1996, 'Alexandria, British occupation of 1807' in Olson, James Stuart; Shadle, Robert (eds), *Historical Dictionary of the British Empire* (London)

Herlihy, Patricia, 1986, *Odessa: a history, 1794-1914*, (Cambridge Mss)

Hore, Peter, 2002, *Seapower Ashore* (London)

Jane, Fred T., 1983, *Imperial Russian Navy* (London)

Kaplan, Herbert H., 1995, *Russian overseas commerce with Great Britain during the reign of Catherine II* (Philadelphia)

Kenney, James J., 'Lord Whitworth and the Conspiracy Against Tsar Paul I: The New Evidence of the Kent Archives' in *Slavic Review*, Jun 1977, vol. 36, no. 2 (Jun 1977), pp.205-219a Available at https://www.jstor.org/stable/2495036

Knight, Roger, 2006, *The Pursuit of Victory: The Life and Achievement of Horatio Nelson* (London)

Labanov-Rostovsky, A.A.,1968, *Russia and Europe 1789-1825* (London)

Lambert, Andrew, 2005, *Nelson: Britannia's God of War* (London)

MacDougall, Philip, 1994, Somerset Place to Whitehall (unpublished Ph.D. thesis) available at https://kar.kent.ac.uk/85965/1/240181.pdf

MacDougall, Philip, 2013, *London and the Georgian Navy* (Cheltenham)

MacDougall, Philip, 2022, *The Great Anglo-Russian Naval Alliance of the Eighteenth Century and Beyond* (Woodbridge, Suffolk)

MacDougall, Philip, 2023, *A Birthday Present for the Emperor Napoleon I – a Naval Complex on the Scheldt* available at www.academia.edu/109671616

Mackesy, Piers (1970) 'Regulations in Troopships: Home Popham and the Russian Expedition of 1799' in *The Mariner's Mirror*, 56:2, pp.229-23

Montefiore, Simon Sebag, 2010, *Catherine the Great and Potemkin: Power, Love and the Russian Empire* (London)

Morin, Marco, F. 2011, 'The Russian "Unicorn" and the Venetian "cannone di nuova inventione"' in *Journal of the Ordnance Society* vol. 23, pp.45-53

Piechowiak, A.B., 'The Anglo-Russian Expedition to Holland in 1799' in *The Slavonic and East European Review* Dec 1962, vol. 41, pp.182-195a Available at https://www.jstor.org/stable/4205424

Pocock, Tom, 2020, *Horatio Nelson: The story of the man who saved Britain from invasion* (London)

Pope, Dudley, 1972, *The Great Gamble: Nelson at Copenhagen* (London)

Radischev, Aleksandr, 2020, *A Journey from St. Petersburg to Moscow*, Columbia University Press (The Russian Library). Translated by Andrew Kahn and Irina Reyfman

Rey, Marie-Pierre, 2012, *Alexander I: The Tsar Who Defeated Napoleon* (Illinois)

Robert C. Sands (ed), 1830, *Life and Correspondence of John Paul Jones, Including His Narrative of the Campaign of Liman* (New York)
Robinson, Eric H., 2004, *Charles Gascoigne* in New Dictionary of National Bibliography available at https://doi.org/10.1093/ref:odnb/40411
Sakul, Kahraman, 2009, *An Ottoman Global Moment: War of the Second Coalition in the Levant* (unpublished dissertation, Georgetown University) available at: https://www.yumpu.com/en/document/read/12003023/an-ottoman-global-moment-georgetown-university
Sozaev, Eduard and Tredrea, John, 2010, *Russian Warships in the Age of Sail 1696–1860: Design, Construction, Careers and Fates* (Barnsley)
Sugden, J., 2014, *Nelson: The Sword of Albion* (London)
Sutherland, Edwards, H., 1885, *Russian projects against India: from the czar Peter to General Skobeleff* (London)
Syrett, David, 2006, *Admiral Lord Howe: A Biography* (Stroud)
Testa, Carmel, *The French in Malta 1798-1800* (Valletta, 1997)
Tracy, Nichollas, 2002, *Nelson's Battles: The Art of Victory in the Age of Sail* (London)
Troyatt, Henri, 1979, *Catherine the Great* (Henley)
Tucker, Spencer, 1981, *Arming the Fleet: U.S. Navy Ordnance in the Muzzle-Loading Era* (Annapolis)
Uythoven, Geert van, 2018, *The Secret Expedition: The Anglo-Russian Invasion of Holland 1799* (London)
Voelker, Tim, 2008, *Admiral Saumarez Versus Napoleon: The Baltic, 1807-12* (Woodbridge, Suffolk)
Waliszewski, Kazimierz, 1913, *Paul the First of Russia, the son of Catherine the Great* (London)
Willis, Sam, 2008, *Fighting at Sea in the Eighteenth Century* (Woodbridge, Suffolk)
Woods, Joanna, 2000, *The Commissioner's Daughter: The Story of Elizabeth Proby and Admiral Chichagov* (Witney)
Woodward, David, 1965, The Russians at Sea (London)

## French Language

Driault, E., 'Les Anglais Devant Constantinople et Alexandrie 1807' in *Revue Historique*, T. 73, Fasc. 1 (1900), pp.24-60
Mitchell, Mairin, 1952, *Histoire Maritime de la Russe* (Paris)
Mourousy, Paul, 1997, *Le Tsar Paul Ier: La Puissance et la Peur* (Paris)

## Russian Language

Arens, E.I., Captain Second Rank, 1899, *History of the Russian Fleet: the Reign of Emperor Alexander I] Handwritten lecture notes, 1898-9*, held by Russian State Naval Academy
[Аренс, Е.И., капитан 2-го ранга, 1899, История российского флота: царствование императора Александра I] available at https://www.prlib.ru/en/item/956758

Dotsenko, V.D., 1992, *History of the Russian Fleet*, vol. 2 (St Petersburg)
Доценко, В.Д., 1992, История российского флота, т. 2 (Санкт-Петербург)

Eliseeva O.I., 2005, *Grigory Potemkin* (Moscow)
[Елисеева О.И., 2005, Григорий Потемкин]

Firsov, I.I., 1992, *Peter's Creation* (Moscow: Young Guard)
[И.И.Фирсов, 1992, Петра творенье]

Kurordov, V.I. (ed), 1999, *History of Naval Art vol.1: History of the Theory of Strategy, Operational Art and the Tactics of the Navy* (St Petersburg, Shipbuilding)
[Курордов, В.И., ред., 1999, *История военно-морского искусства, т. 1: История теории стратегии, оперативного искусства и тактики флота*]

Lebedev, A.A., 2013, 'Dardanelles and Athos: Behind the Scenes of a Famous Victory' in *Gangut*, vol. 28, pp.28-35
[Лебедев А.А., Дарданеллы и Афон: за кулисами извеснтbіх победы (Гангут)]

Lebedev, A.A., 2020, *Naval Battles: Russian Sailing Fleet, a Complete Guide* (St Petersburg)
[Лебедев, А.А., 2020, *Морские сражения: Русский парусный флот, полное руководство*]

Mikhailov, S.S., 1957, *The Medical Service of the Russian Fleet in the Eighteenth Century: Materials Towards the History of Russian Medicine* (Leningrad)
[Михайлов, С.С., 1957, Медицинская служба Российского флота в XVIII веке: материалы к истории российской медицины]

Monakov, M.S., and Rodionov, B.I., 2006, *History of the Russian Navy in the light of world politics and economics* (Kronstadt)
[Монаков, М.С., и Родионов, Б.И., 2006, История российского флота в свете мировой политики и экономики]

Pronkin, I.S. (ed), 1990 reprint of 1907 edition, *Regicide, 11 March 1801: Notes on participants and contemporaries* (St Petersburg)
[Пронькин, И. С., (редактор), Переиздание 1907 года 1990 года, Цареубийство 11 марта 1801 года]

Rakovsky, Leonty, 2020, *Admiral Ushakov* (Moscow: Alfa-Kniga)
[Раковский, Леонтий, 2020, *Адмирал Ушаков*]

Satsky, G., 2002, Fyodor *Fedorovich Ushakov* in Voprosy istorii. 2002, no.3, pp.51-78 available at Вопросы истории 03. Фёдор Фёдорович Ушаков - Сацкий А.Г. - 2002
[Сатский, Г., Фёдор Фёдорович Ушаков в Вопросах истории. 2002. № 3. С. 51-78]

Skritsky, Nikolai, 2013, Admiral Senyavin (Moscow)
[Скрицкий, Николай, 2013, Адмирал Сенявин]

Stanislavskaya, 1962, *Russia-English Relations and Problems of the Mediterranean (1798-1807)* (Moscow)
[Станиславская, 1962, Русско-английские отношения и проблемы Средиземноморья (1798-1807)

Taras, Anatoly, 2007, *Battles and Campaigns of the Russian Sailing Fleet: 1696-1863* (Minsk)
[Тарас, Анатолий, 2007, *Битвы и кампании русского парусного флота: 1696-1863*]

Tarle, E.V., 1948, *Admiral Nelson in the Mediterranean Sea, 1798-1800* (Moscow)
[Тарле, Е.В., 1948, Адмирал Нельсон в Средиземном море, 1798-1800]

Tarle, E.V., 1966, *Three Expeditions of the Russian Fleet* (Moscow: Ministry of Defence of the Union of the SSR)
[Тарле Е.В., 1966, Три экспедиции российского флота]

Vaylov, Alexander, 2021, *Ushakov and Nelson: Two Admirals in the Era of the Napoleonic Wars* (Moscow)
[Вайлов+, Александр, 2021, Ушаков И Нельсон: Два адмирала в эпоху наполеоновских войск]

Veselago, Feodosy Fedorovich, 1872, *Russian Warships from 1668 to 1860* (St Petersburg)
[Веселаго, Феодосий Федорович, 1872, Русские военные корабли с 1668 по 1860 год]

Yulin, Vladimir Alekseevich, 2018, *Admiral Pavel Chichagov, Fatherland's Loyal Son: Life Story and Fate* (Moscow)
[Юлин, Владимир Алексеевич, 2018, Адмирал Павел Чичагов. Отечества верный сын: история жизни и судьбы]

## Turkish Language

Yilmaz, Özgür, 'Some new information about the Russian attacks on Trabzon and Akçaabat during the Ottoman-Russian War of 1806-1812' in *Journal of Black Sea Studies: Spring 2019*; (26): pp.461-490
[Yilmaz, Özgür, 1806-1812 Osmanli-Rus Savaşi'nda Ruslarin Trabzon ve Akçaabat Saldirilarina Dair Bazi Yeni Bilgiler]

# INDEX